Uncertain Citizenship

Uncertain Citizenship

Everyday Practices of Bolivian Migrants in Chile

———

Megan Ryburn

中

UNIVERSITY OF CALIFORNIA PRESS

University of California Press, one of the most distinguished university presses in the United States, enriches lives around the world by advancing scholarship in the humanities, social sciences, and natural sciences. Its activities are supported by the UC Press Foundation and by philanthropic contributions from individuals and institutions. For more information, visit www.ucpress.edu.

University of California Press
Oakland, California

Library of Congress Cataloging-in-Publication Data

Names: Ryburn, Megan, author.
Title: Uncertain citizenship : everyday practices of Bolivian migrants
   in Chile / Megan Ryburn.
Description: Oakland, California : University of California Press, [2018] |
   Includes bibliographical references and index. |
Identifiers: LCCN 2018014113 (print) | LCCN 2018017092 (ebook) |
   ISBN 9780520970793 (ebook) | ISBN 9780520298767 (cloth : alk. paper) |
   ISBN 9780520298774 (pbk. : alk. paper)
Subjects: LCSH: Bolivia—Emigration and immigration. |
   Immigrants—Bolivia—Social conditions. | Foreign workers,
   Bolivian—Chile—Social conditions. | Bolivians—Chile—Social
   conditions.
Classification: LCC HD8268.5.B65 (ebook) | LCC HD8268.5.B65 R93 2018
   (print) | DDC 305.868/84083—dc23
LC record available at https://lccn.loc.gov/2018014113

27   26   25   24   23   22   21   20   19   18
10   9   8   7   6   5   4   3   2   1

For Liz Ryburn, and in memory of Murray Ryburn

CONTENTS

ILLUSTRATIONS

MAPS

FIGURES

TABLES

ACKNOWLEDGMENTS

First, I want to express my most sincere thanks to all those who participated in the research that became this book. I cannot name you here, but please know that the stories and knowledge you shared with me have been my constant motivation during the long process of completing this project. *Mil gracias.*

The project began with my doctoral research at the School of Geography and School of Politics and International Relations at Queen Mary University of London. My heartfelt gratitude goes to Cathy McIlwaine, now at King's College London, whose expertise and research experience have been, and continue to be, a true inspiration. Her invariably insightful comments on my work during the PhD and beyond, and her kindness, generosity, and mentoring, are deeply appreciated. Very many thanks also to James Dunkerley, who gave valuable feedback throughout my doctoral research, and whose breadth of knowledge and passion for his work I greatly admire. Thanks also to Kavita Datta, whose helpful commentary at the progression stage informed my subsequent approach "in the field" and after. I was additionally very fortunate to have such thorough and constructive examiners in Jasmine Gideon and Davide Però, who helped convince me to pursue writing this book. At Queen Mary, I was lucky enough to undertake the PhD journey with a brilliant cohort. The animated discussions, many curries, and marathon completion (literal and metaphorical) shared with Hayley Peacock, Victoria Pickering, Suzanne Solley, and Annabelle Wilkins are especially acknowledged. The research would not have been possible without a Queen Mary Principal's Studentship and additional funding for fieldwork from the Queen Mary Postgraduate Research Fund and the Society of Latin American Studies. I am grateful for their support.

As an LSE Fellow in the Department of Geography and Environment at the London School of Economics and Political Science, I have found an ideal place in which to complete this book. My colleagues in the Urbanisation, Planning and Development research cluster and in the wider department have been so welcoming and encouraging. I owe a particular debt of gratitude to Sylvia Chant, Ryan Centner, Gareth Jones, Claire Mercer, and Austin Zeiderman for the advice and suggestions they have generously given.

It has been an absolute pleasure to work with my editor Kate Marshall at the University of California Press, whose many contributions include guiding me to elucidate much more clearly the argument at the heart of the work. Thanks too to editorial assistant Bradley Depew and to the rest of the editorial, production, and marketing teams. The comments of the three anonymous reviewers and the depth of their engagement with the manuscript could not have been more appreciatively received. Their astute comments and observations have made this a far better book. I am grateful also to the member of the University of California Press Editorial Committee who reviewed the revised version of the manuscript.

Sarah Abel, Lauren Harris, and Rachel Randall were there when this all started with our fantastic MPhil year at the Centre of Latin American Studies at the University of Cambridge and have been there ever since. And without Diana Crossan, those initial postgraduate studies would not have happened. Helen Lyttelton, my partner in crime and fellow writer, read this manuscript in its entirety in an early iteration. "Coach" Kirsten Mander has unflaggingly cheered me on. Many other dear friends across four continents have also been an important part of this, and I am sorry not to be able to do justice to you all.

I am indebted to all those who shared their homes with me in Chile and Bolivia, in particular Daniela Jadue, Katherine Despot, Juan Despot, Patricia Ulloa, María Rosa Garcia, and Álvaro Zapata. And of course thank-you to Nora Núñez and Basilio Torres, Alejandra Torres, Adelmo, Rocío, Camilo, Joaquín, and Catalina Muñoz for welcoming me always with open arms and delicious vegetarian *asados*. On the other side of the world, Lizzie Jones and Philip Greenstone; Rodrigo Torres and Alexandra Tzirkoti; Ruth, Paul, Jess, and Maya Denyer; and Helen Wensley have put me up and put up with me in London over the past six years. Along with Sue, Robin, and Ben Wensley, and Irene Horner, they have played an enormous role in making England feel like home again and enabling me to complete this endeavor.

To my brother and sister, Finlay and Caitlin Ryburn, your courage and humor on our family's own migration journey helps keep me going. Thank-you. And my deepest thanks to my husband Pablo Torres for his support throughout all that this has entailed. It would take many more pages to fully acknowledge the magnitude of your contribution. But perhaps it is somewhat encapsulated in that verse from Mario Benedetti's poem: "si te quiero es porque sos / mi amor mi cómplice y todo

/ y en la calle codo a codo / somos mucho más que dos." Finally, to my mum, Liz Ryburn, and my dad, Murray Ryburn, who instilled in me through actions and conversations a concern with social justice: Dad, how I wish you were here to see this published and to shed a proud fatherly tear, as no doubt you would. Mum, there aren't words to express how present you have been through all of this. Suffice it to say, this is dedicated to you both.

Introduction

Luz María was nineteen when I met her. When she was in the last months of her second pregnancy, she would invite me to visit in the afternoon in her cramped, windowless room. She would apologize for the lack of seating and offer me cups of herbal tea, boiling water on the stove attached to a gas cylinder in the open-air communal courtyard surrounded by rooms like hers. As she talked, she would conjure for me images of a verdant place far away from that run-down Santiago tenement housing. What she enjoyed most was to tell me in intricate detail about the little rituals of this green, back-home place, of the food and decorations she would prepare with her mother, sisters, and aunties for birthdays, christenings, Christmas, and All Saints' Day. Yet through the cracks in the narrative I also caught glimpses of what had often been a life of poverty, hardship, and frustration at the thwarting of her aspirations. This is what had compelled her to move from Bolivia to Chile. Luz María longed for the sacrifices she had made by migrating to enable her to return, with her new baby, to a nostalgic future. Here, her parents and in-laws would be in good health, her possibility of continuing with education would be secure, and she would not have to worry about where the next meal and the next rent payment were coming from.

She had come to Santiago in April 2013 with her partner, Wilson. They were both from the tropical lowland *departamento* of Santa Cruz, Bolivia; Luz María's family lived in Plan 3000, a poor, peri-urban neighborhood on the outskirts of the city of Santa Cruz. Wilson, who was twenty-two, was originally from Mairana, a small town on the edge of the densely forested Amboró National Park, but had moved to Plan 3000 in his late teens because there was little work to be had in Mairana. They met when Luz María was in secondary school and had a child shortly afterward, in 2012. They both had ambitions; Wilson wanted to start a moto-taxi business, and Luz María wished to complete the vocational studies that she started when their little boy was a few months old.

But by early 2013 they were in debt to informal lenders after borrowing money to cover health-care costs for Wilson's chronically ill mother and to pay for a motorbike so Wilson could start his business. In April that year they discovered that Luz María was pregnant again. Very worried about the debt, as well as about telling their families they were going to have another child, they felt compelled to leave Bolivia for somewhere with greater economic opportunities. They hoped to pay off the loan and make enough money to support their young family. Without telling anyone about the pregnancy, they left their one-year-old in the care of Luz María's mother and embarked on the fifty-hour bus journey to Santiago, Chile. They had heard rumors that things were good there; you could earn a decent salary and send money home.

Once in Santiago, both started working for contractors: Luz María as a cleaner, and Wilson in construction. The hours were long, and the pay was less than the minimum wage. Luz María spent much of her day bending and lifting, breathing in the fumes of powerful cleaning fluids. Both she and Wilson were in the country on tourist visas and therefore working unauthorized, which gave their employers leverage to exploit them. The couple were shocked by the cost of living in Santiago and could barely afford the rent for the unfurnished room that they found downtown. When Luz María was dismissed from her job after her pregnancy began to show, the situation became critical. Any money they managed to save was sent back to support their young son in Bolivia and to keep the debt collectors at bay. Even living on just rice and vegetables, they could not afford to pay for the MERCOSUR temporary resident visa (MTRV) that would allow them to work legally and in better conditions. Scared of the authorities, they did not know where to turn for help. Luz María spent the first five months of her pregnancy too afraid to seek medical care, unsure where she would give birth. And yet despite all this insecurity, they still found moments of joy in the everyday—sharing the rare treat of a fizzy drink with their neighbors in the evening, visiting Santiago's parks on Wilson's day off—and drew on all their resources to doggedly pursue their goals.

UNCERTAIN CITIZENSHIP

Eating as little as they could, sleeping in a room with a bare concrete floor and no heating through the cold Santiago winter, working in precarious employment, and without legal status, in Chile Luz María and Wilson were living outside the bounds of some of the most basic conditions for inclusion in society. In Bolivia, too, they had experienced multiple exclusions, which had eventually led to their migration. Throughout this book I offer an understanding of why and how the manifold, overlapping exclusions experienced by migrants like Luz María and Wilson are occurring within and across nation-state borders in this global South context. I also explore how migrants—sometimes with the support of migrant rights advocates—seek and aspire to greater inclusion, as Luz María and Wilson did.

Thinking in terms of migrants' *citizenship* allows for exploration of these complex patterns of exclusion and inclusion, given that citizenship is one of the most powerful mechanisms for indicating belonging. Citizenship has increasingly been understood as encompassing both possession of formal, legal status *and* the ability to access substantive rights (such as the rights to shelter and health care). By examining migrants' access to legal status and the degree to which they are able to exercise substantive rights on a day-to-day basis, it is possible to build a picture of how and why they may experience marginalization transnationally, and of how this may be challenged.

Some important work that examines migration and citizenship together in order to map these patterns of inclusion and exclusion has already been done (see chapter 1). It has, however, been overwhelmingly centered on contexts of migration from the global South to the global North. This book responds to an urgent need to further examine migration outside the context of flows from South to North. The predominant focus to date on South-North migration prevents full understanding of the intricate global processes shaping the movement of people in today's world. What is particularly concerning is that many migrants in the global South, like Luz María and Wilson, are subject to human rights abuses that remain largely concealed because of the lack of attention paid to the topic. By contrast, in South-North contexts—and especially regarding Latin American migration to the United States—significant strides have been taken toward uncovering such abuses in the everyday, although certainly much more remains to be done.[1]

Following in this vein, *Uncertain Citizenship* exposes the empirical reality of migrants' lives in an underexplored South-South context. It also does broader conceptual work. I suggest that it is necessary to find new modes of thinking about the shifting and uneven ways that migrants in different parts of the world live citizenship in the everyday. To date, migrants' citizenship has often been parsed in binary terms; they are either citizens or they are noncitizens. And if not in binary terms, then their citizenship has been characterized as falling somewhere within a triadic formation; that is to say, they can be categorized as citizens, as noncitizens, or as fitting into a third space in between. Neither of these approaches, however, quite seems to convey the cross-border entanglement of fluctuating, multiple, and simultaneous exclusions from some aspects of citizenship but inclusion in others that many migrants live. This book proposes that one way in which migrants' citizenship can be comprehended is by considering their relationships to different *transnational spaces of citizenship*: legal, economic, social, and political. In what ways are migrants—simultaneously and multiply—excluded from or included in these spaces across borders? How are exclusions produced? How do migrants pursue greater inclusion?

In many cases the complex array of shifting inclusions and exclusions from citizenship experienced by the migrants with whom I worked could best be captured by viewing them through the lens of uncertainty. It is the notion of uncertainty that encapsulates the sense of past and present instability, as well as future possibility, that Luz María expressed in the long conversations we had. Uncertainty indicates the temporal and spatial mind-set triggered by migration, particularly when that migration has been compelled. It is the mind-set of being here and not-here, of constantly "going," constantly "becoming," of the present as a means to the future. Uncertainty also articulates the emotional timbre of migration: the jumble of fears, anxieties, and hopes that it generates. Uncertainty, however, does more than just capture something of the psychology of migration. In both Bolivia and Chile, Luz María had so often been living on a knife-edge, poised between slipping further into marginalization and reaching for greater security. This is the balancing act in which many migrants and potential migrants engage daily. Excluded from some dimensions, included in others, and in a constant state of flux, their everyday citizenship becomes characterized by uncertainty.

SITES AND METHODS FOR MAPPING UNCERTAINTY

The stories of uncertain citizenship that this book tells have been gathered over an extended time across different sites. They have their foundations in the part-time voluntary work I undertook in Santiago de Chile from 2010 to 2011 with the organization that I refer to here by a pseudonym as the Asociación para Migrantes, or simply the Asociación. This organization offers a range of free support services, such as legal advice, for vulnerable migrants, and also engages in wider advocacy campaigns for migrants' rights. With its members I learned a great deal about the low-wage work and xenophobia that were the daily reality for many migrants in Chile. I also realized that, although there were notable exceptions, there was a scarcity of research that drew together reflections on these daily realities. There was a particular paucity of work addressing the experiences of Bolivian migrants, even though they were the third or fourth largest group of migrants in the country and had been identified as potentially the most marginalized.[2]

Trying to uncover something more about the lived realities of low-wage Bolivian migrants, and specifically their transnational experiences of citizenship, was my guiding motivation when I returned to carry out fieldwork in 2013 and 2014. I realized that it was necessary to take a methodological approach that was responsive and agile; it was difficult to gain access to a population who often suffered discrimination and labor exploitation in Chile, which understandably made them wary of the new and untested. Some migrants had irregular legal status as well, and naturally this too made them reluctant to speak to me. In addition, the places in which they lived and worked were often isolated and hard to get to (see chapter 2).

Multi-sited ethnography provided the flexible approach that I needed. Like "classic" ethnography, in which the researcher works in one site, multi-sited ethnography is grounded in participant observation. A concern with what people are *actually doing* makes participant observation a method that, as Mike Crang and Ian Cook put it, is able to effectively "engage . . . with 'real world' messiness."[3] As a consequence, participant observation is particularly appropriate for researching people's everyday engagement with citizenship. Moreover, its emphasis on spending extended periods of time in the research context enables the building of relationships of trust, which is especially important when working with marginalized groups. Ethnography also allows, however, for the incorporation of methods other than participant observation, most commonly interviews. Interviews are particularly useful for understanding *why* people might engage in the practices that they do, offering an opportunity to learn more about people's personal narratives and identities.

While both approaches use the same methods, the difference between single-sited and multi-sited ethnography is that the latter is especially concerned with acknowledging the multitudinous connections of places across space and time. First developed by anthropologist George Marcus, it is an approach "designed around chains, paths, threads, conjunctions, or juxtapositions of locations in which the ethnographer establishes some form of literal, physical presence, with an explicit, posited logic of association or connection among sites."[4] This can be established by "following" people, things, or ideas, and thus it is a methodology that permits (and requires) a degree of flexibility.[5] Consequently, multi-sited ethnography is well suited to studies of migration. It reflects a transnational social spaces perspective on migration because it understands space as socially constructed and not necessarily bound to the nation-state (see chapter 2). As Anna Amelina and Thomas Faist contend, multi-sited ethnography therefore allows for a more holistic understanding of the different cultures, contexts, and identities that influence migrants' daily lives.[6] It also provided me with the tools for mapping uncertainty as I pieced together what I realized was the defining logic linking together migrants' experiences of the places I spent time in (see chapter 2).

I began my research in Chile's capital, Santiago, before heading to Arica in the very North of the country on the border with Bolivia and Peru (see map 1 for an indication of my field sites). There are large numbers of Bolivian migrants in both Santiago and Arica. From Arica, I traveled twice to Bolivia to get a better sense of the places of origin of the migrants I was meeting in Chile and of their lived experiences of citizenship. I met some of their family members and friends in La Paz, El Alto, and Santa Cruz, and in Oruro I discovered a great deal about how claims to citizenship may be expressed through carnival dance, a practice of citizenship that Bolivians take with them across borders. In addition to participant observation in these sites and the everyday engagement with migrants that this entailed, I carried out sixty formal interviews with migrants in Chile: twenty in Arica and twenty in Santiago.

MAP 1. Fieldwork sites in Chile and Bolivia. Credit: Edward Oliver, Queen Mary University of London, 2015.

I also worked closely with the Asociación throughout this time, volunteering for about twenty hours a week in the group's offices in Santiago, Arica, and El Alto, doing whatever I could to be useful. In Santiago I also rehearsed and performed with the Bolivian migrant dance fraternity Corazón de Tinkus (a pseudonym). Finally, I conducted interviews and had many informal conversations with representatives of various migrant organizations, local government, and the Bolivian consulate, among other institutions. In this book I have given pseudonyms to all of the people whom I interviewed and spoke with, as well as to the migrant organizations with which I had contact. I have also been deliberately vague in providing geographic identifiers of some of the places to which I refer, to further protect the identity of those who participated in this research. Quotes and observations are based on taped audiorecordings and my typed and handwritten notes. All translations are my own unless otherwise indicated.

It is important to note that throughout this book I try to pay attention to the specific, context-dependent ways in which participants referred to their social identities (e.g., class) and to the ways in which they spoke about experiences of discrimination, when this was relevant. Overlapping hierarchies of race, class, and gender remain deeply embedded in both Chile and Bolivia. While race, class, and gender are socially constructed systems that are the product of particular histories, the consequences of their construction are real and material.[7] By reflecting the language of identity that participants used, I hope to better capture the complexities of how people understand and present their social identities and what this means in relation to stratified systems of race, class, and gender. Therefore, for example, if someone actively self-identified as Aymara, or as being *de clase media* (middle class), I state this. If, however, people expressed their identity through describing themselves as speaking some Aymara and having Aymara parents, or as coming from a family *de bajos recursos* (with limited resources), I note that fact.

My *own* social identities, of course, had an impact on my interactions with participants and therefore ultimately on the knowledge produced in the course of the research. A white woman of New Zealand and British nationality, how I identified myself, and the ways in which my identities were categorized by others, affected the relationships I could build with organizations and participants in multiple ways. The most straightforward relationships I built, and built on, were those with the Asociación. Having been a volunteer in the Santiago office, I already knew several of the people who worked there, and they were quick to introduce me to others and connect me with those in Arica and in the Bolivia office in El Alto. Moreover, the staff and volunteers shared progressive values and a commitment to research-led, reflexive, and multiscalar practice that focused on directly supporting individual migrants; advocating for migrants' rights at the highest levels of government; and working with public officials, health-care workers, and teachers who interacted with migrants daily. The relationships we built were ones of learning and mutual respect, and the practical and intellectual support that so many members of the Asociación across all three offices offered me was invaluable.

The relationships I could build with other organizations and individuals were more varied. It is difficult to comprehend and convey the multifaceted ways in which one is perceived by others. Nevertheless, there were certain responses from people associated with other migrant organizations, from those in government and relevant institutions, and from employers of migrant workers, as well as in other everyday encounters, that were particularly salient. First, my whiteness and foreign nationality afforded me privileged access to certain people and spaces, most notably the offices of government or municipal workers, both in Chile and Bolivia. This was apparent when, having had no success contacting the Bolivian consulate in Santiago by e-mail or telephone, I went in person to try to arrange an appointment to speak to someone. Upon entering the building, I was ushered straight to the reception desk, even though there were other people—mainly Bolivian—waiting to be seen. After I introduced myself and explained the purpose of my visit, one of the consuls cleared time to speak to me then and there. I felt very discomforted by this obvious indication of the power of white, foreign privilege; looking sheepishly at the people waiting in the queue, I asked, "But, are you sure? If you're busy, I can come another day, no problem." The motive behind my question was not understood by the consul or the receptionist, however, and resulted in confusion about *my* availability, leading me to hurriedly say, "No, no, it's fine, let's talk now," and follow the consul to his spacious, wood-paneled office.

On other occasions, when speaking to male representatives of some organizations or to some male employers of migrants—as well as in ordinary exchanges in my day-to-day life—I was assessed as naive and in need of assistance. This reflected certain attitudes toward women more generally but seemed to be made more acute by the fact that I was foreign and by my slightly accented Spanish, with the occasional misspoken word. I was commonly referred to as "gringa" or even "rubiecita" (little blonde) by such interlocutors. Being thus perceived as ingenuous and perhaps malleable meant that I was exposed in an especially overt way to the discriminatory discourses and stereotypes that shape hierarchies of race, gender, and class. I learned that when a sentence began with "Mira, yo te cuento la verdad" ("Look, I'll tell you the truth") in a tone that dropped below the normal conversational register, what followed would often expose ugly prejudices. In Chile I would be told, for example, that Bolivians are "sumisivos" (submissive) or "un poquito más lento" ("a little bit slower"), which is why "les cuesta integrarse" ("it is hard for them to integrate").

In addition to the perceptions of gendered näiveté that invited this kind of comment, it also clearly had to do with perceptions of my race and class, whereby my whiteness, and the way in which this situated me in relation to my own countries' legacies of colonialism, racism, and oppression, was interpreted as a sign that

I would be willingly complicit in such confidences.[8] It is worth noting that there were occasions on which women as well as men expressed such sentiments to me, but this was not as common—which isn't to say that some women did not hold these prejudices, just that they were not as forthcoming in expressing themselves to me in this way. I found these attitudes and comments deeply offensive, as they flew totally in the face of my personal antiracist and feminist beliefs, and I struggled with how to respond. This was particularly challenging in an interview situation because I was grateful for the time taken to speak to me, and it was also important for my research to comprehend the attitudes of the representatives of organizations, institutions, and employers of migrant workers, even when these were offensive to me. I would try hard not to acquiesce with nods or murmurs to views I found reprehensible, maintaining a neutral expression when I could, although I was never comfortable doing this, feeling as though I were compromising my values.

Outside of an interview context, in an "everyday" setting, I did try to challenge the discriminatory views I encountered as far as I could, but again, this was always tinged with a sense of insufficiency. One weekday afternoon, I was putting up posters on behalf of the Asociación on lampposts and fences outside the bus terminal in Arica, having checked with the terminal authorities that I was allowed to do this. The posters advertised the support services available through the Asociación and expressed a positive message about migration. One of the fences I had selected was next to a taxi rank, where there were five male drivers leaning on their cars, waiting for passengers. There was no one else around. They watched me intently as I set to putting up the posters, and one finally said loudly to the other, "¿Qué hace esa gringa poniendo posters sobre los inmigrantes?" ("What's that gringa doing putting up posters about immigrants?"). Then another turned and addressed this question to me, before he and two of the others let rip with a tirade of antimigrant vitriol.

Shocked, I gave a stuttering explanation of the services the Asociación offered and why it offered them, stating that the terminal authorities were supportive of the posters. Then I turned around and continued putting up the poster I had been pinning. The most aggressive driver taunted me, saying, "We'll just rip them down." Trying not to show I was affected, I finished what I was doing and walked into the bus terminal without turning around. Shaken and tearful, I also felt impotent and inadequate. I knew that no matter how unpleasant this incident had been, it was nothing compared to the everyday racism to which many of the migrants I worked with were subjected, which I could never comprehend, given my white privilege. I felt I should have done a better job of defending my antiracist principles and given a less tongue-tied response.

A very different response generated by perceptions of my race, class, and gender, and of the research I was doing, was wariness, particularly on the part of some migrant organization representatives. This was the case during my initial encounters with Corazón de Tinkus, the migrant dance fraternity with which I ultimately rehearsed and performed. The group leader, Antony, was extremely troubled by the difficulties and discrimination faced by Bolivian migrants in Chile and was unwilling to engage with me on the issue of Bolivian migration to Chile until he was certain that I shared his views on and sensitivity to the issues migrants faced. He also questioned whether my project would be beneficial to me but not to those I worked with. I thought, and still think, that this was an admirable and valid concern, one that I must continually try to address. At the time—and in general in my conversations with those who were involved in the research—I explained that realistically the short-term, direct benefits would be small, and that I hoped that there might be longer-term (if still limited) outcomes through the eventual sharing of the results of the project with academics, migrant organizations, and policy makers. I also told Antony about my connection to the Asociación, explaining that I always passed on information about it to migrant participants who did not know about its services. In this way, I tried to ensure that my encounters with migrant participants would have some direct potential benefit for them if they were in need of legal or other assistance.

In terms of the relationships I formed with migrant participants more broadly, above all these were colored by the great kindness, openness, and trust with which I was received, once any first concerns about confidentiality and anonymity had been addressed. We would laugh and joke together, and I would share experiences of my life, too. The terms of address in initially reserved relationships would move from the formal *Usted* to the informal *tú*, and women who had started off calling me *señorita* came to refer to me instead by the affectionate *amiga* or *mamita*. Nevertheless, there were still moments that served as important reminders of the differences between our life situations. I remember drawing in a sharp breath at the end of one exchange with Magdalena, who worked as a live-in *nana* (maid). A serious conversation had evolved into kidding around about managing relationships and juggling commitments, and we were both laughing when suddenly she said, touching my arm, "Hey, I know! I could come and work as your *nana* and look after your children [when you have them]!" Struck by how easily she said this, I laughed awkwardly and made a mumbled comment about how I wouldn't have a *nana*, and the conversation moved on. The truth inherent in her observation about our vastly different circumstances stayed with me, however.

I feel very fortunate to have been invited to glimpse the lives of the migrants I worked with and to have been trusted to share the stories told to me. These stories, and the living and working conditions I witnessed, often moved me profoundly and certainly stood in stark contrast to my own privilege. I do not see either this emotional response, or awareness of the power implications of my own positionality, as things to be written out of these pages in a mythical pursuit of "objectivity."

Rather, my analysis is led by my sense of how wrong it is that these imbalances and injustices can exist.

ORGANIZATION OF THE BOOK

I structure this analysis primarily around the four spaces of transnational citizenship I identified in the research: legal, economic, social, and political. I consider migrants' relationships to each through the lens of uncertainty and take into account the overlaps among them. Prior to this, however, chapter 1, "Citizenship, Migration, and Uncertainty," expands on the conceptual framing of the book, bringing together literature from political philosophy, on citizenship in Latin America, and from migration studies. In doing so, it also sketches histories of citizenship and migration in Chile and Bolivia. This is complemented by chapter 2, "Places of Uncertain Citizenship," which moves from this more theoretical discussion to focus on lived experiences of uncertain citizenship. In it, I construct detailed ethnographic accounts of six "places of uncertain citizenship" inhabited and passed through by the migrants whose stories form the center of this book. These places were nodal points within overlapping transnational spaces of citizenship; they were physical manifestations of what it means to live uncertain citizenship. This embodied understanding of the lived reality of uncertain citizenship, articulated through particular places, provides the jumping-off point for exploration of migrants' relationships to transnational spaces of citizenship.

Chapter 3, "*Papeleo*," begins this exploration by examining migrants' multiple transitions between (ir)regular legal statuses as they are excluded from, and seek inclusion within, the transnational space of legal citizenship. Centered around the motif of *papeleo* (paperwork/red tape), the chapter examines how this transnational space of legal citizenship and migrants' positions within it are constructed. It suggests that this occurs through interactions between legislation as it exists "on paper," its (often discriminatory) application by officials "through paper," and the practices of "presenting papers" in which migrants engage, sometimes with the support of a migrant organization.

Leading on from this, chapter 4, "*¿El Sueño Chileno?*," is concerned with economic citizenship and the quest for *el sueño chileno* (the Chilean dream).[9] Taking a transnational perspective on economic citizenship and comprehending it as more than just access to decent work, it seeks first to capture the economic marginalization in Bolivia that often acted as a catalyst for pursuing *el sueño chileno*. The latter part of the chapter reflects on the degree to which *el sueño chileno* was realized after migrants crossed the border. It has a particular focus on employment experiences in wholesale garment retail, agriculture, and domestic work and includes reflections on a case of trafficking for labor exploitation uncovered in the course of my fieldwork. The chapter considers the ways in which both structural processes and the agentic practices of migrants contribute to their ability to access the space of economic citizenship across borders, and thus to their experiences of uncertainty.

The emphasis on both structure and agency carries over into chapter 5, "*Solidaridad*," which uncovers the degree to which those with whom I worked are often excluded transnationally from social citizenship. The transnational space of social citizenship is defined in terms of tangible rights to shelter, education, and health care, but also encompasses the less tangible right to family life and the necessity of having "social support." Migrants' experiences in relation to each of these domains are discussed, highlighting the worrying tendency toward a lack of *solidaridad* (solidarity) from Chilean service providers; a case study of six migrant women's experiences of pregnancy and birth in Chile attests to this particularly.

Chapter 6, "*¿De Dónde Somos? ¡De Bolivia!*," provides a rather different angle on migration and political citizenship. Emphasis has often been placed on migrants' formal political practices (e.g., voting) or on informal political practices that fall more within global North concepts of "the political" (e.g., union participation). The Bolivian migrants in Chile whom I encountered did not generally engage in these kinds of practices, as this chapter outlines. Through an account of my time with Corazón de Tinkus I reveal, however, the ways in which performing Bolivian carnival dances in public spaces in Chile can be read as a transnational citizenship practice within the realm of the political. So, while migrants were excluded from political citizenship in the sense in which it is often understood, dancing in public spaces, accompanied by the cry "*¿De dónde somos? ¡De Bolivia!*" ("Where're we from? From Bolivia!"), allowed them a politicized means of expressing their hope of greater future inclusion across borders. This use of dance is indicative of the germ of possibility contained within the notion of uncertainty, the proposition that animates the conclusion. It widens the scope of the book, suggesting that living uncertain citizenship is not uncommon for many migrants globally. It finds, however, that this analytic allows for both recognition and promotion of incremental steps that can be taken toward increased inclusion in transnational spaces of citizenship.

1

Citizenship, Migration, and Uncertainty

Predicated on being a "full member of a community," citizenship acts to include and exclude.[1] Citizens must be constructed in opposition to an "other," and frequently that "other" has been a migrant. Nevertheless, the boundaries between citizen and migrant are, and always have been, blurred. As Engin Isin argues, "[C]itizenship and otherness are . . . really not two different conditions, but two aspects of the ontological condition that makes politics possible."[2] In this chapter I am interested in how these two aspects have been understood as fitting together. I trace the origins of citizenship, examine critiques of the classic liberal interpretation, and explore iterations of citizenship in Latin American contexts. I then similarly outline how interpretations of the processes lived by migrants have changed over time, also providing a brief account of migration in and from Bolivia and to Chile. This serves to enable the final discussion, which draws together perspectives on citizenship and migration with work on uncertainty to develop the twin concepts of *transnational spaces of citizenship* and *uncertain citizenship*.

CITIZENSHIP

Broadly speaking, there have been two main politico-philosophical schools of citizenship: the liberal and civic republican traditions.[3] The foundations of the liberal tradition of citizenship can be found in John Locke's *Two Treatises of Government* (1689), as well as in the US Bill of Rights (1789) and the French Declaration of the Rights of Man and of the Citizen (1789). This tradition holds at its core the values of individual liberty—conceived of as "negative freedom," or the freedom to do what one likes as long as it does not impede others' right to do the same—and the right to property. Participation of the citizenry in the running of society is largely through voting and the payment of taxes. This liberal notion of citizenship was reformulated in the mid-twentieth century in T. H. Marshall's seminal work *Citizenship and Social Class*.[4] While maintaining a focus on the individual, he incorporated the idea of "social rights" as being crucial to citizenship in addition to civil and political rights. As those before him had, he saw the state as bestowing these rights on those it governs. He contended that the provision of rights had expanded progressively from civil to political to social rights.

In contrast to the liberal tradition, the civic republican tradition highlights the collective rather than the individual. Its roots can be traced back further than those of the liberal tradition, to Aristotle and the Athenian city-state.[5] While both traditions conceive of the individual as preexistent to and choosing to enter into society, in the liberal tradition the individual then has minimal responsibilities, and political engagement occurs through representation. In the civic republican tradition, by contrast, direct political participation is vital; as Stephen Castles and Alastair Davidson put it, this is a tradition "based on popular wisdom" through the active engagement of all in the creation and upholding of laws.[6]

In the twentieth century, communitarianism emerged as a "cousin" of civic republicanism, and its followers further developed arguments about the importance of community and the collective in order to challenge the individualistic focus of liberal interpretations of citizenship.[7] Crucially, communitarians, perhaps most notably Michael Sandel, call into question the liberal notion that the individual is "unencumbered"—that is, rational, autonomous, and self-sufficient.[8] Rather, they argue, the individual is very much "encumbered" by community because, as Alison Assiter writes, humans are "social beings."[9] Thus our actions as citizens are influenced by our relationships to our community and cannot be separated from them (in other words, the individual is not preexistent to society). While considered to offer valuable contributions regarding how we might better comprehend citizenship, communitarianism has not been without its critics.[10] Indeed, both the broadly liberal and broadly civic republican traditions and their offshoots have been strongly critiqued from a variety of theoretical perspectives, not least a feminist one.

The feminist critique of both liberal and civic republican traditions of citizenship is founded on an analysis of *who* the citizen is supposed to be. Feminist interrogations of this question expose the answer to be, as Ruth Lister explains, "a definitely male citizen, and a white heterosexual, non-disabled one at that" under the "universalist cloak of the abstract, disembodied individual."[11] The supposedly universal, gender-neutral citizen is in fact profoundly gendered because of the classic binary created between public and private spheres, whereby the rational and abstract is associated with the public sphere and masculinity and the emotional and embodied with the private sphere and femininity.[12] The citizen acts in the public sphere and so must be rational, capable of abstraction, and therefore masculine.[13] Moreover, as those working in the communitarian tradition had identified, this rational, autonomous citizen fits within a highly individualistic concept of citizenship. While a communitarian perspective did attempt to overcome the individualistic approach of liberal citizenship and, to a lesser extent, civic republicanism, feminist theorists such as Iris Young criticized communitarianism for its reification of the idea of community and therefore its failure to admit difference.[14]

More recent understandings of citizenship, such as Ruth Lister's, have highlighted the fluidity and multiplicity of identity and group belonging while maintaining the ideal of universal rights for all.[15] Through a focus on agency, she proposes a synthesis of the liberal and civic republican traditions:

> Citizenship as participation [civic republican tradition] represents an expression of human agency in the political arena, broadly defined; citizenship as rights [liberal tradition] enables people to act as agents. Moreover, citizenship rights are not fixed. They remain the object of political struggles to defend, reinterpret and extend them. Who is involved in these struggles, where they are placed in the political hierarchy and the political power and influence they can yield will help to determine the outcomes. Citizenship thus emerges as a dynamic concept in which process and outcome stand in a dialectical relationship to each other.[16]

Thus, Lister is advocating an understanding of citizenship as both "being" and "doing," as a status and a practice. Furthermore, she argues that citizenship occurs on multiple levels, blurring the perceived gap between public and private and giving prominence to the idea that the experience of citizenship is not limited to state-level interactions but also includes participation in more "informal" arenas, such as collective participation in community organizations. As Luin Goldring indicates, Lister is also highly aware of the impact of social identities, such as gender, on the ability of individuals to act at different levels.[17]

Iterations of Citizenship in Latin America

In the Latin American context, Bryan Roberts, though not writing from an overtly feminist standpoint, has taken a similar approach. He understands citizenship as "always negotiated[,] since by their participation citizens can change their rights and obligations and, equally, governing elites may seek to limit or influence these changes as a means of consolidating their power."[18] Roberts traces the history of citizenship in Latin America back to the aftermath of the wars of independence, a period that saw the adoption of liberal constitutions in many Latin American countries, often directly modeled on those of the United States or France. He argues, however, that following these liberal beginnings, "the evolution of citizenship in Latin America is not linear, nor did the extension of one set of rights, whether civil, political or social, necessarily entail the extension of others."[19] He is also cognizant of the different ways in which citizenship in Latin America is and has been experienced according to gender and ethnic identities, and he emphasizes particularly the significant exclusions suffered by indigenous populations. Thus, Roberts disrupts Marshall's argument regarding the linear way in which the provision of citizenship rights expanded, in addition to arguing for an understanding of citizenship much more akin to Lister's.[20]

Indeed, Roberts argues that in the majority of Latin American countries, from the 1940s to the 1970s *social* rights were the first "set" of rights to be extended to the population in a relatively comprehensive fashion, although there were still significant gaps in provision. He suggests that this reflected the priorities of both the growing urban poor, for whom education, health, and other social welfare provisions were of obvious importance, and the state and the elite, with whom the developmentalist theories of the time, with their emphasis on health and education as the keys to development, resonated strongly. Moreover, the expansion of social rights represented a way for the state and elite to quell and co-opt potential discontent from the working classes. Bolivia arguably fits within this assessment to a considerable degree, and Chile to a lesser extent (as Roberts acknowledges).

The 1930s and 1940s in Bolivia were a period of deep unrest and turbulence after the 1932–1935 Chaco War with Paraguay, which was a disaster for Bolivia. Huge swathes of Bolivian territory were captured, and the human cost was staggering.[21] By the end of the war many of the men who had fought were disgusted with the corruption, racism, and classism of the military elite, and more broadly with the Bolivian oligarchy and social inequalities in the country. This sentiment hardened into political resolve, spawning various movements and parties. The one that ultimately came to the fore in 1952 was the Movimiento Nacional Revolucionario (National Revolutionary Movement), led by a coalition of members of the urban middle class and workers. A coup d'état was staged, which overthrew the established order.

From these beginnings the revolution burgeoned in the coming years into an attempt at fairly sweeping social and economic change as increasing numbers of more radical miners and peasants joined the movement. One of the consequences of the revolution was agrarian reform, and large haciendas in the western altiplano were seized and redistributed to the indigenous population. Another key consequence was the expansion of health care and provision of education. Civil and political rights were also expanded, most notably through the enfranchisement of indigenous people and women. Nevertheless, the eventual outcomes of the revolution were mixed, and the degree to which it produced a lasting social change has been debated.[22] In particular, serious violations of indigenous peoples' civil rights very much persisted, and politics continued to be highly volatile in Bolivia.

The Chilean context was somewhat different, and until 1973 Chile had one of the strongest democratic traditions in Latin America. There was a well-developed party system and high levels of political participation among large sectors of the population, particularly from the 1930s onward as enfranchisement gradually expanded; universal suffrage was achieved in 1947 when women won the right to vote. During this period there was marked investment in health, education, and social services, which did bear some fruit, although much of the population still lived in poverty.[23] Throughout the 1960s, during the presidencies of the right-wing independent Jorge Alessandri (1958–1964) and particularly that of the centrist Christian Democrat Eduardo Frei (1964–1970), political awareness and discontent with the status quo, especially the serious social inequalities within the country, increased dramatically. The Frei government did bring about some not insignificant changes, including the expansion of state ownership of the copper mines and a program of agrarian reform. However, there was a sense of frustration that change had not been deep enough nor sufficiently far-reaching.[24] During the late 1960s, many who were disillusioned found in the Unidad Popular (UP, Popular Unity)—a coalition of left-wing parties led by Salvador Allende—a party that expressed these frustrations and offered a solution: the "Chilean road to socialism."

Elected by a narrow margin in 1970, Allende and the UP initially fostered a heady sense of optimism among their supporters. This rapidly deteriorated, however, as the country became riven by division and anger. The coup d'état of September 11, 1973, irrevocably changed the course of Chile's history and the fabric of its society.[25] As is well-known, the subsequent seventeen years of dictatorship under General Pinochet saw massive human rights abuses, including the murder or disappearance of more than 2,200 people by government agents and the torture of nearly 30,000.[26] It also resulted in the exile of approximately 200,000 people, 2 percent of Chile's 1973 population.[27] Civil and political rights were effectively entirely repressed. In addition, Chile became the first testing ground for neoliberal ideology and was thus subject to particularly extreme versions of policies of privatization, deregulation, and cuts to social spending. This stalled Chile's progress in terms of social welfare and had a deleterious impact on equality in the country.[28]

Similar regimes took over throughout the Southern Cone in this period. Nor was Bolivia unaffected. Indeed, the 1970s and early 1980s was an especially chaotic and brutal epoch in Bolivian politics. From 1971 to 1978 the country was under the dictatorship of General Hugo Banzer. Then, over just four years, from 1978 to 1982, there were three different regimes: a transitional military regime following the Banzer dictatorship, a brief period of civilian rule, and then the forceful installation of a military junta initially headed by General Luis Garcia Meza. A period of extreme violence and repression, it left the economy devastated due to corruption and mismanagement by both the state and private sectors. Democratic, civilian government returned in 1982 under the presidency of Hernán Siles Zuazo, swiftly followed by Víctor Paz Estenssoro in 1985, who assumed the presidency for the third time. In his first year back in power, Paz Estenssoro—infamously—implemented Decreto Supremo no. 21060. In keeping with what was at that time common economic policy in the region and globally, it incorporated a series of tough, orthodox measures intended to bring the economy under control, thus ushering in an era of neoliberalism in Bolivia as well.[29]

Roberts contends that throughout the 1970s and 1980s, with this movement toward neoliberal economic policies throughout most of the region, the emphasis in terms of citizenship rights shifted to the civil and political. This was in part because, as indicated, the rollout of neoliberal policies entailed cuts to social service provisions; subsequently, "by throwing more of the responsibility for social and economic welfare onto the populace, states, both directly and indirectly, promote[d] the independent organization of citizens."[30] Moreover, in the dictatorships of the Southern Cone during these decades, groups began to organize—often putting themselves in great danger—to defend their civil and political rights. They played a key role in the eventual return to democracy in Chile in 1990 and in the rest of the Southern Cone.[31]

The legacy of dictatorship has been long-lasting, however. One respect in which this has made itself felt in the Chilean context (and others) is that, as Patricia Richards argues, "the imposition of neoliberal reform represented a transformation of the content of citizenship."[32] The key elements of this transformation, she continues, are that it has reduced "the role of citizens . . . to voting, consuming, and participating in community projects to make up for the loss of state services, rather than making demands on the state."[33] Throughout the 1990s and into the 2000s, this change has gone hand in hand with a shift toward "multiculturalism" in many Latin American countries, resulting in what has been critically referred to as "neoliberal multiculturalism."[34] Under the policies of such a framework there may be official recognition of cultural differences, for example, through celebration of the more "folkloric" elements of indigenous culture. This is not, however, accompanied by serious attempts to redress the severe social, political, and economic disadvantages faced by indigenous peoples and other historically oppressed groups. While falling within the paradigm of "neoliberal multiculturalism," as Richards argues, Chile has been a "particularly reticent" case with respect to enacting *both* policies of cultural recognition *and* policies that would have substantive impacts on indigenous populations.[35] Around 9 percent of the Chilean population self-identifies as belonging to one of Chile's nine officially recognized indigenous peoples, 84 percent of whom self-identify as Mapuche.[36] They continue to suffer serious discrimination.[37]

Until the election of Evo Morales in 2005, Bolivia was also considered a clear, if different, example of neoliberal multiculturalism.[38] This changed, however, following Morales's extraordinary victory after several years of turmoil and unrest. Protests had centered on indigenous rights and access to natural resources, and they reached a crisis point in conflicts that came to be known as the Guerra del Agua (Water War) in Cochabamba in 2000 and the Guerra del Gas (Gas War) in El Alto in 2003. Morales's rise to power during this period was greeted with jubilation by those on the left in Bolivia, and globally, and was hailed as opening up new "post-multicultural" possibilities for citizenship.[39] The reality has been somewhat different. As Nancy Postero outlines, there *have* been significant changes under the Morales government.[40] In Bolivia, 40 to 60 percent of the population self-identifies as belonging to one of thirty-six indigenous peoples—Quechua, Aymara, Chiquitano, and Guaraní are the largest groups—and indigenous peoples have suffered centuries of oppression.[41] The symbolic importance of having an indigenous president has therefore been huge, as has that of the 2009 constitution, which proclaims Bolivia to be a plurinational, communitarian state and establishes particular rights for indigenous peoples. Nevertheless, as Postero indicates, "the emancipatory language about indigenous rights in the constitution obscures the more important results of the constitution: the overarching power of the central state in the new model" and the restrictions placed on indigenous autonomy.[42] Moreover, the continued pursuit of hydrocarbon extraction as a strategy for economic growth has been strongly criticized, as have other projects (such as the road to be built through the TIPNIS national park and protected area) that have serious environmental consequences and negatively affect certain indigenous groups.[43]

Bryan Roberts's astute assessment of the evolution of citizenship in Latin America as uneven and complex continues to ring true, at least in the cases of Chile and Bolivia. Ongoing struggles over its meanings and contents abound. This is increasingly reflected in a rich and growing body of work—such as that by Teresa Caldeira, Daniel Goldstein, James Holston, Sian Lazar, and Patricia Richards—that examines how traditionally marginalized groups seek to express an alternative vision of citizenship and/or demand the substantive rights that are so often denied them, in spite of their nominal formal citizenship status.[44] This scholarship explores how nonstate actors may play a crucial part in shaping and pushing the boundaries of citizenship in a process that is, as Étienne Balibar notes, always "*imparfaite*."[45] Nevertheless, it also considers the ways in which the top-down ideas—or "regimes"—of citizenship prevalent in each nation-state also have a fundamental role in this process, as do the actions of state actors, who will interpret these "regimes" in different, nonmonolithic ways.[46]

Both this work on the anthropology and sociology of citizenship in Latin America and the synthesis of the two traditions of citizenship from a feminist perspective that comes from within political theory have influenced how I think about citizenship in this book. Citizenship is a process that is constantly under construction. It is built in part "from below" through the everyday practices of ordinary people who, irrespective of their uniform possession of formal citizenship status, have differentiated access—contingent on their social identities—to the substantive rights of citizenship. Their practices may either support or contest the hegemonic narrative of citizenship promoted by the state; this is a narrative that will vary according to history and location, as will the practices in which ordinary people may engage. Already complex, the ways in which citizenship is lived and constructed in the everyday are further complicated by the movement of people across nation-state borders.

MIGRATION

I understand migration across nation-state borders from a transnational perspective. That is, I take the view that, in the words of Linda Basch, Nina Glick-Schiller, and Cristina Szanton-Blanc, "immigrants forge and sustain multi-stranded social relations that link together their societies of origin and settlement."[47] This now widely accepted approach to the study of migration emerged in the late 1980s and early 1990s to counter prior understandings of migration as entailing a definitive cutting of ties with the country of origin.

As migration increased in the late nineteenth century, the process experienced by migrants upon arriving in a different nation-state was predominantly understood as one of assimilation. The "melting pot" analogy was used to indicate how the majority group would remain largely unchanged by the absorption of the new migrant minority group, and the minority group would only retain some limited features of "ethnic" identification.[48] Heralded particularly by Nathan Glazer and Daniel Moynihan's 1970 publication *Beyond the Melting Pot*, it was gradually recognized, however, that not all migrants were assimilating.[49] Many were, in fact, retaining features of the cultures of their countries of origin. One reaction to this was the emergence of multiculturalism as an approach to migration in academia and the policy arena. Approaching migration from the perspective of multiculturalism, difference is recognized and acknowledged, and migrants are encouraged to maintain cultural practices from their countries of origin. However, they are encouraged to do this from a position that is embedded within the "settlement country," thus forming a "cultural mosaic" or "tapestry" as opposed to a "melting pot."[50]

While purporting to be very different, in a certain sense assimilation and multiculturalism are two sides of the same coin.[51] They are both based on the notion of the nation-state and society as being one and the same.[52] From both perspectives, migration is understood as a discrete event, a decisive break in the life of migrants as they move from one nation-state to another. Migrants renounce their ties to their countries of origin and enter into some form of integration process in the settlement country. It is not possible to remain part of more than one geographically bounded society. In the case of assimilation, migrants adapt completely to a new way of life. In the case of multiculturalism, they retain aspects of their cultural heritage but nonetheless focus on doing so within the context of the settlement country, and as mentioned above with respect to indigenous peoples, the focus is usually on the retention of the "folkloric" aspects of their culture.

By contrast, a transnational approach suggests that migrants maintain a thick web of networks that connect them to both countries. These connections play a vital role in their daily lives. It has become increasingly common to think about migrants' experiences of moving and "settling" from this viewpoint. Nevertheless, the concept of transnationalism has not been without its critics. The extent to which migrants really do maintain transnational ties has been debated, with some suggesting that it has been exaggerated.[53]

This is because transnationalism has sometimes been understood in terms of the practices in which individual migrants engage, such as visiting their countries of origin.[54] This certainly does lead to a fairly limited definition of what constitutes engagement in transnationalism; there may, for example, be extended periods during which individual migrants do not visit their countries of origin.[55] But that is not to say that they do not *think* about their countries of origin and engage in other, less tangible, activities that nevertheless reproduce and reinforce their connections across borders. These might be things like socializing with conationals or decorating their homes in a way that incorporates the aesthetics of the places they have come from. Reflecting on these types of practices has led others to a different conceptualization of transnationalism. This interpretation understands international migration as a process occurring within, and creating, "transnational social spaces."[56]

Peggy Levitt and Bernadette Jaworsky define "transnational social spaces" as "arenas" that "are multi-layered and multi-sited, including not just the home and host countries but other sites around the world that connect migrants to their conationals and coreligionists. Both migrants and nonmigrants occupy them because the flow of people, money, and 'social remittances' (ideas, norms, practices, and identities) within these spaces is so dense, thick, and widespread that nonmigrants' lives are also transformed, even though they do not move."[57] Expanding further on the idea, Levitt and Jaworsky explain that even though few people may engage in intensive transnational activity, many more take part in occasional activities. Over time "their combined efforts add up and can alter the economies, values, and practices of entire regions."[58]

Thus, the idea of transnational social spaces challenges the "methodological nationalism" that would equate geographical, physical space with societal space.[59] It is an idea founded on the tenets that space is actively socially constructed and is a fluid and changing process.[60] A transnational social space exists beyond, and indeed may contest, the boundaries of the "national container society."[61] Nevertheless, the importance of the state in forging, shaping, and restricting the creation of transnational social spaces cannot be overlooked.[62] Not only individual migrants and nonmigrants, but also states, institutions, and businesses at the local, national, and international levels are involved in the construction of transnational social spaces. Furthermore, the degree to which individual migrants (and nonmigrants) can negotiate and control the construction of transnational social spaces is highly contingent on their gender, race, socioeconomic status, and other social identities. It is therefore important to consider migrants' relationships to transnational social spaces from an intersectional perspective.[63]

In addition to the perspective on citizenship previously discussed, a transnational social spaces approach to international migration forms one of the conceptual building blocks of this book. It is an approach informed by an understanding of space as a fluid, multidimensional process constructed through interrelations among varied actors. These actors may be states and institutions or migrant and nonmigrant individuals. Individual actors' ability to move within and manipulate transnational social spaces will be profoundly impacted by their intersecting social identities. As I explain at the end of this chapter, I transfer this spatial understanding of migrant transnationalism to the concept of citizenship in order to better comprehend how and why migrants are excluded from some aspects of citizenship but included in others across nation-state borders. Recognizing the importance of history and place to the development of specific transnational spaces of migration, prior to this I turn, however, to outline approaches to migration studies taken in South-South contexts and examine migration flows specifically in the Bolivian-Chilean context.

South-South Migration

Katja Hujo and Nicola Piper point to a "dearth of knowledge on the dynamics of migration between countries in the South" and in general a profound lack of research on the topic.[64] Arguably largely responsible for the scarcity of work on South-South migration is the northern bias of academia more widely.[65] Susanne Melde and colleagues remind us that most funders are located in the North, resulting in relatively little support for research that examines migration *within* the global South, given the many northern anxieties surrounding migration flows to the North from the South.[66] This is in addition to the more generalized tendency for migration research to focus on short-term projects that will offer solutions to "migration problems," which leads to a subsequent lack of study of the "nature, causes, and consequences of migration," as Mohamed Berriane and Hein de Haas maintain.[67]

Nevertheless, a slow but steady series of attempts have been made to seriously address the flows that conform what is estimated to be nearly half of all international migration.[68] Much of this work has focused on the "migration-development nexus," and there has been a tendency to address the potential for migrants to be "agents of development"—for example, through remittance sending. This focus can be to the neglect of the many other important aspects of the everyday lived experiences of migrants addressed in the transnational studies literature, which looks predominantly at South-North migration.[69]

Still, there *is* some research that is beginning to address these lacunae, as in the case of the important, incipient work on migration in Chile and from Bolivia, with which I engage throughout this book. While I agree wholeheartedly with Hujo and Piper and others that there is a severe paucity of research on South-South migration, I suggest that they may potentially fall into one of the traps of northern academic bias through neglect of some research on the subject published *in* the South, often in languages other than English.[70] Additionally, some research that could be considered to address "South-South migration" does not identify itself as such, preferring instead to refer specifically to the countries under study. This is understandable given the problematic nature of the terms "global South" and "global North" and the homogenizing effect they can have.[71] However, greater use of the term "South-South migration" as one way of categorizing such studies may assist with knowledge sharing and construction. In doing so, somewhat paradoxically, it may aid in promoting understanding of South-South migration as a heterogeneous phenomenon, but with marked points of difference from South-North migration—as this book endeavors to do.

The Bolivian-Chilean Context

An overview of the particular migration context under study is therefore important to understand both its specificities and the ways it fits within broader trends. In terms of Bolivian migration, it is estimated that around 706,000 Bolivians, or 6.8 percent of the Bolivian population, currently reside outside the country, although some estimates put the figure as high as 14 to 23 percent of the population.[72] While historically Bolivia pursued policies of encouraging (white, elite) immigration in order to populate what was portrayed as an "uninhabited country," for many years now it has been a country of negative net migration. This has been combined with a continuous flow of internal migration from rural to urban areas since the 1952 revolution.

As previously indicated, the effects of the revolution were complex, and its lasting impacts are debated. What is clear, however, is that the processes it set in motion sparked the beginning of a significant increase in rural-urban migration, predominantly from Aymara and Quechua communities in the western altiplano. While the agrarian reform—which was one of the major changes wrought by the revolution—did make most rural indigenous families into landowners, plots of land were not large, and they became further reduced through fragmentation due to inheritance and the population growth that followed the revolution. Combined with the increasing importance of a cash economy, the smaller size of plots made it difficult for rural indigenous inhabitants to make a living. This was particularly the case for young women, who were not necessarily favored in inheritance arrangements. They also had the greatest chance of making an income in the city, often as domestic workers, but in addition as market and street vendors. Many therefore ventured to the city as part of a family livelihood diversification strategy, or sometimes to seek a degree of independence. Thus, although both men and women left their rural communities for urban areas in large numbers from 1953 onward, young women in particular migrated.[73]

Internal migration increased particularly from 1971 to 1978, during General Hugo Banzer's dictatorship. Almost one-third of those from the rural altiplano who moved to La Paz between the years 1953 and 1980 did so in this period.[74] It was an era of massive modernization of urban areas, not just in the west of Bolivia but notably in the eastern Santa Cruz region as well. While the population had previously been clustered in the west and around the cities of La Paz, Potosí, and Oruro, people began to move eastward, with the importance of the cities of Cochabamba and Santa Cruz growing significantly. Rural-urban migration in Bolivia has continued through the present day. According to the last census in 2012, 67 percent of the population was classified as urban, compared to just 26 percent in 1952.[75] These changes in population distribution within the country have been accompanied by mass out-migration beginning in the 1970s during the political upheaval of that decade and continuing into the 1980s following the implementation of neoliberal economic policies under President Paz Estenssoro.

The immediate impact of the measures Paz Estenssoro and his government implemented could be categorized to some degree as short-term "political and fiscal successes."[76] Nonetheless, the longer-term impact was a lack of economic growth and increased social injustice. Unemployment rose to 20 percent, particularly due to the collapse of the tin industry, which also severely impacted organized labor. Working conditions became increasingly precarious for many.[77] The economic uncertainty in this period led to a marked increase in out-migration, especially to Argentina.[78]

During this period, Buenos Aires rose to prominence as a favored destination for Bolivian migrants to Argentina. Here, many migrants—predominantly women—found employment in garment manufacturing, working in small sweatshops that were generally informal and unregulated. They labored sewing precut garments for contractors for around twelve hours per day and sometimes more. Food and board were provided, but living conditions were usually poor. Moreover, workers' freedom of movement was restricted, and wages were low, particularly in the first few months, when migrants owed "debts" to their employers, who paid for their transport from Bolivia to Argentina in many cases.[79]

There are still significant numbers of Bolivians residing in Buenos Aires, and many continue to work in garment manufacturing. Following the 2001 Argentinean crisis and the devaluation of the Argentine peso, however, those Bolivians who were compelled to migrate began to look to other destinations as well, and the Bolivian population resident in Argentina declined, although in 2011 there were still approximately 345,272 Bolivians resident in Argentina.[80] Outside Latin America, Spain became a popular destination for Bolivian migrants with the resources to leave the continent.[81] This was motivated in large part by the fact that it was not necessary for Bolivians to have a visa to move to Spain until 2007. The United States was also an increasingly appealing option for those with the means to get there. From 2001 to 2008—the period during which many Bolivians moved to Spain and the United States as well as other destinations outside Latin America— the amount of money sent back to Bolivia in remittances boomed, reaching 7.4 percent of Bolivian gross domestic product (GDP) in 2007.[82] Of the remittances sent back to Bolivia in 2007, 46.2 percent came from Spain and 21.7 percent from the United States.[83]

There were many Bolivians on lower incomes, however, who could not afford to leave the continent for places like Spain and the United States, but who nonetheless still considered it vital to leave the country. While there had been marked improvements in access to health care and education since the 1970s, as Bolivia entered the twenty-first century it remained one of the poorest countries in Latin America, having suffered years of economic turmoil and neoliberal policies unfriendly to those not in the upper echelons of society. In the early 2000s, 29.7 percent of the population lived on less than US$1.90 per day, and 66.4 percent of the population lived below the national poverty line. Life expectancy at birth was just fifty-five years, and the infant mortality rate was eighty per one thousand live births.[84]

For Bolivians with limited economic resources and little formal education who were seeking better opportunities, Brazil, and particularly São Paulo, increased in popularity as a destination within Latin America from the early 2000s onward. In São Paulo as in Buenos Aires, many migrants have found work in garment manufacturing, working under similar conditions to those in Buenos Aires.[85] Demonstrating the increase in the Bolivian migrant population in Brazil, the 2010 Brazilian census recorded 38,816 Bolivian migrants resident in the country, compared to 20,394 in 2001.[86] It is likely that this significantly underrepresents the Bolivian migrant population, however; in 2011, it was estimated that there were between 50,000 and 80,000 Bolivians resident in São Paulo alone, many of whom held irregular status and were thus not recorded in the census.[87]

Further indicating the growth of the Bolivian population in Brazil, remittances sent back to Bolivia from Brazil have increased notably, from 0.6 percent of the total in 2007, to 3.8 percent in 2013, to 10.4 percent in 2017. By contrast, remittances coming from Spain decreased to 33.8 percent of the total in 2017, and those from the United States to 17.1 percent.[88] This change can be attributed to a considerable degree to the impacts of recession and austerity on Spain and the United States since the 2008 crisis, which have played a role in reducing migration to these countries and encouraging those intending to migrate to consider destinations within Latin America.[89]

The other major shift in Bolivian migration away from Argentina within Latin America has been to Chile, although there is far less information available on Bolivian migrants in Chile than on their counterparts in Brazil and Argentina. This is in spite of the significant numbers entering Chile, especially when one considers the markedly smaller population of Chile in comparison to Brazil (17.8 million and 200 million, respectively).[90] The most recent Chilean CASEN (Caracterización Socioeconómica Nacional, National Socioeconomic Characterization Survey) data estimated the Bolivian population in Chile to be 47,100 in 2015, showing a significant increase from an estimated 24,116 in 2009.[91] The remittance data for flows from Chile to Bolivia is also telling. In 2007 remittances from Chile to Bolivia accounted for just 1.6 percent of total remittances to Bolivia; by 2013 this had increased to 6.1 percent, and in 2017 this figure reached 9.5 percent.[92] As is the case for Bolivian migration flows generally, Bolivian migration to Chile is highly feminized, and in 2014 54.5 percent of all Bolivian migrants were women.[93]

The flow of Bolivian migrants into Chile seems set to continue and potentially to increase further as part of a rapidly shifting landscape of migration patterns within Latin America. As for why this may be so from the Bolivian perspective, as already outlined, the economic, social, and political outcomes of the period under Evo Morales since 2005 have been mixed, and in different, complex ways, they may contribute to the continuation of Bolivian migration. First, there have been some very marked improvements in key poverty indicators in Bolivia in the past decade. The number of those living on less than US$1.90 per day had decreased to 6.8 percent by 2016, and the number of those living below the national poverty line had also decreased, to 38.6 percent. Life expectancy at birth has increased to sixty-six years, and the infant mortality rate has decreased to thirty-eight per one thousand live births.[94]

It would be reasonable to assume that these improvements might make Bolivia a more attractive place to remain. In one of the apparent paradoxes of migration, however, there is evidence that—broadly speaking—as poverty in a country decreases, out-migration increases. This is because growing numbers of people have the necessary resources to leave the country for somewhere that is still better off than the home country (out-migration then decreases again once a country hits a certain economic level).[95] As will be made clear throughout this book, although the migrants with whom I worked were generally from lower socioeconomic backgrounds, and many came from contexts of multidimensional poverty, they were not the very poorest in society (see particularly chapter 4). As this sector of the population in Bolivia expands, it could be expected that so too would out-migration flows. Other factors may also contribute to continued migration flows from Bolivia, however, and as Hein de Haas reminds us, while "economic forces often play an important role as one of the root causes of migration . . . this alone cannot explain the actual shape of migration patterns."[96] In the Bolivian case, one sociopolitical factor that may have an impact is the sense of dissatisfaction among a growing proportion of the population who think that change under Morales is not happening fast enough, or that it is not the type of change they hoped for (see chapters 4 and 6).

In terms of Chile as a migration destination, as indicated above, part of the story behind the reduction in migration to Spain and the United States and the concurrent increase in intraregional migration in Latin America to countries such as Chile has been the impacts of recession and ongoing austerity measures. Within South America, the unrest in Brazil due to the ongoing corruption scandal at the highest levels of politics and the severe economic downturn, in addition to ongoing economic instability in Argentina, may well position Chile as an increasingly popular destination for those migrating in search of economic opportunity and relative social and political stability.

This would be consonant with the general shifts in migration to and from Chile over the past forty years. As a consequence of the exile of tens of thousands during the Pinochet dictatorship, the number of Chileans outside the country grew rapidly in the 1970s and 1980s, increasing what was already a negative net migration trend. Furthermore, very few foreigners moved to Chile during this period. While Chileans who had been in exile did gradually return following the end of the military regime, in 2005 it was estimated that over 850,000 Chileans resided outside the country.[97]

Today Chile remains a country of negative net migration, but the number of migrants residing in the country has increased exponentially since the 1990s. In 1992 there were an estimated 114,597 foreigners living in Chile, or 0.9 percent of the total population. This number has more than quadrupled, with conservative estimates putting the migrant population at 465,319 in 2015, around 2.7 percent of the population.[98] The majority—90 percent—are from other Latin American countries, and there is increasing diversity in the range of migrants' countries of origin. As already indicated, the increase in migration to Chile can largely be explained by the relatively steady economic growth and the political and social stability that Chile has experienced since the fall of the dictatorship.[99] Moreover, once a certain number of "pioneer migrants" select a destination such as Chile, their social networks across borders facilitate the arrival of more people at the same destination.[100]

Chile became a member of the OECD (Organisation for Economic Co-operation and Development) in 2010 and was the first (and to date, only) South American country to join. Thus, in some respects it is perhaps more comparable with countries considered part of the global North than with those of the global South, and this is undoubtedly part of its allure for migrants from other parts of Latin America. Nevertheless, Chile is consistently well below average with respect to many OECD social indicators.[101] The effects of years of neoliberal polices continue to reverberate; while experiencing sustained economic growth, Chile has a Gini coefficient of 0.49, making it the most unequal country in the OECD and average within Latin America.[102] Public social spending is also very low, and 14.4 percent of the population lives below the national poverty line.[103] It is thus situated in an ambiguous position between global North and global South. Migrants, and particularly Bolivian migrants, are some of the most marginalized and discriminated against people in this highly unequal society and often do not reap the benefits of living in a country considered to be one of the thirty-four most "developed" in the world.[104] While this is also true for many migrants from the global South living in the global North, it is arguably especially acute in a country like Chile that is so glaringly unequal.

The unique, in-depth qualitative perspective offered in this book sheds light on the everyday lived experiences of migrants in this context. In the chapters that follow, the similarities and differences between this and other migration destinations in both the global South and North are highlighted. By marrying perspectives on citizenship from feminist political theory and sociological and anthropological studies of Latin America with insights drawn from studies of migration that take a transnational, intersectional approach, the book also offers a fresh conceptual approach, as I explain in the next section.

CITIZENSHIP, MIGRATION, AND UNCERTAINTY

Within migration studies, there is a growing body of work that—mirroring the approach taken in the scholarship on citizenship in Latin America previously discussed—focuses on citizenship in practice in order to comprehend how it is actually experienced in the everyday as opposed to how it is normatively represented.[105] Such analyses have sometimes struggled, however, to consider holistically the "formal" and "substantive" aspects of citizenship in a way that accounts for the interactions between them, how they are produced within and across nation-state borders, and the multiple ways in which migrants may be simultaneously included in and excluded from citizenship.

A spatial perspective on citizenship and migration has been adopted by some in attempting to make such an analysis because, as Lynn Staeheli and colleagues put it, citizenship "is inseparable from the geographies of communities and the networks and relationships that link them."[106] While they have made extremely important advances, the complexity of inclusion and exclusion is not fully recognized by the approaches taken to date because spaces of citizenship have been conceptualized as binary (as spaces of citizenship/noncitizenship) or triadic (as spaces of citizenship/noncitizenship with a third space in between).[107] Where attempts have been made to overcome these binary and triadic interpretations, the focus has been on the politico-legal dimensions of citizenship, not its other substantive components.[108] The multitude of simultaneous in/exclusions from different aspects of citizenship that migrants may experience transnationally is not, therefore, as wholly accounted for as it might be.

I suggest in this book that to better capture the dynamism of migrants' citizenship, it can instead be thought of in relation to overlapping *transnational spaces of citizenship*. This reflects the approaches to migrant transnationalism and citizenship explained above. Transnational spaces of citizenship are produced through interactions between individual migrants and nonmigrants, in addition to processes initiated by states and their actors and sometimes interventions by international organizations such as the International Labour Organization. Groups within civil society, such as migrant organizations, also play a role in their production. These interactions are shaped by history and are both impacted by, and have an impact on, place. Thus, to think in terms of transnational spaces of citizenship is to take a profoundly geographical approach to comprehending the production of citizenship across nation-state boundaries in terms of both structural processes and agentic practices. Individuals' relationships to these spaces are deeply influenced by their social identities.

Reflecting on the lived experiences of migrants I worked with, I found it most useful to think about transnational spaces of citizenship as representing citizenship's legal, economic, social, and political elements, consequently reflecting both its formal and substantive components and giving due weight to each. Clearly these four spaces reference Marshall's thinking about the civil, political, and social spheres of citizenship.[109] They also build on it, however, reflecting feminist approaches to the political theory of citizenship, perspectives on the lived realities of citizenship that come from those working on and in Latin America, and the rich contributions to understandings of citizenship that have emerged from migration studies.

Primarily, the idea that these spaces are constructed through structural and agentic processes encourages thinking about citizenship not just in terms of the passive reception of rights by subjects, but also in terms of active participation, because of the emphasis on the everyday citizenship practices of migrants and other actors. Additionally, rather than thinking in terms of a linear progression of rights acquisition as Marshall did (from civil to political to social rights), this approach considers that migrants may have simultaneous, uneven access to many of these spaces of citizenship. Finally, following other feminist scholars such as Alice Kessler-Harris, Carole Pateman, and Yvonne Riaño, I expand on the definition of the social to distinguish between social and economic citizenship.[110] While Marshall considered protection from poverty a social right, he did not expand further on the economic aspect of citizenship. It has been argued, however, that economic incorporation through equal access to paid employment is fundamental to women's ability to participate as citizens, and thus the economic must be given greater weight in studies of citizenship.[111] This argument can be expanded to include other disadvantaged groups, such as migrants, given the powerful impact that nationality and migratory status, as well as gender and other identities, can have on equal access to paid employment.[112]

The complex and dynamic ways in which migrants in this research were both excluded from and included in these distinct but interwoven spaces of transnational citizenship (legal, economic, social, and political) are best captured through the analytic of uncertainty. Uncertainty, and how it is navigated, has increasingly been used as an optic in other social science research, and it is noticeably present in some recent ethnographic studies carried out in the global South.[113] While these works may have disparate foci, they coalesce around a common conceptual understanding. There is a shared sense that uncertainty conveys the insecurity, precariousness, and sometimes fear generated by economic, social, and political processes occurring in the countries under study, and that it also elucidates the ways in which these are materialized in everyday life, becoming a normalized part of its texture. Uncertainty also, however, is comprehended as allowing for—and to a degree enabling—anticipation, aspiration, planning, and action. As Austin Zeiderman and colleagues contend, we can therefore understand "uncertainty as something that is both produced and productive."[114] Its temporal mode is thus foregrounded; Elizabeth Cooper and David Patten view uncertainty as "best approached as a theory of action in the 'subjunctive mood.'"[115] The subjunctive mood, as they explain, quoting Susan Whyte, "is a doubting, hoping, provisional, cautious, and testing disposition to action."[116]

Uncertainty grasped in this way manages to encompass multiple aspects of migrants' lived experiences in relation to transnational spaces of citizenship. It is suggestive of the way in which these spaces, and migrants' places within and outside of them, are constructed through dynamic, multiscalar processes. And it expresses a lived reality of doubt, insecurity, and ambiguity. It also, however, reflects possibilities of hope and aspiration.

CONCLUSION

The approach developed by bringing together the perspectives on citizenship, migration, and uncertainty addressed in this chapter allows comprehension of how at any one time a migrant may be positioned differently, and multiply, in each of a range of overlapping transnational social spaces of citizenship. Her different positions within these spaces are highly contingent on power relations and her social identities—both in terms of how she is perceived and how she perceives herself—and also grounded in place and historical context. Perhaps she is on the very periphery of legal citizenship in one nation-state—holding a tourist visa, for example—while in full possession of legal citizenship in another where she does not currently reside. In terms of the political, she exercises her right to extraterritorial voting and also is a grassroots activist in the country where she is living, but she cannot vote there.

With respect to social citizenship, she had better access to health care in the country she has left than in the country where she lives at present. She has left one country because she could not find waged employment there and is precariously employed in the other. Almost all of these aspects of her citizenship could shift and change depending on both her exercise of agency through everyday citizenship practices (such as applying for legal residency, perhaps with support from a migrant organization) and structural factors (such as changes to immigration law, perhaps precipitated by recommendations from an international body). A change in one may result in a change in another, although not necessarily.

In this way, many migrants are neither entirely citizens nor "noncitizens," nor are they in a clearly delineated "third space" of citizenship. Rather, as the stories that unfold in the pages ahead illustrate, there is an unpredictable quality to their experiences of citizenship across multiple dimensions. In relation to each of these dimensions, and spanning them, there is a sense of ambiguity, of instability, and sometimes of fear, but also a whisper of possibility. They live uncertain citizenship.

2

Places of Uncertain Citizenship

In the room where my niece lives you can fit a double bed and a single, and nothing else. And we all squashed in there, and we lived four grown-ups and a little girl. Five people. . . . In the single bed, there was my husband, me, and we put a soft toy or something alongside so that if we rolled off, we'd fall on that. I mean, it's not a bed, it's a mattress on the floor. We were like that for March, April, May, about two months while we looked for another room. April was when my sister arrived. Then in that same room it was my niece, her husband, my husband and me, my sister, and two children. There were seven of us.

—DIANA, AGE TWENTY-EIGHT, FROM SANTA CRUZ, BOLIVIA

As the late, great Doreen Massey contended, "If space is . . . a simultaneity of stories-so-far, then places are collections of those stories, articulations within the wider power-geometries of space."[1] That is to say, places do not preexist but rather are formed and reformed through social interactions and interventions by institutions.[2] They are not abstract. They are made manifest through embodiment, understood and created through the physical, experiential, and emotional.[3] Places are consequently comprehended in a variety of ways by different people, but they also have shared meaning.

For Diana and many others, there were certainly particular places—like the inner-city tenement housing she describes in this chapter's opening quotation—that were tangible expressions of their collected migration stories-so-far. It is imperative to grasp a sense of these places in order to comprehend how uncertain citizenship affects migrants in their daily lives. So prior to embarking on a discussion in the rest of the book of the construction of and interactions between the "wider power geometries" of spaces of citizenship, this chapter provides a grounding in the lived reality of uncertain citizenship.

Combining migrants' accounts with my own participant observation through an iterative process, I slowly began to map the connections among what I came to understand as "places of uncertain citizenship," six of which I discuss here.[4] All, to borrow from Rob Shields, are places on the margins—in some cases literally on the geographic periphery, such as on the border at Lago Chungará, and in other cases figuratively peripheral to the center of society, as with the *migrant cités* (tenement housing) located in the heart of the capital city.[5] They are places that perform a clever trompe l'oeil, being at once invisibilized and yet highly visible. And thus they are places of liminality, full of "ambiguity and paradox."[6]

THE BOLIVIAN-CHILEAN BORDER
AT LAGO CHUNGARÁ

The physical geography of Lago Chungará marks it as somewhere outside normal paradigms. One of the highest lakes in the world, it sits at forty-five hundred meters above sea level. The altiplano landscape that surrounds it is splendidly dramatic, covered in pampa and snowy peaks; grazed by llama, alpaca, and vicuña; and a feeding ground for flamingo. I approached the Chungará–Tambo Quemado border crossing on my first journey there for this research in a fog of dizziness after briefly passing out on the bus due to our rapid ascent from sea level in Arica. My altitude sickness on that journey contributed to the sense of almost surreality engendered by the contrast between the dark green militarization of the border guards and the impossible blueness of the sky and the beauty of the place. Chungará seemed a shimmering mirage perched in the cordillera, yet it also was a place where weighty decisions regarding the movement of people were being enforced every day.

As a nexus point on the *triple frontera* (triple frontier) joining Chile, Peru, and Bolivia, its present is imbued with a history of conflict and unease. It is part of a borderland that holds deep importance in the national imaginaries of these three neighbors. The boundaries of Chile, Peru, and Bolivia were drastically redrawn following the War of the Pacific (1879–1883), and the consequences have been far-reaching. The war was a product of tensions among the three nations that evolved in conjunction with the discovery around the 1840s of rich guano deposits and *salitre* (sodium nitrate) on the Pacific coast and in the Atacama Desert in what was then southern Peru, Bolivia's littoral territory, and the top of northern Chile (see map 2). Tensions escalated to crisis point in February 1879. The Chilean government occupied the port of Antofagasta—at that point part of Bolivia—with the ironclad vessel *Blanco Encalada* in response to a fierce dispute over Bolivian taxation of a Chilean nitrate exploitation company operating in Bolivian territory. Shortly thereafter Bolivia declared war on Chile. As a result of signing a "secret" pact with Bolivia in 1873, Peru became embroiled in the conflict on the Bolivian side following a failed attempt to mediate, and in April 1879 war was declared on Bolivia and Peru by the Chilean congress.

The war was long and protracted, with neither the Chilean side nor the Peruvian-Bolivian alliance willing to back down. While Bolivia had effectively exited the war by 1881, Peru continued fighting until 1883. Peru negotiated the Treaty of

MAP 2. Territorial boundaries of Chile, Peru, and Bolivia before the War of the Pacific. Credit: Bill Nelson, 2017.

Ancón with Chile that same year, following extended Chilean occupation of Lima. In 1884 Bolivia and Chile reached an official truce, and they signed the Treaty of Peace and Friendship in 1904, essentially confirming the conditions of that truce. Under these agreements Chile took possession of Bolivian and Peruvian territory up to and including Arica and Tacna, thus leaving Bolivia landlocked and increasing the size of Chile by one-third (see map 3). In the Treaty of Peace and Friendship it was agreed that Bolivia would have access to the now Chilean ports of Arica and Antofagasta, that Bolivian imports through these ports would not be taxed, and that Bolivia could establish its own customs houses there. A railroad would also be built by Chile to link Arica to La Paz; this was completed in 1913.[7]

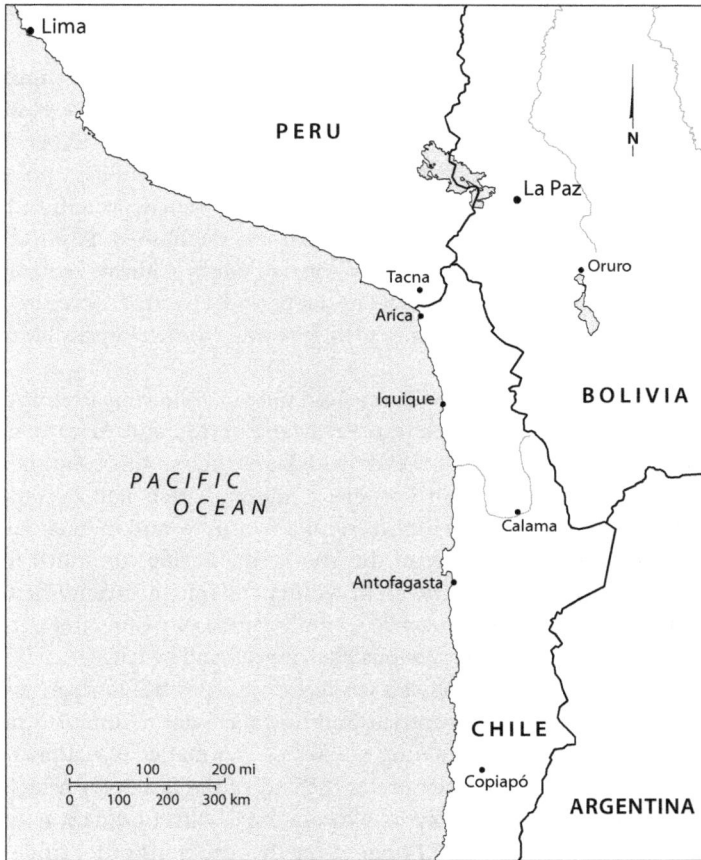

MAP 3. Contemporary map of Chile, Peru, and Bolivia. Credit: Bill Nelson, 2017.

Part of the agreement laid out in the Treaty of Ancón was that a plebiscite would be held in 1893 to decide the future of Arica and Tacna, according to the wishes of those residing there. This date came and went, however, with no attempt made at a vote. After years of discussion, in 1925 plans were finally made for a plebiscite, to be overseen by representatives from the United States. This was canceled in 1926 by the US representatives after what was described by plebiscitary commissioner general William Lassiter as a "state of terrorism" descended on the region in the period preceding the planned vote.[8] While violent acts were committed by both Peru and Chile as they sought to establish their national identity in the area, much of the violence was perpetrated by Chile. Effectively since the signing of the Treaty of Ancón, but increasingly during the period from 1910 onward, Chile had begun a process of "Chileanization" in the region.

The Chilean national identity that such actions sought to affirm promoted the homogeneity of Chile based on the "whiteness" of Chileans as opposed to the "Indian" or "mestizo" Peruvians, who were cast as an inferior Other. Peruvian schools, churches, and press outlets were closed; the Chilean military presence was augmented; approximately forty thousand Peruvians were deported; and a policy of colonization by Chileans from farther south was established. Physical assaults, rapes, and murders were not uncommon, carried out by Chilean vigilante groups but also by police. Violence increased in the period directly before the vote was due to be held, and thus a free and fair plebiscite was deemed impossible by the US representatives.[9]

The Tacna-Arica issue was finally resolved in 1929, following arbitration by the United States. Tacna passed back into Peruvian control, and Arica remained in Chilean control, with no plebiscite ever held. Nevertheless, this solution was only partial. Xenophobic antagonism between Chile and Peru had become deeply entrenched during the previous fifty years, and racism toward indigenous peoples had been reinforced. The specter of the War of the Pacific continued to rear its head throughout the rest of the twentieth century and into the twenty-first through repeated displays of this antagonism.[10] A similar animosity came to exist between Chile and Bolivia, and its repercussions likewise can still be felt.

Most notably, the issue of Bolivian sea access was, and still is, a serious bone of contention between the two countries, and they have not maintained full diplomatic relations since 1962. Regaining sea access is a matter of national pride in Bolivia, and the country commemorates the Day of the Sea every March 23 with parades, chants, and songs, led by its navy. In 2013 Bolivia brought a case to the International Court of Justice (ICJ) requesting that the court order Chile to negotiate the issue of Bolivian sovereign access to the sea (as opposed to the more limited access it currently has via the ports of Arica and Antofagasta). Much to Chile's chagrin, the ICJ ruled in 2015 that it would hear the case, and it is likely that a judgment will be issued in 2018 or 2019.

Whatever the conclusions that might be drawn about the causes of the sea access dispute and how it might be resolved, matters have not been helped by the aggressive public acts and comments of certain politicians on both sides. As a recent example, Evo Morales has insisted on playing Bolivia's "Naval March" in the presence of Chilean delegations to the country. Among other things, the lyrics contain a line indicating that Antofagasta, as well as other Chilean cities, will be returned once again to Bolivia (*otra vez a la patria volverá*). Bolivian minister of defense Reimy Ferreira has also recently compared former president Michelle Bachelet's government with that of General Augusto Pinochet. Bachelet was a victim of torture under the Pinochet regime. On another recent occasion, following a spat over a border infringement by Bolivian public officials, former and now again incumbent Chilean president Sebastián Piñera tweeted that President Evo Morales should "shut up stop lying and comply with the 1904 Treaty" (*mejor que se calle deje de mentir y cumpla Tratado de 1904*).[11]

At the border crossing at Lago Chungará, the ongoing tensions of the past century and a half can at times make themselves felt. This was revealed to me through the responses to a questionnaire survey that I assisted the Asociación in conducting with forty-six Bolivian truck drivers in the port of Arica. Employed by Bolivian companies, these drivers come largely from the *departamentos* of Cochabamba, Oruro, and Potosí, crossing into Chile at Lago Chungará to deliver their goods to the port before reloading and making the return journey. The drivers never had a good sense of how long a return journey would take them because there were often delays with the loading and unloading of cargo and at the border crossing, which the drivers attributed to the geopolitical tension between the two countries. Thus the journey could take them anywhere between two weeks and a month, with delays resulting in lost wages because of the high cost of accommodations and food in Arica. A member of staff at the port confirmed that proceedings were sometimes less than efficient and that the underlying cause was at least in part the fraught relations between the two countries.

Moreover, application of the law on the Chilean side of the border as individuals cross over from Bolivia can be arbitrary and discriminatory. Here Bolivians' right to freedom of movement and to migrate may be questioned, although there is often no basis for such questioning under Chilean law. Under the MERCOSUR visa agreement among Argentina, Bolivia, Brazil, Chile, Paraguay, and Uruguay, since 2009 Bolivians should be able to cross freely with only their identity cards and enter Chile as tourists (see chapter 3).[12] The MTRV to allow migrants to work is acquired once in Chile. Other than their identity cards, Bolivians crossing into Chile may be required at the border to show "proof of solvency," a concept for which I have struggled to find a clear definition. What is notable with regard to this point is that questioning about funds often appears to be arbitrary, and it seems that those crossing the border may be asked about their financial situation—or not—on the basis of their appearance. Those who appear to be indigenous are more likely to be questioned, as well as searched.

On my journey back across the border from La Paz to Arica, the woman in front of me in the customs queue, who was dressed *de pollera* (wearing Aymara or Quechua indigenous dress), was made to unpack all of the belongings she was carrying in her *aguayo* (woven cloth used to carry items) and zippered, blue-and-white-striped plastic bag. My equally large backpack passed unremarked. Of course this could have been an anomaly, the whim of the customs officer on that particular day. This seems unlikely, however, given that many participants in my research, particularly those in Arica and especially those who identified as indigenous and had lower levels of education, had experienced discrimination at the border. Sometimes this was relatively low-key—such as being subjected to more searches—but sometimes it resulted in being prohibited entry into Chile. Migrant organizations in the region confirmed that this type of discrimination and arbitrary decision making is a reality at the Chungará border, and at times people become stranded as they try to cross into Chile, sometimes struggling to cope with the altitude and relative lack of services.

Kevin, age forty-eight, an Aymara Bolivian who has lived in Arica for twenty-three years and has Chilean permanent residency, narrated to me a recent experience of crossing the border:

> Of the forty-five or so who were on the bus, at least ten to fifteen returned. They said to you, "Well, and where are you going?"
>
> "Arica," you replied.
>
> "To do what?" It was enough to hesitate about something, turn around, and they made you go back, even if you had money [i.e., could prove financial solvency].
>
> And you know that those who speak Aymara, most of us are from the countryside, and, how can I say this, sometimes they don't express themselves well. They don't explain themselves properly. . . . And well, last week I was crossing and they say, they ask me, "Where are you going?"
>
> "To Arica," I replied.
>
> "To do what?"
>
> "My family's there."
>
> "How long have you lived there?"
>
> They start to ask you things.

The prickly relations between Chile and Bolivia—the product of the old and still unhealed wounds of the War of the Pacific—impact the lives of ordinary people who set out to cross the border at Chungará. Deeply engrained discrimination toward indigenous peoples means that greater barriers to entry may be faced by some than by others. This literal borderland in the upper reaches of the Andes is, then, a place of tensions and exclusions, a place of uncertainty. The places subsequently discussed are in many ways figurative borderlands. They are there and not-there, hidden in plain sight, on the margins; they too are pervaded by tensions and exclusions, which at least in part are the product of histories of discrimination.

THE *MIGRANT CITÉ*, SANTIAGO

The term *cité* has more than one meaning in modern Santiago. When it first came into use in the late nineteenth century, it referred to the housing created for the urban working class, generally by the philanthropic arm of a business for its workers or through Catholic Church funding.[13] A *cité* typically consisted of two rows of small, terraced houses facing each other across a narrow passageway, which served as a communal outdoor space for the inhabitants of the houses. Each house had its own toilet, washing, and cooking facilities. This was in contrast to the *conventillos*, which were simply rooms off an outdoor passageway or courtyard with shared facilities.[14]

There is now a certain romanticizing of the old *cité* and the notion of community life that it seemed to promote. Indeed, in parts of downtown Santiago, such as Barrios Yungay and Brasil, the old *cités*—which were constructed up until about the 1950s—are undergoing a process of gentrification, with campaigns to save and restore them. The *conventillos*, on the other hand, have been to a considerable degree expunged from public memory. The places in which the migrants with whom I worked were living have far more in common with the old *conventillos* than with the *cités*. In popular parlance, however, these migrant dwellings are also referred to as *cités*, perhaps to veil their unhappy reality.

To be consistent with the language of home and housing used in Santiago but also recognize the stark contrast between the traditional *cité* and the residences discussed here, I refer to the latter as *migrant cités*. Almost half of the forty migrants whom I interviewed in-depth in Santiago lived in such places, compelled to do so by the multiple difficulties migrants face when trying to rent on the private market, not least discrimination by landlords (see chapter 5). They were men and women from various *departamentos* of Bolivia. A few identified as Quechua or Aymara, and others referred to having Quechua- or Aymara-speaking family. The majority had finished secondary school but had no further education.

A typical *migrant cité* consists of several rooms—around ten—off a central passageway, which is sometimes covered by a roof but quite often exposed. The façades of the houses look bare but reasonably maintained, and from the street their size gives the impression that each house must be occupied by one family. However, this belies the reality in whole blocks in downtown Santiago *comunas*. The rooms in these *migrant cités* are not normally single occupant; rather, they are shared among couples, families, or sometimes nonfamily groups. There is often serious overcrowding, as well as constant movement of people, as the extract from the interview with Diana at the beginning of this chapter indicates.[15] She had already moved through various similar places, including the sweatshops and *villas miserias* of Buenos Aires. Diana eloquently sketched how it felt to live in a place like that: it was to be "amontonados, como ratitas" ("piled on top of each other, like little rats"). Her most dearly held dream was to be able to one day build a little house on the outskirts of Santa Cruz, where she was from, and finally have space and security.

Not only are conditions crowded in *migrant cités*; basic needs go largely unmet. Diego, age twenty-one, also from Santa Cruz and working in construction, shared

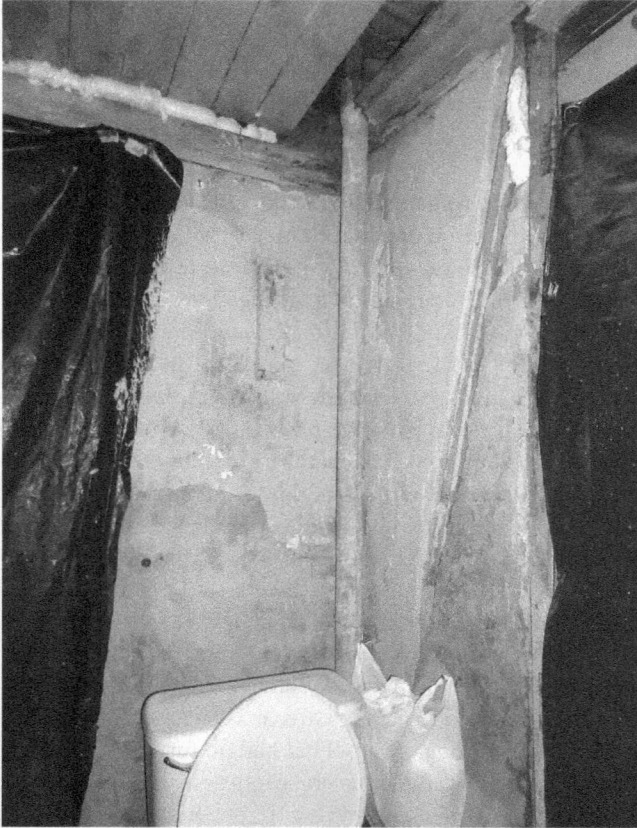

FIGURE 1. Bathroom, Cristina's *migrant cité*, Recoleta, Santiago, 2013. Photo by author.

with three other men a room that was two by three meters square. When he first arrived, he wore all his clothes while sleeping and lay on several sheets of cardboard, as he could not afford bedding or a mattress. For Rosa, twenty-nine and from Sucre, one of the worst aspects of living in a *migrant cité* was sharing a bathroom with ten other people and having no hot water. This was especially difficult as she tried to care for her newborn baby.

Temperatures in Santiago can drop to several degrees below zero in the winter, making a lack of hot water even more unpleasant at this time of year. Furthermore, *migrant cités* are unheated and frequently have ill-fitting roofs that let in wind and rain. Cristina, age thirty-seven, who like Diana had lived in other marginal places, including on the streets in Cochabamba, Bolivia, described the

FIGURE 2. Cooking facilities, Cristina's *migrant cite*, Recoleta, Santiago, 2013. Photo by author.

winter conditions in her *migrant cité* (see the bathroom and kitchen facilities in figures 1 and 2):

Megan: And are there leaks?

Cristina: Water, yes. Actually, the roof fell in and ever since, every year I've been saying [to the landlord], "Don Guillermo, please fix the roof because it's letting in water."

Megan: Of course. [Indicating ceiling] Well, there are also exposed cables, so it could be dangerous.

Cristina: "Yes," he says, "let's just cover it with some bin bags," and, well, that's it. The water really flows in badly here. No, here it fills up with water.

Megan: And is it cold in the winter?

Cristina: Yes, it's cold. Ugh, in the winter you truly get cold. It's horrible, we walk around numb from cold.

As I noticed in the passageway outside Cristina's room, exposed electric cables hanging in the passageways are another common feature of many *migrant cités*. This is because rather than being officially connected, it is common for the residents to *colgar de la luz* (hang off the mains), circumnavigating the system in order to pirate electricity. These cables, drooping slightly above head height, can pose a serious fire hazard, not only because they may get wet but also because inhabitants must cook over open gas flames in their rooms or in the passageway and hang up their clothes to dry here as well. These multiple hardships—cramped conditions, lack of the most basic facilities, intense cold, and the potential for flooding or fire—become the daily bread of many migrants who live uncertain citizenship in Santiago. But these are places of quiet deprivation, unknown to the average passerby because they blend so seamlessly into the scruffy but respectable downtown streetscapes.

WORKING *PUERTAS ADENTRO*, SANTIAGO

Nana puertas adentro (live-in maid/nanny) is a job description set out in a turn of phrase that seems to be peculiar to Chile. While of course the concept of domestic workers "living in" is widespread throughout Latin America and much of the rest of the world, it appears that the term *nana puertas adentro* is a Chileanism. *Nana* is the word generally used in Chile to refer to female domestic workers. There is a less demeaning term—*asesora de hogar* (loosely, female household employee)—but I use *nana* here deliberately because of the connotations of gendered and racialized power relations that it conveys. Moreover, the sense of "behind closed doors" implied by *puertas adentro* makes the phrase unwittingly appropriate given the exploitative labor and living conditions to which many women working as *nanas* are subjected.

As has been discussed more extensively in a US context, in crucial ways women (it is almost invariably women) in these roles "have been denied full citizenship —that is, they have not been recognized as fully independent and responsible members of the community, entitled to civil, political, and social rights," as Evelyn Glenn writes.[16] Gender, race, and class have all played a central role in constructing and enabling these exclusions, which are rooted in a history of slavery and servitude. In the colonial era and on into the period of independence prior to the abolition of slavery, in many countries in the Americas the role of domestic workers was commonly filled by African and Afro-descendant slaves. Indigenous women in conditions of servitude, who were frequently unpaid, also performed these roles.[17] The long shadow of this oppression has been cast into the twenty-first century. Women of indigenous or African descent still predominate in domestic work in many contexts in the Americas. Many of these women are migrants—both internal and transnational—from low-income backgrounds. Labor exploitation and discrimination continue to characterize this type of work.[18]

In Bolivia many of the women working as live-in domestic workers have been, and continue to be, of indigenous descent. As indicated above, many have migrated from rural communities to cities like La Paz to engage in such work. Lesley Gill provides a powerful indictment of the racism and classism that permeated labor relations between Aymara female domestic workers and their employers (who are generally white-mestizo, although sometimes wealthy urban Aymara) in La Paz over the course of the twentieth century. As Gill argues, the "most enduring feature" of domestic work is that workers "are drawn from groups considered inferior by those in power. . . . [T]he women who carry out paid household labour invariably represent a subordinate race, class, ethnic group, or nationality."[19] Although Gill was writing in the mid-1990s, her analysis continues to resonate. In spite of the progress that Bolivia has made in indigenous rights (see chapter 1), within private homes domestic workers continue to face gender and racial discrimination.[20]

There are strong parallels with the Chilean case, as documented by Carolina Stefoni and Rosario Fernández in their analysis of domestic worker and employer relations in Santiago historically and in the present.[21] In the past in Chile, women in these roles in Santiago were likely to be internal migrants from the South, and they were of indigenous descent (mainly Mapuche) or mestiza. In the present, Chilean women who are employed as domestic workers are still largely mestiza or of indigenous descent. But in the past two decades the Chilean women who carry out domestic work have been joined by growing numbers of transnational migrant domestic workers, initially predominantly from Peru but increasingly from countries such as Bolivia and Colombia as well. Indeed, 12.3 percent of the total foreign-born population in Chile is employed in domestic work, compared with 6.1 percent of the Chilean-born population.[22] Migrant women from other Latin American countries have proven to be a "natural fit" in a labor niche that, as Gill and Stefoni and Fernández indicate, serves to reproduce a hierarchical social order because it is filled by those considered to be of lower social standing based on gender, race, and/or nationality. Those who fill these roles are excluded from full citizenship, in both symbolic and substantive terms.

As in the *migrant cités*, in the houses where women work *puertas adentro*, migrants' multiple exclusions from spaces of citizenship become articulated in place. Of course the big houses—typically in the wealthy eastern suburbs of Santiago—where women employed as *nanas* work and live are vastly different from the *migrant cités* in terms of the material comfort they offer. Nonetheless, as in the *migrant cités*, the very private sphere of the family home in which *nanas* work and live is hidden from public view. *Nanas* in these places are cut off from family, social networks, and normal, everyday social life. Although all work in Chile, caring work included, is nominally subject to public sphere regulations (see chapter 4), in the houses where migrant women work as *nanas* a liminal borderland is created as private and public, work and life are blurred. This was made starkly apparent to me when I interviewed Magdalena, age thirty-eight, from El Alto, near the house where she worked and lived.

Like Magdalena and the vast majority of migrants who participated in this research, I did not have a car and was dependent on public transportation. To travel from the center of Santiago to the house where Magdalena was a *nana puertas adentro*, I had to take the metro and then two buses, the second of which ran only once every sixty minutes. The journey by public transportation took an hour, not including time spent waiting for the bus, after which I walked for fifteen minutes to reach the house in Alto Macul, in the foothills of the Andes in the southeast part of the city. The house was in a gated community with a small plaza. The properties had high walls and fences, and many were guarded by large dogs that growled at me from within the confines of manicured gardens.

In the plaza I sat on a bench with Magdalena while we talked. She couldn't invite me into the house and wouldn't, in any case, have wanted to host me in her small bedroom off the kitchen. The position of her bedroom within the home was typical of the floor plan of houses in Chile's upper-middle- and upper-class neighborhoods. They continue to be built with a *dormitorio y baño de servicio* (domestic worker's bedroom and bathroom) next to the kitchen and laundry, which speaks strongly to the position occupied by *nanas puertas adentro* within the household and wider society. One can easily connect the dots backward in time to the location of the servants' or slaves' quarters in colonial houses.[23]

Such comparisons do not end with the layout of houses in contemporary Chilean condominiums. Magdalena only had forty minutes for our interview because, although it was 7:00 p.m. and she had started her working day at 8:00 a.m., her employer required her to finish cooking the evening meal and then clear up. She worked Monday to Saturday but thought she might look for a job in another house on Sundays because of living and working in such an isolated place. As she had little chance of forming a social life in her time off, she thought she might as well spend it working.

The great irony, of course, is that it was Magdalena's vital participation in the fabric of another family's social life that disallowed her own. Naturalized and normalized by generations of gendered and racialized labor relations within the homes of the upper social classes, this contribution was barely recognized. Indeed Magdalena, like many other *nanas puertas adentro*, faced the constant worry of losing her job without notice and having nowhere to go. Insecurity becomes a feature of the daily lives of *nanas puerta adentro*, as does the cloak of invisibility from the outside world that such a role confers.

BODEGAS, SANTIAGO AND ARICA

In October 2013 I interviewed the Bolivian consul in Santiago, pressing him to tell me what he knew about the labor conditions of his compatriots in the capital city. In response to my queries, he recommended I visit the wholesale clothes shopping arcades along Santiago's main avenue, La Alameda, where it traverses the *comuna* of Estación Central. The day after our interview I did just that. In the very first arcade I entered, in a shop toward the back, I met a young Bolivian woman who was prepared to chat with me. She was looking tired and disconsolate, leaning on the shop counter, with her straight black hair nearly sweeping its surface.

Her name was Cata; she was twenty-five and from El Alto. It transpired that she was working twelve to sixteen hours a day, six days a week, and had not been paid for five months. Moreover, she had been lured to Santiago on false pretenses. She was living with several other people in what she referred to as a *bodega* (warehouse, storage space) near the clothes shop where she worked. The ease with which I found Cata, and subsequent interviews and conversations with other migrants, made it clear that this area of the city abounded with such places of marginality and exploitation. It is potentially comparable, though on a smaller scale, to the sweatshops of São Paulo and Buenos Aires in which Bolivian migrants labor (see chapter 1).

Kinberley, age twenty-six, from La Paz, whom I interviewed soon after meeting Cata, had previously been working and living in similar circumstances in an arcade almost adjacent to the one where Cata was. Kinberley's "room" was provided for "free," and she was required to live there as one of the conditions of her employment. She described the experience of first arriving at her new sleeping quarters:

> It was a room and beside it was the warehouse. But there were some people who slept in the warehouse, they slept like that.
>
> "Ooh," I said, "What should I do?" Because the first time I arrived and entered the house, the house was dirty, and I said to myself, "Where have I ended up?"
>
> I went upstairs. I don't know, I didn't like it. Now, "What should I do?" Like that. I'm here but I can't go back.

This was a place that made her fearful, but she felt she could not leave. Cata and her fellow worker, Marta, age thirty-five, from a rural community in the *departamento* of Oruro, also described feeling trapped; they were generally only able to leave the building where they were living on Sundays. Moreover, there was a sense of danger and clandestine activity in the area. Like the facades of the *migrant cités*, the shopping arcade and house fronts along La Alameda in this part of the city hid the reality within. In the small shopping arcade where Cata and Marta worked, most of the shops sold clothing at wholesale prices. Cata informed me—and I could verify—that nearly all the shops were staffed by migrant workers. She told me that most of them lived and worked in conditions like her own.

Furthermore, in the same arcade there was a *café con piernas* (literally, café with legs), a euphemism for a café where the waitstaff are women wearing minimal clothing. In the mildest of these cafés, the women wear blouses and very short skirts. At the other end of the spectrum, such establishments are essentially strip clubs. *Cafés con piernas* are a fairly accepted and normalized part of Santiago culture, and most are openly advertised. There are, however, some that are not openly advertised and that may be fronts for brothels, which are illegal in Chile. The *café con piernas* in the arcade where Cata and Marta worked seemed highly likely to be one of the latter. It was hidden away at the back of the arcade, and the door and windows were blacked out. Cata and Marta said that the women working there were mainly Colombian migrants, and they thought that they were involved in sex work.

There are clear gendered, racialized stereotypes of different nationalities at work in Chile, which have an impact on migrants.[24] Colombian and Central American women in particular can be seen as an exotic and sexualized Other; the continuation of a long history of racist, gendered stereotyping of Afro-descendant and mestiza women as sexually available, which can increase their vulnerability to sexual exploitation in Chile.[25] While the women in the *café con piernas* in the arcade where Cata and Marta worked may have been there voluntarily, given the circumstances in which others in the arcade were working, there was a distinct possibility that they were being sexually exploited. Overall, within the arcade there was a sense of a sordid twilight world in which migrant workers were effectively trapped, day and night.

In Arica, sisters Isabela, age twenty, and Antonia, age twenty-five, were also hidden in plain sight in similar conditions. The flower stall where they worked in El Agro, Arica's main market, was an enchanting mass of colors, scents, and neat, orderly displays (much like that in figure 3). However, Isabela and Antonia labored there up to sixteen hours a day, six days a week, and then went to sleep in a room off one of the warehouses behind the market. Just as for the women in Santiago, the room was provided as part of the job. There they slept three to a mattress, with no cooking facilities and a rudimentary bathroom. There was no lock on the door, leading to a profound sense of unease for the women; they had been robbed on more than one occasion. Yet the commercial bustle of shops and markets camouflages these places in both Arica and Santiago, ensuring that they remain unregulated and unnoticed.

PARCELAS, ARICA

The fertile Valle de Azapa, which spreads out to the southeast of Arica, provides much of the produce that is sold in El Agro, where people like Isabela and Antonia work. The Valle de Azapa itself is also home to places of uncertain citizenship and has a long history of being so. Arica and the Valle de Azapa were part of Peru prior to the War of the Pacific, after which they became Chilean territory. For many centuries before the conflict, the Valle de Azapa and parts of what is now southern Peru were agricultural heartlands of the Viceroyalty and then the Republic of Peru. Until abolition in 1854, much of the agricultural work was performed by African slaves.

The history of slavery in the area is today memorialized in the "The Slave Route," a thirty-kilometer trail through Arica and the Valle de Azapa established by Afro-descendants in the region, officially recognized by the Chilean Ministerio

FIGURE 3. Flower stall, El Agro, Arica, 2014. Photo by author.

de Bienes Nacionales (Ministry of National Heritage) in 2009. Viviana Briones Valentín explains that, rather than the large plantations and haciendas of other areas of southern Peru, the Valle de Azapa was characterized by smaller units of production worked by fewer slaves than on the large plantations. Of the slave population in the region, she says: "Attempts to marginalize them from all social, official and economic recognition, from cultural and religious duties, had an immediate and everyday effect (Mellafe, 1964). But, on the other hand, we know that in spite of these measures, the black community managed to reinvent itself time and time again from this 'no place.'"[26] Today in the Valle de Azapa, the ghost of the colonial slavery regime seems to linger on in more than just the memorial sites along trail. So too does the legacy of racism that was a product of the "Chileanization" of the region following the War of the Pacific.

The model of small units of production as opposed to large-scale industrial operations continues to predominate on what are known as *parcelas* in Azapa. Here some of the crops of colonial times are still produced: olives and cotton, to give just two examples. Tomatoes, peppers, sweet corn, cucumbers, avocados, and mangoes, among other fruit and vegetables, are also cultivated. Many *parcelas* are chiefly worked by migrant laborers. In general, those who work there also live there. As with the *bodegas* or working *puertas adentro*, the provision of accommodation is part of the work agreement. Each *parcela* is run by one owner, referred to by the workers as the *patrón*, a term of address with its roots firmly planted in colonial times. Beneath them are overseers. On the *parcelas*, workers I spoke to labored for nine to twelve hours per day and often had only one half-day off per week. They earned less than the minimum wage, did not have contracts, and were encouraged by their employers to remain on tourist visas, which exacerbated their job insecurity. The very long hours worked meant that they were cut off from society and had few means of accessing information about labor rights, health services, or education. The living conditions were also extremely poor.

One evening in March 2014 I went to interview Luisa, age twenty-five, from rural Oruro, on the *parcela* where she lived. We walked down a long driveway shaded by mango trees to get to the shelter occupied by Luisa, her husband, their two boys, aged six and five, and Luisa's sister. It was built of plywood and corrugated iron and had a dirt floor. There was a bedsheet separating the two "rooms," where they slept on mattresses on the floor. A covered area outside served as a kitchen, where Luisa did the cooking squatting beside a small camping stove. They shared a bathroom, a fifty-meter walk from their shelter, with the twenty other workers on the *parcela*, using buckets of cold water to wash.

Curious about this stranger talking to their *mamá*, Luisa's boys peered at me around the corner of the entrance to the shelter. Egged on by his elder brother, the youngest, barefoot, eventually ran over to where Luisa and I were sitting on a low bench. He reached his hand out to stroke my face and looked straight into my eyes. Luisa laughingly explained to me that he was intrigued "porque tienes los ojos muy claros y eres tan blanquita" ("because your eyes are very clear [blue or green] and you are so white"). Rarely have I felt so acutely the many power imbalances in my relationship with the migrants with whom I work or such an emotional response to the injustices to which I was bearing witness.

In addition to awareness of my own positionality, I was deeply cognizant of the ways in which migrant workers' positions within racialized hierarchies of power played a fundamental role in their exclusion from spaces and places of citizenship. Nearly all the workers on the *parcelas* were of Aymara or sometimes Quechua descent. Some, particularly the women, spoke limited Spanish and had not finished their schooling. Nearly all who lived on *parcelas* were originally from rural communities in the departments of Oruro and La Paz, which they said were very poor. Racial and class-based discrimination certainly seemed to contribute to making participants more vulnerable to living and working in such harsh conditions, as an overt example of racist talk indicated. The *patrón* on one of the *parcelas* that I visited—who, according to the Asociación, was one of the more responsible employers in the Valle de Azapa—told me about his trials and tribulations employing migrant workers. He explained that Aymara Bolivians were "medio lentos, y nunca toman la initiativa" ("pretty slow and they never take initiative"). Perpetuated by centuries of discrimination, places of uncertain citizenship remain a hidden feature of the Valle de Azapa.

PLAN 3000, SANTA CRUZ DE LA SIERRA, BOLIVIA

Uncertain citizenship is embodied in place not only on the Chilean side of Lago Chungará, but also on the Bolivian side. Roughly a thirty-hour bus ride east from Chungará is Plan 3000, in the city of Santa Cruz. Many *cruceño* (resident of Santa Cruz) migrants I interviewed had originally come from here. When the Amazonian River Piraí, on the northwest side of Santa Cruz, burst its banks in 1983, three thousand people were left homeless. They were relocated to the southeast of the concentric circles that form the center of Santa Cruz, and Plan 3000 was born. This peri-urban area is now home to around 300,000 people, the vast majority of whom are first- or second-generation internal migrants from other areas of Bolivia. Most identify as indigenous, principally Aymara, Quechua, and Guaraní.

Plan 3000 is considered a dangerous district by other inhabitants of Santa Cruz, especially for a white foreigner like myself. The first time I visited I arrived by taxi. The driver was concerned when I gave him the address, confirming several times that I knew where I was going. Having crossed the sixth ring road encircling the city, we turned off Avenue Tres Pasos al Frente, one of the main arteries out of the city, down unpaved streets identified only by numbers. Conscious of the potholes and concerned about the taxi's rather rickety suspension, I offered to walk, as I knew I was close to the community center where I had a day's activities planned. But the *taxista* insisted on taking me right to the door, valiantly zigzagging around various obstacles and waiting until he saw someone come and greet me.

While the taxi driver's anxiety was overstated, there is no doubt that there *are* quotidian dangers that threaten life in Plan 3000. At a session of a youth group at the community center, the young people present (many of whom had parents working in other countries) were discussing where to host an event aimed at promoting a positive image of young *cruceño* street artists and rappers. There was concern about holding it within Plan 3000, as they feared it might spark turf wars between rival gangs. I thought this was a teenage exaggeration, but it was confirmed by the group leaders. They were longtime residents of the neighborhood

FIGURE 4. Luz María and her family's street, Plan 3000, Santa Cruz, Bolivia, 2014. Photo by author.

and said that it was certainly wise to be very cautious after dark and to keep an eye on personal belongings in the daytime as well.

This threat of human violence exists alongside threats from more "natural" causes.[27] As I experienced on another occasion, heavy rains, frequent at certain times of year, have a disastrous effect on Plan 3000's dirt roads. They become unpassable, and when they do eventually begin to dry out, residual water gathers in large puddles that become breeding-grounds for mosquitos. Dengue fever is more or less endemic. Typhoid is also not uncommon, no doubt because access to clean drinking water and adequate sewerage is by no means guaranteed in the more peripheral areas of Plan 3000.

Indeed, Luz María and Wilson (the couple referred to in the introduction) had passed a worried few days in their *migrant cité* in Santiago when their two-year-old son, in the care of his maternal grandparents back in Plan 3000, had a bout of typhoid. I visited Luz María and Wilson when they were back at her parents' in Plan 3000 for a visit, their newborn son in tow. Wilson and his eldest son—now very bonny and healthy—picked me up from the bus stop on Wilson's motorbike, and we bounced the few blocks along the unpaved roads to Luz María's family home. The house was a big, solid brick construction on a fairly well-established street (see figure 4). The faces and bodies of Luz María's parents, however, spoke of the struggle to build that house and to make do day to day. Luz María's mother wasn't much over forty, but her face was wizened, and she had lost most of her teeth. Her father was now unemployed because his work as a bricklayer had left him with severe back pain.

In the sweltering heat, we sat out in front of the house, eating takeout pizza bought especially for me and drinking orange fizzy drink while we chatted and members of the extended family came to visit. Soon I noticed that a handful of people in white lab coats were wandering up and down the street, carrying clipboards. Seeing my puzzled look, Luz María's father, rolling his eyes slightly in their direction, said, "Oh, they're from the municipality, vaccinating animals in the neighborhood against rabies." When they came near his property he grabbed a ginger cat that was lingering in the front yard and proffered the scruff of its neck for injecting. After confirming the address, giving his name, and signing a sheet of paper on the municipal worker's clipboard, he sat back down with a wry smile, indicating that his actions should keep them happy.

That brief interaction seemed indicative of the ways in which institutions may intervene in places like Plan 3000, shaping and reshaping them. Inhabitants are identified as a risk/at risk in some respect (in this case, because they may be keeping unhealthy animals) and therefore are acted upon in order to control the danger. And so in some way they are "counted" and they, and the place they inhabit, become—to borrow from Partha Chatterjee—part of the governed *population* in a legal-administrative sense.[28] Yet in most respects they remain cast out from *citizenship*, scraping a living as best they can, without sufficient access to health care, education, and at times basic needs such as clean water, not to mention lacking representation in the political arena. Such uncertainty of citizenship can sow the seeds for many reactions, not least political mobilization; like El Alto above La Paz, with which it has been compared, Plan 3000 has at times been a site of contestation of government policies and actions.[29] And of course this uncertainty may also spark a different kind of movement of people: transnational migration in search of more certain citizenship.

CONCLUSION

The irony is that upon embarking on their journeys to try to get *away* from places of uncertain citizenship, many migrants are likely to encounter more such places that are linked by liminality, privation, fear, and insecurity. If they venture to Chile, they must cross a border such as that at Lago Chungará and may face interrogative questions, searches, and the palpable prospect of being sent back. If they make it across and go only as far as Arica, they may well end up on *parcelas*, or in *bodegas* if they are particularly unlucky. Or perhaps they will become *nanas puertas aden-tro*, isolated in the capital city, or inhabitants of its cramped *migrant cités*.

To return to Doreen Massey, these six places I have sketched are, as she says, "articulations within the wider power-geometries of space." I endeavor in the rest of this book to interrogate more thoroughly the "wider power-geometries of space" by examining distinct but overlapping transnational spaces of citizenship and migrants' relationships to them. What should be clear already from this chapter, however, is that these spaces are structured and contoured by different forms of discrimination that have a deep-rooted history. The War of the Pacific and its aftermath entrenched xenophobia and distrust between Chile and Bolivia. The subsequent, related process of "Chileanization" reinforced the negation of indigenous, Afro-descendant, and mestiza identities, the origins of which oppression can be found still further back in the colonial era. This did not just occur in Chile, however. Across the border in Bolivia, similar processes were also at work. And intertwined with a legacy of racial discrimination in both countries is also one of strong patriarchy. These are the histories, then, that in part shape the transnational spaces of legal, economic, social, and political citizenship that are the focus of the subsequent chapters in this book. The places of uncertain citizenship discussed in this chapter are nodal points at which the lived realities of exclusion from many of these spaces are made manifest.

Yet in all this, it is important not to lose sight of the fact that within these places people cope, and aspire, and move forward. Indeed, Doreen Massey writes of how we must consider the ways in which individuals exercise agency within the power geometries of space. After all, the very act of migration, however much compelled by circumstance in somewhere like Plan 3000, is still a decisive, agentic undertaking. It takes grit and determination to make the long bus journey via a crossing like Lago Chungará, confronting complex border bureaucracy perhaps for the first time. And maybe in the places on the other side of the border, money will be made, friends met, babies born, and claims staked in a more stable future, thus revealing the incipient possibilities of inclusion that are also contained within uncertainty.

3

Papeleo

Beimar, age twenty-eight, was one of the few migrants I interviewed who had lived in both Arica and Santiago. When I met him, he was working loading and unloading produce coming in from the *parcelas* in the Valle de Azapa to be sold in El Agro, Arica. Wending my way through the labyrinth of the entirely male-dominated produce loading bays at the back of El Agro, trying to find Beimar at the end of his shift, I certainly made an incongruous sight. Several unhelpful comments later, I eventually located him, and we began a lengthy and informative conversation. Perhaps because I had met him through a mutual friend, Beimar was particularly candid with me about his complex entanglements with legal citizenship and their evolution over time.

Beimar was from Oruro, Bolivia, and there he had undertaken some technical studies after completing his military service. He first came to Chile in 2010 for a three-month period over the Chilean summer. He arrived on a tourist visa and spent his time traveling around Arica, Iquique, and finally Santiago, where he stayed with his brother. He returned to Bolivia but was drawn back to Chile the next summer, thinking it would be good to make some money in Santiago. Again he entered on a tourist visa, but this time he went straight to stay with his brother in the capital. His brother found him a job working in a market garden on the outskirts of the city. While strictly speaking he was not "undocumented" because he possessed a tourist visa and had a passport, to work on such a visa was irregular.

Beimar moved further into irregularity as he overstayed his tourist visa. He switched jobs and began working in a *fuente de soda* (fast-food diner) in one of Santiago's international bus terminals, flipping hamburgers for long hours each day. His employer knew about his irregular migratory situation and used it to his advantage. He promised to pay Beimar cash at the end of a six-month period, giving him only small *adelantos* (advances) in the meantime. Beimar, trusting his employer, saw this as a means of saving. The amount promised was US$230 per month, far below the minimum wage. Nonetheless, Beimar was happy to settle for this because he knew he would not get the minimum wage unless his migratory situation was regular. And his brother and friends kept dissuading him from applying to regularize, saying, "hay mucho papeleo" ("there's a lot of red tape/paperwork"). The end of six months' hard work arrived, and to Beimar's shock, his employer only handed over the equivalent of two months' salary. When Beimar complained, his employer said the money had run out and then threatened to report him to "Extranjería."

Unsure what to do and cowed by the threat of being reported to the Departamento de Extranjería y Migraciones (DEM, Department of Immigration), Beimar left Santiago for Arica, hoping there would be better opportunities there. He began working in El Agro, Arica's largest market, for a wage of around US$6 per day cash in hand. He continually demonstrated that he was reliable and hard working, and gradually his wage improved. He then changed employers on the promise of a better salary paid to him monthly. After several months of working in this job, Beimar persuaded his employer to grant him a loan to pay the cost of a visa application and the fine accrued through being in an irregular migratory situation.

Beimar managed to regularize his situation, moving to an MTRV. Through careful study of the rather challenging requirements, he worked hard over the next year to comply with the conditions for application for permanent residency. At the time of our interview, his application for permanent residency was being processed. Beimar's negotiation of the intricacies of legal citizenship did not, however, end there. When I interviewed him, his girlfriend, who is from Bolivia, had just moved to Chile on a tourist visa to be with him. She was four months pregnant. If she did not manage to change her migration status to temporary or permanent residency by the fifth month of pregnancy, there was a real possibility that their child might be born *hijo de transeúnte* (child of transient parents). This generates a series of legal difficulties for the child and parents and had happened to Beimar's nephew, born in Santiago.[1] Although we also spoke of other things during our conversation, these worries over shifting irregular and regular migratory status, not only for himself but also for his family, were very much at the forefront of Beimar's mind.

LEGAL CITIZENSHIP: DEBATES AND DEFINITIONS

As Beimar's story illustrates, and as is very well established, migrants' position in relation to legal citizenship is highly significant in their everyday lives. It therefore deserves our attention. Nonetheless, the disproportionate focus of policy makers and the media on migrants' legal status may at times lead to a distorted emphasis on this particular aspect of citizenship, to the neglect of its other components.[2] This book attempts both to acknowledge the importance of legal status for migrants in this chapter, and in subsequent chapters to recognize more fully the other—interconnected—facets of their experiences of citizenship.

A discussion of terms is an important starting point for a chapter that deals with not only the lived realities of daily negotiations of migratory status, but also their wider ideological implications. *Illegal* has tended to be, and continues to be, the term employed by the state and the popular media to define that which is not legal citizenship.[3] Stories regarding "illegal immigration" score easy political points and sell more papers; they fuel the popular discourse that creates certain types of migrants as "Non-Citizens" or "Failed Citizens."[4] The criminalization of the subject that *illegal* implies, however, means that it has generally been discredited by academics and to a degree in wider society in some contexts—for example, in some Canadian cities where the "No One is Illegal" movement has been particularly strong.[5] This still leaves a variety of options; *unauthorized, undocumented, non-status,* and *irregular* are some of the most common.

Unauthorized can be criticized for having similar, although milder, connotations as *illegal*; a sense of deliberate rule-breaking activity is still implied. *Undocumented* is preferred by some scholars and has been replaced with *non-status* by others.[6] Arguably, *undocumented*, while free of negative associations, is unclear, as many migrants who could be classed as such do possess some documents, genuine or not.[7] I likewise argue that *non-status*—borrowed from migrant social movements and admirable in its political objective to be an inclusive term denoting all those without permission to permanently remain in a country—is nonetheless somewhat lacking analytically.[8] It is too broad, is too general, and could refer to too many types of status, in fact, to the point of unintentionally stripping migrants of agency by declaring them to have "no status." *Irregular* is the term used by the majority of scholars, although it is acknowledged that this too has its limitations.[9] I suggest that it should be deployed in the context of describing a person's *migratory situation* rather than the person (so not *irregular migrant* but *migrant with irregular status*). Thus it is clear that it is not the defining feature of an individual, but rather describes one aspect of her circumstances at that moment.

This concern with the selection of terms is not mere semantic pedantry. Rather, our choice of language is profoundly indicative of how we understand the production of legal citizenship and migrant "illegality." As Nicholas De Genova contends, migrant "illegality" cannot be fully comprehended if it is only explored as a policy problem to be "solved" from on high without delving into the everyday lived realities of migrants with irregular status. On the other hand, we mustn't swing entirely the other way, focusing solely on the daily lives of migrants experiencing irregularity, ignoring the legal and policy dimensions that generate its very possibility.[10]

State legislation, its application by state actors, and the everyday experiences and actions of migrants in relation to their legal status must all be considered.[11] It is also important to understand the historical conditions that have led to particular legislative frameworks and migration policies.[12]

There has also been increasing recognition of the need to move beyond creating a dichotomous binary between those who have regular migratory status and those whose status is irregular.[13] As Beimar's story indicates, such a binary does not reflect the complex reality of migrants' many transitions between different types of regularity and irregularity. Luin Goldring and Patricia Landolt recognize the problems inherent in either/or (citizen or noncitizen) models of migrant legal citizenship, as well as those that offer a tripartite interpretation of migrants' legal status.[14] They propose instead a model in which *noncitizenship* is understood as an "assemblage" that "invites attention as to how non-citizenship is assembled over time and across space, presenting a dynamic conceptualisation of the chutes and ladders of legal status."[15] This is similar to Cathy McIlwaine's "webs," a conceptualization of migrant (ir)regularity that is likewise concerned with "captur[ing] the dynamism of migrant irregularity over time, space and scale as well as a degree of migrant agency."[16]

I build on these proposals in this chapter and further enhance them later in the book through consideration of how the legal interacts with other aspects of citizenship—something that does not fall within the scope of McIlwaine's webs of (ir)regularity or Goldring and Landolt's assemblage of legal noncitizenship.[17] I understand legal citizenship as a transnational, dynamic, three-dimensional space that is also intertwined with other spaces of citizenship. As migrants attempt to access and move through the space of legal citizenship, they may be classed as holding a wide variety of irregular and regular migratory statuses. Very frequently, their legal status is characterized by insecurity and uncertainty. The transnational space of legal citizenship is constructed through processes occurring at a legislative level, through migrants' own practices, and sometimes through those of migrant organizations.

In the pages ahead I reflect migrants' frequent use of the term *papeleo* (paperwork/red tape) to reference the day-to-day "doing" of negotiating legal citizenship. I consider migration law in the Bolivian-Chilean context as it exists 'on paper"; I address its implementation by state actors "through paper"; and I discuss the ways in which migrants negotiate their legal citizenship by "presenting papers," sometimes with the intercession of a migrant organization. How do these complex processes and practices of *papeleo* contribute to the construction of a transnational space of legal citizenship? How do migrants become differentially positioned within and outside this space? And—to be considered in subsequent chapters— how does a migrant's position within or outside the space of legal citizenship impact her experiences of other facets of citizenship?

MIGRATION LEGISLATION "ON PAPER"

Maximiliano, lawyer for the human rights division of the Corporación de Asistencia Judicial (Legal Aid Agency), explained to me in impassioned tones that Decree Law 1094, the most important legal instrument governing migration in Chile, "is a norm dictated under the state of exception in the year 1975, which establishes a police regime . . . with regards to foreigners in Chile. Let's start with that; that is our premise." A prevailing concern with protecting Chile from "subversive" elements generated this law and saw the expulsion of many foreigners from Chile, as well as the exile of approximately 200,000 Chileans (see chapter 1).[18] Modifications to Decree Law 1094 have since been made, in 1993, 1996, 1998, and 2000, and at first glance the processes by which Bolivians and migrants of other nationalities now enter the country and acquire visas seem straightforward and unremarkable; indeed, they may seem far easier than for migrants in the United States or Western Europe. Nevertheless, the logic of exclusion that provided the ideological foundations of Decree Law 1094 is still pervasive. It is not, however, immediately apparent; as will prove to be the case throughout this chapter, the devil is in the details.

Under the MERCOSUR agreement, the ethos of which is to promote more ready freedom of movement in addition to free trade, since 2009 Bolivian, Uruguayan, Paraguayan, Argentinean, and Brazilian citizens have been able to enter Chile—an associate member of MERCOSUR—as tourists and then apply for an MTRV before their permission to stay as tourists expires (see figure 5). For a national of these countries, in order to enter as a tourist, it is necessary to present a national identification card, and, technically, to be able to provide proof of "financial solvency."[19] To obtain an MTRV, applicants in Santiago must send by registered post a photocopy of their passport, including the page with their entry stamp into Chile; a photocopy of the tourist card given to them when they entered the country; and three photographs. Applicants in all places other than Santiago must go to their provincial government office and present in person their passport and two photocopies, their tourist card and two photocopies, and two photographs.[20]

The MTRV allows the bearer to undertake any employment or other legal activity in Chile. After holding an MTRV for one year, it is possible to apply for permanent residency. In order to apply, applicants must be able to show that they are currently formally employed with a contract and that they have been paying health and pension contributions for a year.[21] They must also present a range of documents in addition to those necessary for obtaining the MTRV, including a letter indicating their motives for wishing to remain in the country.[22] After holding permanent residency for five years, it is possible to apply to naturalize and become a full Chilean citizen. This process sounds simple and linear and indicates a hierarchical conceptualization of different citizenship statuses on the part of those responsible for the creation of the system.[23] On closer examination, however, there

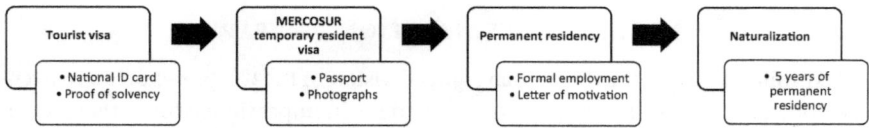

FIGURE 5. Regular migratory status acquisition for Bolivian migrants in Chile. Created by author.

are some anomalies that indicate, even "on paper," an underlying tendency toward exclusion and discrimination.

"On paper" one of the first noticeable anomalies is that it is only necessary to have a national ID card to enter Chile if you are from a MERCOSUR country; however, it is necessary to possess a passport to apply for the MTRV. This information is not widely publicized in Chile, and certainly not in Bolivia. Typically, poorer Bolivians will not have a passport because of the cost of obtaining one. Therefore, they may enter Chile with an ID card, only to find that they need a passport in order to obtain an MTRV. If they are in Santiago, they can apply for a passport via the Bolivian consulate located there, although the cost is higher than if they had applied in Bolivia. If they are in Arica (and the north of Chile more generally), they are not permitted to apply for a passport via the consulate, but rather will have to return to Bolivia in order to apply; this will, of course, incur some considerable cost. This first bureaucratic obstacle to regular migration targets—whether deliberately or not—Bolivians intending to migrate to the north of Chile. Those in this group frequently come from rural, indigenous communities in Bolivia where poverty is widespread.

A second incongruity apparent "on paper" is found within the fee structure for visa applications. The amount payable by each nationality upon applying for an MTRV in Chile is indicated in table 1. The fee is supposed to be reciprocal and so comparable to the fee payable by a Chilean applying for a similar visa in the partner country. During the period in which this research was conducted, the fee for a Chilean to apply for a similar visa for Bolivia was US$85. Prior to September 2013, the fee for a Bolivian to obtain an MTRV in Chile was US$150; it increased to US$283 that month. While I could not find an official explanation for the rise in the fee, staff at migrant organizations thought that it was likely to be for geopolitical reasons—namely, Bolivia's decision to take Chile to The Hague over the land and sea access dispute stemming from the War of the Pacific (see chapter 1). It appears to be a deliberate attempt to exclude Bolivians from the country, again targeting poorer migrants especially. The monthly minimum wage in Bolivia is approximately US$200, and in Chile it is approximately US$334; this gives some idea of what US$283 means in real terms to many migrants (who often do not earn even the minimum wage, as Beimar's case illustrates).

TABLE 1. Fees for MERCOSUR Temporary
Resident Visa by Country*

Country	Cost (US$)
Argentina	100
Brazil	100
Bolivia	283
Paraguay	312
Uruguay	65

SOURCE: Megan Ryburn, 2017.

*Additional information can be found at Ministerio del Interior y Seguridad Pública, "Resolución Exenta No. 64819," June 10, 2014, http://www.extranjeria.gob.cl/media/2013/09 /Valores-Visas.pdf.

Finally, the requirements for an application for permanent residency also seem to have a negative impact on poorer Bolivian migrants. Migrants must be formally employed in order to apply for permanent residency. As will be discussed, however, it is beneficial to employers *not* to formally contract migrants, particularly those employed in manual labor, who are inevitably earning low wages. If they are not formally employed and their MTRV is due to expire, migrants can apply to renew it for a further year. The cost, however, is the same as the cost for the original MTRV (US$283), whereas the cost for permanent residency is approximately US$95. Again, the fee structure seems to chiefly disadvantage migrants working in low-end jobs. These incongruities speak to the fact that the exclusionary and discriminatory ideological roots of Chile's migration law still underlie the foundations for policy today. Moreover, they provide conditions propitious to positioning migrants outside the bounds of legal citizenship, as high visa costs encourage migrants into irregular status positions—be it through working on a tourist visa, overstaying a tourist visa, or failing to renew an MTRV. This is further exacerbated by the ways in which migration law is applied "through paper" on a daily basis.

"THROUGH PAPER": MIGRATION LEGISLATION APPLIED

Although I am of a generation that remembers an era before the ubiquity of the internet in the global North, it goes without saying that it is now a major part of my life, as it is for 93 percent of the UK population. This is also the case for 78 percent of the Chilean population, who can access the internet at home. In Bolivia, only 41 percent of the population has home internet access.[24] There is an abundance of *cibercafés*, but despite this the number of people with regular internet access and know-how is certainly smaller than in neighboring Chile. Corroborating this point, in the early stages of my research I volunteered in a computer literacy course for migrants in Santiago. There were twenty participants, almost all under age forty-five, with the majority in their twenties and thirties, and most were Peruvian and Bolivian women. I had been told that this eight-week course was extremely popular and ran several times a year. I had been given no other prior indication of the nature of the course, however, and so imagined that we might be mastering the basics of Excel or practicing advanced searches on Google. I was surprised, then, to find that we were working on how to use a mouse and how to open and save a document.

Further reinforcing this initial impression of low levels of information and communications technology (ICT) knowledge among the migrant population in Chile, throughout my research I encountered many Bolivians in their twenties and thirties who did not have email or social media accounts and had very little knowledge of the internet. Moreover, even among those who had finished or partially finished school, literacy levels were frequently low (see chapter 5). This led me to reflect on how inordinately difficult it must be for many Bolivian migrants in Chile to access information regarding migration legislation as it pertains to them. The main source is the website of the DEM. Compounding the problem of its being online, the language used is dense and the layout unintuitive. The other major means of obtaining official information—by going in person to the DEM—is likewise not straightforward. The queue to ask for information or to make visa applications is one and the same; the offices open on Monday through Friday at 8:30 a.m. and close at 2:00 p.m., but by 6:00 a.m. there will be a line snaking halfway around the block. There is now an online booking system for visa appointments to try to cut waiting time, but obviously this doesn't help if you can't use the internet.[25]

The complexity of obtaining information about migratory status in Chile is unlikely to be a mechanism designed to deliberately discriminate against certain populations. Nevertheless, the impression conveyed is of a lofty state, communicating in a register distant from the language of ordinary people. Following James Ferguson and Akhil Gupta, it is an illustration of how the metaphor of the state as both vertical and encompassing is produced through "the routine operation of state institutions," thereby becoming our commonsense understanding of how a state should, and does, operate.[26] It is pervasive or encompassing because it can be present in internet cafés or in one's living room. It is also, however, a vertical state, inaccessible to those without certain social and cultural capital; those without internet must go as supplicants to stand outside for long hours in the hope of getting five minutes of face-to-face communication.

If a lack of accessible information on migration legislation can be classed as unintentionally discriminatory and unwittingly operating to construct a certain vision of the state, the attitudes of some border agents and other public officials involved in the application of migration legislation cannot. Diana reflected on the treatment she received at the DEM:

[They] attend you very badly in all honesty and it makes you not want to ask anything.... I think that people who are going to do those things to do with migrants should have more training in how to *atender* [help/serve/deal with others], you know? I mean, in how to treat people. How can I explain it? There are people from my country who maybe don't know how to read, how to write, they should be patient with those people.

In addition to a generally negative attitude toward some groups of migrants, there was evidence of specific instances of discrimination and arbitrary decision making by public officials. As discussed in chapter 2, Bolivians identified by border agents as "indigenous" and "poor" would often be asked for additional information as they crossed into Chile. Nebulously defined "proof of financial solvency" were required of some Bolivians but not others, as was information on their plans in Chile. Furthermore, Gabriela, lawyer for the Asociación in Arica, informed me that border agents would sometimes refuse to stamp certain Bolivians' passports as they entered Chile. The lack of a stamp means that it is then impossible for those people to apply for the MTRV, as they do not have proof of entry into Chile.[27] Indicating a by now familiar pattern, this practice seems to disproportionately affect Aymara Bolivians from rural backgrounds who intend to work in agriculture in the north. Thus, before even entering the nation-state, certain bodies are inscribed as unfit for entry into the space of legal citizenship.

Migration legislation is also sometimes applied in an arbitrary and discriminatory fashion once across the border. According to staff at the Asociación in both Santiago and Arica, immigration officers would on occasion ask migrants for additional documentation not required by law, such as, when applying for the MTRV, requesting to see an employment contract, which is not a requirement (see figure 5). When migrants were unable to produce this documentation, their application would be denied. It was noted by Gabriela, herself a white-mestiza Bolivian, that the processing time for Bolivians' visa applications, notably permanent residency, was also often significantly longer than the processing times for applications from migrants of other nationalities. This was so not only for service users to whom she provided legal advice, but in her own case as well, indicating that in this instance discrimination may have occurred on the basis of nationality rather than along more complex racial and class lines.

A further practice of the state, Gabriela informed me, was the enforcement of the temporary work permit in Arica. Technically, while the MTRV is being processed, if an applicant wishes to work during this period (approximately one hundred days), she should apply for a temporary work permit, the cost of which is US$150 for Bolivians. In Santiago, this is not enforced. In Arica, however, when Bolivians go in person to the provincial government office to make their application for the MTRV, they are automatically required to also obtain a temporary work permit. This means that the cost of the MTRV is effectively US$433 for a

Bolivian in Arica, compared to US$283 in Santiago. Again, it would seem that this has a particular impact on Aymara Bolivians from rural backgrounds, as they are the group who predominantly migrate to work in this part of Chile.

This collection of arbitrary and discriminatory practices by state actors, combined with the difficulties of obtaining easily digested information regarding migration legislation, augments the exclusionary characteristics already present in Chilean migration legislation "on paper." Those who are from lower socioeconomic backgrounds and those who are indigenous are the most affected. Here we have further evidence of the processes that contribute to the construction of the Bolivian-Chilean transnational space of legal citizenship and the selection of those deemed worthy for inclusion within it.

Employers also play an important role in the construction "through paper" of the space of legal citizenship. As has been observed for many decades in contexts of South-North migration, irregularity acts as an excellent structural enabler for maintaining a cheap workforce.[28] Irregularity may enable employers to avoid giving their workers contracts, paying them the minimum wage, ensuring they are enrolled in health and pension plans, and so forth. They can cajole their workforce through presenting themselves as benevolent protectors willing to give an irregular migrant a chance, but also coerce workers using the threat of reporting them to the authorities should they be noncompliant (see also chapter 4).

In Chile, active encouragement of irregularity occurs particularly in the construction and cleaning sectors, and above all in the *bodegas* and *parcelas* in Arica. In Arica, instead of applying for the MTRV, workers are often encouraged by employers to exit and enter Chile every three months in order to remain perpetually on tourist visas. Thus, they are not "undocumented" per se but are in a highly irregular migratory status position, which is beneficial to their employers for the above-mentioned reasons. All migrants I spoke to who were living and working on *parcelas* or in *bodegas*, and several working in other sectors, had been in this situation. Many had been working like this for over a year and even more than three.

In Santiago, due to its distance from the border, this is generally not a viable strategy. Migrants are still often encouraged to work on their tourist visas in their first few months in the country but then are more likely to regularize by applying for the MTRV. Some, however, overstay their tourist visas with encouragement from their employers. Kinberley, who as mentioned in chapter 2 had been briefly working in wholesale clothing retail and living in a *bodega*, reported that when she enquired about obtaining an MTRV because she did not want to overstay her tourist visa, her employer replied, "But what do you need that for? . . . Because we're going to . . . when you leave [Chile] we're going to pay your fine."[29] Kinberley explained that employers in such places would sometimes refuse to allow employees to leave their workplace or living quarters during working hours, thus ensuring that it was nearly impossible for them to obtain the MTRV. She indicated that this was part of a coercive strategy to keep employees entirely dependent on employers and in fear of being reported to the authorities should they complain about working conditions.

More common, however, is for employers in Santiago to facilitate employees' applications for the MTRV by granting them time off work to complete the process. By allowing this, employers ensure that they are employing "documented" workers and therefore are not at risk of being fined for the employment of an "undocumented" workforce should they be subject to an inspection by the Departamento de Trabajo (Department of Labor). This does not mean, however, that employers necessarily then provide a contract, pay health and pension contributions, or even pay the minimum wage. The lack of these requirements makes it difficult for migrant employees to obtain permanent residency. Keeping migrants in a constant state of temporary residency is beneficial to employers because the uncertainty it generates often makes the migrants less likely to seek employment elsewhere, as they are frightened of ending up jobless and with only temporary legal status. Employers clearly possess a great deal of power to manipulate migration legislation to their advantage through the demanding and withholding of particular papers. When combined with other processes of applying migration legislation 'through paper,' the effect is stark discrimination against particular groups of migrants.

PRESENTING PAPERS: MIGRANT NEGOTIATIONS OF LEGAL CITIZENSHIP

It is not, however, only these processes from above that produce the space of legal citizenship and differentiated access to it. In the concern to address the structural elements that can be neglected in some qualitative studies of (ir)regularity, it is crucial not to let the balance slide the other way into disregard for the role of migrant agency.[30] Bridget Anderson and Martin Ruhs have written convincingly of the need to avoid "oversimplifying a vision of irregular migrants either as 'victims' of exploitation or as 'villains' who broke the law," by fully acknowledging migrant agency.[31] This echoes arguments about recognizing agency that have largely come from ethnographic accounts of everyday citizenship practices.[32]

Specifically in relation to legal citizenship and migration, I argue that, in line with Mcilwaine and Goldring and Landolt, it is also detrimental to focus only on those migrants in situations of irregularity, as this may run the risk of contributing further to the erroneous idea of an irregular/regular binary.[33] Transition between different migratory statuses is fluid and shifting; there is no "end-state," as the next several paragraphs indicate.[34] I explore here the ways in which migrants, sometimes with the support of a migrant organization, exercised agency in negotiating their legal status position and thus played a part in the construction of the transnational space of legal citizenship. First I address irregularity and temporary residence in Arica, then in Santiago. Finally, I discuss permanent residency and naturalization.

Irregularity and Temporary Residence in Arica

As already established, the physical geography of Arica led to employers, particularly on the *parcelas*, encouraging their migrant employees to remain perpetual "tourists," entering and exiting Arica every three months in order to renew their tourist visas. This was one of the principal forms of irregularity I encountered. In the vast majority of cases, Bolivians do not enter Chile unauthorized. Rather, as should be clear by now, if irregularity occurs it is because they move into irregular status positions after entering in a regular fashion, which is often the case with respect to irregular migration in other parts of the globe, too.[35]

Migrants with irregular status on the *parcelas* in Arica are not, however, always simply victims of their employers' demands. Some migrants, particularly initially, do not see the value of the MTRV. The cost is prohibitive, and they believe they will have more freedom simply coming and going as 'tourists." Interestingly, some also think it gives them a modicum of power over their employer on the *parcela*. Julieta, age forty-two, now a full-time mother but with several years' previous experience working on the *parcelas*, succinctly explained the potential relationship between the *patrón* and the worker on a tourist visa:

> Because [the worker] doesn't have papers, the *patrón* he says to the worker, 'Where are you going to go and complain? I'm not going to pay you" or "I'm not going to worry about your health, where are you going to go?"
>
> And so the worker says as well, "Because I have no contract, I can just go, I mean, I can do what I like for the *patrón*, if I want to do it, I do it; if I don't, I don't."
>
> There are neither rights nor obligations.

This fits with Alice Bloch and Milena Chimienti's argument that "looking at agency allows us to see irregularity as something that can be envisaged by some groups as a resource in a particular context."[36] The degree to which remaining on a tourist visa could be categorized as indicating a more profound form of resistance to powerful actors and structural factors is, however, debatable. As Cathy McIlwaine suggests in her discussion of practices used by Latin American migrants in London to negotiate (ir)regularity, "the everyday realities of living in a state of irregularity which so often entails multiple exclusions make is difficult to conceive of such practices as resistance when viewed through the eyes of migrants."[37] Indeed, as Julieta and others who had worked on tourist visas on the *parcelas* in Arica explained, it slowly became apparent that being in this situation was actually far more beneficial to the *patrón* than to the worker.

Nevertheless, participants still found the MTRV expensive and also restrictive. Some wanted to spend less than a year at a time in Chile and to be able to freely come and go between their home communities in Bolivia and the *parcelas* in the Valle de Azapa, reflecting the seasonal nature of much of the work in which they were engaged; during the visa application process, however, it is necessary to remain in Chile. Some people found this problematic, as this process can last a hundred days or more. A further underlying factor that may have motivated people on the *parcelas*—the vast majority of whom were Aymara—not to apply for the MTRV was its incongruity with an indigenous perspective on the geography of the area—namely, the artificiality of the borders that carve up what would once have been land freely and frequently traversed.[38] Furthermore, the isolation of the *parcelas* makes access to information on migration legislation even more difficult than in urban areas, which is compounded by the fact that ICT and literacy levels among workers in these places are often low, and Spanish is frequently not their first language.

I found that two migrant organizations—the Asociación in Arica and Radio Andina (also a pseudonym)—played an important role in enabling migrants on the *parcelas* to obtain information regarding visa applications. In 2013 the Asociación in Arica had conducted a survey on the *parcelas* to find out about migrants' working conditions. In order to gain access, they had had to negotiate with the owners of the *parcelas*. Their strategy had been to explain the benefits of employing workers in regular migratory situations to the owners, highlighting in particular the fines to which they could be subjected for noncompliance. They then offered to assist the owners with free legal advice for them and their employees in return for access to conduct the survey. Once access had been gained, the Asociación in Arica was able to give migrant workers information about the MTRV and their labor rights both orally and in the form of brief, easy-to-read pamphlets while conducting the survey. The Asociación in Arica has also focused on building strong relationships with schools in the Valle de Azapa. Here they hold workshops about the MTRV application process and free legal advice "clinics" at times of day when migrant workers on the *parcelas* are most likely to be able to attend.

Radio Andina is a local radio station that transmits to Arica and the surrounding area. The focus of the radio station is on promoting indigenous Andean cultures, in particular Aymara culture, and many of its programs are in Aymara. Every weekday from 10:00 to 11:00 a.m., they broadcast *An Hour with Bolivia*. This program is particularly targeted at the Bolivian migrant population in Arica and the surrounding area and is presented in a mixture of Aymara and Spanish. One of the key focuses of the program is conveying information about visas and labor rights to the migrant population.

Luisa, whom I mentioned in chapter 2, had come and gone between Oruro and the Valle de Azapa as a tourist since 2007. In recent years her journeys had been made with her partner and two small children in tow, who were similarly all in possession of tourist visas. However, she had come to see working on a tourist visa

as extremely precarious, saying that it gave employers the power "to enslave you
. . . you're afraid, you don't have the right to demand anything." She began to listen
to Radio Andina as she worked in the fields picking tomatoes, and it was here in
2013 that she heard information about the MTRV and the assistance with the *papeleo* available at the Asociación in Arica. It was a great help that the information was
given in Aymara, her first language, as her Spanish, though very good, was not
completely fluent.

Armed with this information, Luisa negotiated several days off work in order to
visit the office of the Asociación in Arica and then from there to complete her
application at the provincial government office. Luisa was earning around US$12
per day—less than the minimum wage—and the US$433 fee she had to pay for the
MTRV application and the temporary work permit required in Arica used up all
of her savings. Nonetheless, she expressed to me that she felt much safer and more
protected with the MTRV and was applying for her children's visas. She also
wanted to help more migrant workers access the visa and offered to put up posters
and hand out leaflets from the Asociación that I had with me when I interviewed
her. This was a brave act, as Luisa was very aware that her employer would rather
employ workers on tourist visas than those on MTRVs, so she ran some personal
risk by publicizing the latter. Her resolve to do this was indicative of the ways in
which migrants would pass information informally through their social and kinship networks in order to assist each other with processes of *papeleo*, in addition to
seeking out the more formal support of the Asociación or other organizations. As
I left, Luisa told me that she knew where she would put most of the posters: on
the fence on the roadside outside her *parcela*. But she would also put one on the
bare walls of the shelter where her family lived, as she liked the message they had
on them: "Somos humanos, no mano de obra" ("We are human beings, not just
laborers").

On another *parcela*, workers had similarly become aware of the MTRV through
the Asociación in Arica and Radio Andina. Rather than going individually to
Arica in order to apply, however, they had organized collectively to petition their
patrón to take them all to the provincial government offices to begin the visa application process. They were also negotiating with him to cover 40 percent of their
visa costs. Marcos was the most senior worker and therefore charged with speaking directly with the *patrón*. However, when I asked another worker, Lisa, age
twenty-five, who did the organizing, she replied with a grin that it was the women
who got things done, just as in her rural community in the *departamento* of Oruro.
While one must be wary of drawing strong conclusions from the experiences of
relatively few people, my discussions with Lisa, Luisa, other workers on *parcelas*,
and staff at the Asociación in Arica did hint at its being women who took the lead
in organizing to regularize their migratory status. This provides an interesting
point of comparison with findings from research undertaken with Latin American

migrants in other contexts, where it has been noted that—sometimes but not always—women have tended to be more involved than men in informal organizing and migrant politics.[39]

Irregularity and Temporary Residence in Santiago

While perpetually working on a tourist visa was the most likely form of irregularity in Arica, in Santiago visa overstaying was more common. Some, like Beimar, were put off by the complex bureaucracy involved in regularizing, but for many, financial difficulties were the primary reason for overstaying a tourist visa or MTRV. They simply could not afford to pay the high visa application cost. As indicated in the introduction, in a conversation I had with Luz María when she was seven months pregnant, she told me that she and Wilson had been eating only rice and vegetables and sometimes going hungry in their attempts to save enough to pay the costs for both of them to apply for the visa. Wilson was working on a tourist visa for less than the minimum wage. Luz María had been also, until she was fired because she was pregnant. In spite of their efforts to save, both moved further into irregularity as they overstayed their tourist visas.

In this situation of irregularity, migrants have an opportunity to pay a fine and then regularize their situation by applying for the MTRV. The amount of the fine is set at the discretion of the immigration officer for the DEM overseeing the case and can vary between one and twenty times the monthly minimum wage (i.e., between US$342 and US$6,840). Generally, the fines are set relatively low; however, even US$342 plus the US$283 for the visa is a very significant sum for a migrant earning at or below the minimum wage.

A scheme set up by the Departamento de Asistencia Social (DAS, Department of Social Welfare) in conjunction with the Asociación exposes some of the contradictions inherent in a state relying increasingly on a cheap migrant workforce to carry out manual labor but requiring them to pay high fees in order to hold regular status.[40] Since 2012 the DAS has been providing the Asociación in Santiago approximately US$38,000 per annum to support "migrants in regular situations." The funding can be employed in a variety of ways, but the majority is used to pay the costs of visa applications for migrants who have overstayed their tourist visas or who are about to overstay. In a Kafkaesque bureaucratic sleight of hand, the Asociación carries out an assessment of the finances of migrants in this situation and negotiates with the DEM to lower the fine payable for overstaying. This can normally be reduced to approximately US$60. The Asociación then uses funds provided by the DAS to cover the costs of the fine and the application for the MTRV.

Between May and November 2013 the Asociación in Santiago assisted thirty-six Bolivians using funds from the DAS, nine of whom I interviewed. In thirty-four cases, the funding was used to pay fees for the MTRV and for any fines. The social worker in charge of administering the DAS funds for the Asociación told me that they had seen a significant increase in the numbers of Bolivians applying for financial assistance since the augmentation of the Bolivian MTRV tariff in September 2013. She was immensely frustrated by the whole system and longed for the DAS funds to be used for other types of desperately needed assistance. Her only short-term option, however, was to continue the absurd exercise of using state funding to pay state-levied fees and fines; otherwise, people would be deported.

I witnessed this absurdity firsthand when, as part of my everyday engagement with the Asociación in Santiago, I assisted a Haitian migrant in completing the *papeleo* necessary to apply for DAS support for fine and visa costs. We spent several hours playing around with the form's family budget declaration to ensure he was sufficiently "poor" to be eligible—this was a man who was unemployed with a family of four to support, and whom one felt really should have been eligible for refugee status given the circumstances of his departure from Haiti. But we had to make sure to *prove* this, to position him as thoroughly "vulnerable" in order for him, in the words of Austin Zeiderman, writing on the politics of recognition in Colombia, "to be visible to legal institutions and government apparatuses" according to their frames of reference.[41]

It had been somewhat easier for many of the Bolivians I interviewed who had overstayed tourist visas or MTRVs and been part of the DAS program to "prove" their vulnerability according to the state's criteria for inclusion and exclusion. Most were women, many had small children or were pregnant, and some had chronic illnesses such as Chagas' disease or hepatitis C. These factors were noted when completing the *papeleo* to justify the need to cover visa and fine costs using DAS funds. I am not, of course, in any way suggesting that they should not have been granted access to the DAS funds. Rather, I wish to point out the ways in which hierarchies are constructed that position some migrants as more "deserving" than others, more amenable to acceptance within the bounds of legal citizenship. These hierarchies may be particularly prejudicial to younger men because vulnerability—which makes one more "deserving"—is generally associated with femininity, childhood, motherhood, and old age.[42] Furthermore, constructions of race and nationality may also play into which migrants can more easily position themselves as vulnerable.

Permanent Residency and Naturalization

Constructions of race and nationality continued to play out strongly for those in regular as well as irregular status positions. As already discussed, a variety of practices and processes "on paper" and "through paper" by public officials and employers often made it difficult for poor, and particularly indigenous, migrants to move from temporary to permanent residency status. The eventual acquisition of permanent residency (Permanencia Definitiva) generated evident relief in those who managed it, and sometimes expressions of pride in having negotiated the complex bureaucratic system. Amanda, age twenty-five, from El Alto, relayed in some detail the back and forth between different offices that the process had necessitated, finishing her account with the affirmation, "Y así fue como lo logré. Sí, así fue como lo logré" ("And that's how I achieved it. Yes, that's how I achieved it"). Generally, permanent residency was obtained with less recourse to migration organizations or other external assistance than the MTRV, given that by this stage migrants already had a grasp of the workings of Chilean bureaucracy. Once in possession of permanent residency, they gained most of the rights of full Chilean citizens, and after five years with permanent residency they could apply for housing subsidies and vote in municipal elections. At this stage, they could also apply to naturalize as Chilean citizens.

It was not particularly common to want to naturalize, however, and the people I spoke to who had naturalized had only done so from the point at which Chile began to accept dual nationality (in 2005). As Kevin, age forty-eight, from La Paz—who was in the process of naturalizing for what he termed "practical reasons"—explained, people had a sense that they were betraying Bolivia upon naturalizing as Chileans due to deep-seated feelings about the War of the Pacific, the ongoing geopolitical rivalry between the two countries, and the racism they and their compatriots had often experienced from Chileans. Kevin informed me that for many years there had been a pervasive myth that upon acquiring Chilean nationality "you had to sing the [Chilean] national anthem and spit and stamp on the Bolivian flag." It was certainly a myth with some currency, repeated to me, for example, by José, age forty-seven, an itinerant market seller in El Agro, Arica, who had moved to Chile as a toddler but still had not naturalized.

So, while practicality and a desire for stability had encouraged participants to apply for permanent residency, naturalizing was viewed as a process that entailed emotional considerations as well as practicalities and was therefore approached with greater circumspection. The emotional clearly should not be neglected in studies of citizenship. As Elaine Ho puts it, considering "emotional subjectivities" can illuminate the ways in which people "emotionally negotiate the power relations of citizenship governance."[43] This certainly complicates the notion of citizenship status acquisition as a linear process with the end goal as nationality and highlights the important role of migrants' agency—the ways in which they decide to "present papers"—in constructing the space of legal citizenship.

CONCLUSION

As Beimar's story at the beginning of this chapter illustrates so clearly, migrants may transition through a wide range of (ir)regular migratory status positions. The concept of linear progression from one (ir)regular migratory status to another is often not applicable. The reasons for which migrants possess and change migratory statuses are many and varied, influenced by both structural and agentic factors. Building particularly on Goldring and Landolt, and McIlwaine, I suggest that it is helpful to conceive of different migratory statuses as part of a fluid transnational space of legal citizenship. The Bolivian-Chilean transnational space of legal citizenship is constructed through complex processes of *papeleo* that feature multiple actors. There are those that produce, and have historically produced, migration legislation as it exists "on paper," influenced by an oppressive and repressive military regime. Thus, the ideology of exclusion of certain foreign Others lingers on in pen and ink, in articles and subarticles. It also, however, pervades the ways in which this legislation is communicated and enacted "through paper" in the everyday by state representatives. The imaginary of an omnipresent yet distant state is generated through the production of information that is at once "universally" available by virtue of being online, but simultaneously very difficult to access for migrants living in poverty, and particularly for those with lower levels of literacy or who do not speak Spanish as a first language.

And when face-to-face communication does occur when papers must be exchanged, it may be colored by a rude and dismissive attitude on the part of officials, if not by outright discrimination and arbitrary decision making. Employers are also often complicit in the demanding and withholding of papers that further contribute to the differential positioning of migrants within, and outside of, the bounds of the transnational space of legal citizenship. These actions of officials and employers *through paper*, in addition to the legislation *on paper*, are both a product of and serve to reinforce racial hierarchies existent in Chile; this is made baldly apparent when geographical variation in practices is observed. While discrimination is rife in Santiago, it is particularly prevalent in Arica, where the majority of Bolivian migrants are indigenous and come from poor rural communities. As has been the case for centuries for many of the indigenous inhabitants of the Americas, through bundles of exclusionary practices the state and its actors cast them to the periphery of legal citizenship. Thus, while migrants may nominally have more options for regularization in Chile than in some South-North migration contexts, a range of subtle exclusions is built into the visa application system (e.g., high visa fees), which when combined with practices of some state actors and employers perpetuates disparities of access to legal citizenship.

The ways in which legal status is produced "from above" cannot, therefore, be overlooked, and must be understood in historical context. Nonetheless, migrants' role in constructing the boundaries of the transnational space of legal citizenship and negotiating their position within it is also of crucial importance. While being in a position of irregularity is largely dictated by structural factors, there is at times an element of choice, as when those in Arica sometimes prefer to work on a tourist visa. Agentic decision making plays a substantial role when migrants engage with organizations such as the Asociación to assist them with their visa applications, and when they pass information to one another through their social networks. While migrants must largely play by the state-made rules of the game, there is some capacity for these to be worked around at times. This might be by representing oneself in a particular way in order to be recognized and admitted within the bounds of legal citizenship, as demonstrated through the use of the DAS funds to pay for visa applications and fines for those deemed "vulnerable."

Migrants' fluctuating legal status across borders so often depends, then, on an exclusionary and somewhat capricious state, but migrants do find ways to negotiate the strictures of the system. Uncertainty is the unifying condition describing most of the varied positions of migrants within and outside the transnational space of legal citizenship, as was often reflected in the questions—some rhetorical, some not—that I was posed. Will I be asked at the border for proof of solvency before being allowed into Chile? Is it best to remain working on a tourist visa as my employer suggests, despite the risks? How on earth am I going to raise the funds to pay for my family's visa costs? Will naturalizing as Chilean make me less Bolivian? The frequency and urgency with which these questions were asked indicates that, although it is important not to overstate the place of legal citizenship in migrants' lives and to fully acknowledge the many other dimensions of citizenship, the legal element is nonetheless of real significance. This is so not least because of its bearing on migrants' position with regard to other spaces of citizenship, as the chapters that follow attest.

4

¿El Sueño Chileno?

For International Women's Day 2015, Alice Volpi, a Brazilian graphic designer residing in Chile who is concerned with migrant rights, produced an evocative homage of images of working migrant women. Reproduced in figure 6, these images speak profoundly to the "migrant division of labor" existent in Chile, the macroeconomic conditions and "global care chains" that produce and are produced by it, and its affective dimensions.[1] While, as the image of the doctor indicates, some female migrants in Chile are able to work in their professions, the majority—regardless of their level of education—are employed in domestic labor, petty commerce, or cleaning. Further demonstrating the gendering of migrant labor, men are often employed in construction or agriculture.

Racialization plays an additional role in creating a hierarchy between and within these divisions. Both female and male migrants in Chile frequently experience labor exploitation, as well as discrimination in the workplace, and are likely to feel unable to reach their full potential in their working lives. The consignment of migrants to "unskilled" labor in Chile through gendered and racialized processes, and in many cases the negation of labor rights, mirrors similar patterns seen in contexts of the global North in relation to migration from the global South.

Migrants' economic exclusion is not, however, limited to difficulties accessing work in the receiving country, although to date this has been the key consideration in discussions of migrants' economic citizenship.[2] As I explain in this chapter, migrants may also struggle to access financial services and may experience hardship as they make sacrifices in order to send money "back home." Furthermore, for many the very reason for migration has been economic marginalization in the home country, caused by a variety of factors. Nonetheless, exclusion is only part of

FIGURE 6. Illustration for International Women's Day 2015, an homage to migrant women in Chile. Source: Alice Volpi, 2015.

the story. As they pursue "*el sueño chileno*" (the "Chilean dream")—a phrase increasingly used (often with a heavy dose of irony) to describe the motivation behind coming to Chile—some migrants may indeed experience greater economic integration in some respects. This may be through remittances or savings, which allow for eventual improvement in the standard of living; through a more fulfilling job than in the country of origin; or through greater disposable income.

These multiple inclusions and exclusions coexist and interrelate across borders, making it fundamental to take a transnational perspective on migrants' economic citizenship. Thinking in terms of a transnational space of economic citizenship enables this and also encourages a focus both on migrants' everyday experience and practice of economic citizenship and on the processes from above that structure and constrain the practices in which they may engage. Bearing this out empirically, in the rest of the chapter I first discuss the economic marginalization in Bolivia that often acted as a catalyst for pursuing *el sueño chileno*, then reflect on the degree to which the dream was realized after crossing the border.

THE FOUNDATION OF DREAMS: ECONOMIC
MARGINALIZATION AS A CATALYST FOR MIGRATION

Adriana offered me her gnarled, arthritic hand, inviting me to touch the calluses on her palm, the embodiment of a lifetime of hard work. She was over seventy, the oldest person I interviewed. We sat on low stools in front of her market stall in El Agro, Arica, sipping herbal tea while she told me her story in an energetic Spanish peppered with Aymara words and grammatical structures. She was from a very small rural Aymara community in the *departamento* of Oruro and had lost her father at the age of three and her mother at the age of eight. She was unable to go to school, and following the death of her parents she survived by going

> from neighbour to neighbour, to aunts (*tías*) . . . who gave me [food] to eat. I helped
> to shepherd animals, livestock and sometimes we also cultivated potatoes . . . and
> like that I grew. Then I was eight, nine, ten. At ten I went to Oruro [the city] to
> work. . . . I looked after a baby, I carried it around. I helped the lady to clean. . . . She
> also made me make *chicha de maní*. . . . I worked there about two months then . . .
> the lady didn't pay me, she left me like that, she didn't give me anything, anything.[3]

Homeless and with no money, ten-year-old Adriana took up the offer of some cousins to help her cross into Chile, where they said there were better economic prospects. She made that first journey by donkey, by bus, and on foot; left to fend for herself on arrival in Arica, she spent several nights without shelter or food. She was eventually taken in by a Chilean *señora* who saw her crying on the roadside, and Adriana initially undertook a combination of domestic and agricultural work on one of the *parcelas* in the Valle de Azapa for a minimal salary. From there she gradually worked her way up to owning a market stall in El Agro.

Things have certainly improved to an extent for most people in rural areas in the Bolivian altiplano today. Still, some of the structural factors that led to Adriana's exclusion from economic citizenship remain present in the Bolivian countryside. Poverty disproportionately affects rural dwellers in the altiplano, the vast majority of whom are indigenous. This is a consequence of a lack of agricultural infrastructure and uneven access to basic services, health care, and education.[4] The inability to maintain even subsistence farming in small communities on the high plateaus has been exacerbated by drought, which has increased in recent years due to climate change.[5] Conversations I had on a trip I took in Bolivia made clear that these factors are propelling out-migration from these communities, as well as the continuing internal migration documented in chapter 1.

A member of the staff of the Asociación para Migrantes in Bolivia, headquartered in El Alto, invited me to travel with her to Patacamaya, a town of twenty thousand in the *departamento* of La Paz, which is a hub for smaller rural communities, whose residents come to trade there (see figure 7). She introduced me to Don Martín, a man of some influence in the local area, who is a businessman but

FIGURE 7. Market day in Patacamaya, where rural communities come to trade, 2014. Photo by author.

also is concerned with migration and migrants' rights. He confirmed that "the earth drying up" has been a key factor influencing migration to neighboring countries, with Chile an increasingly popular destination. As he showed us around the town and we spoke to various people, I learned that those in the town were doing fairly well economically, because they were generally involved in the burgeoning dairy industry or in the production of quinoa for export, as well as in trade in the *zona franca* (free trade zone) with Chile (see figure 8). Those from the small, rural communities were missing out, though, as they could not afford the expensive irrigation systems now required to grow their crops, so the young people were migrating in greater and greater numbers, leaving behind the elderly and young children.

For those from the cities, the processes causing exclusion from economic citizenship were different. As has been reported in relation to South-North migration, those who migrate from Bolivia's urban areas tend not to be the very poorest in society and may be well educated and from middle-class families (see also chapter 1).[6] In the Bolivian-Chilean context, the definition given by Isabela, age twenty-five, from La Paz, of her family's socioeconomic position and class was one that

FIGURE 8. The *zona franca*, Patacamaya, 2014. Photo by author.

applied in many cases. She explained, "We are from a humble family (*familia humilde*): we are not from a middle-class family, but neither a lower-class family." Indeed, the majority of migrants I worked with had had some kind of employment in Bolivia, generally "unskilled" or "semiskilled"; however, it was commented upon by the majority who had been living and working in urban areas that the salaries were insufficient to ensure a reasonable standard of living. Constanza, age thirty-two, from Sucre, explained succinctly that "in Bolivia the salaries are very low. They barely give you enough to eat, and not even to eat well."

One of the key issues for many was that although the salaries they earned might yield enough for subsistence, they did not provide enough to save, buy land or a house, support their children if they wanted to go on to higher education, or generally "look to the future" in the words of Aimy, age thirty-four, from Cochabamba. This situation was exacerbated if there was any kind of difficulty within the family, as Amanda's case illustrated. Amanda, age twenty-five, was from El Alto. Throughout her childhood and teens her family had been in a similar economic position to Isabela's. She explained:

> [M]y family has always had limited resources (*siempre ha sido de bajos recursos*), not so much, but we've always had economic problems because of my dad's illness. My

dad couldn't work and I, as I am the eldest daughter, I looked after my mum a lot. I worked while I was at school, I helped my mum, and upon leaving school I put myself to work (*me puse a trabajar*). . . . I would have liked to keep studying, but it wasn't possible. Because I wanted to help my family.

Amanda became employed as a full-time domestic worker upon leaving school, earning around US$100 per month. Combined with her mother's income, they had just enough to get by, with the support of extended family with whom Amanda's family lived, paying lower rent than on the private market. Amanda's family entered into crisis, however, when an argument with the extended family resulted in their eviction.

In such situations, lack of savings or a safety net of comprehensive social security led some participants to take out loans with high interest rates, which they realistically had little chance of paying off with the salaries they were earning in Bolivia.[7] For example, Magdalena, age thirty-eight, from El Alto, had taken out a high-interest informal loan after the landlord increased the rent on the small shop from which she sold clothes. She could not manage to keep up with the loan repayments, however, and quickly became heavily indebted. She was forced to close her shop, and in desperation, came to Chile to work as a *nana puertas adentro* in the hope of becoming solvent again.

Migrants who came to Chile from both urban and rural areas identified the various factors that prevented them from participating as full economic citizens in Bolivia as structural. Their narratives indicated that they viewed themselves as hard workers who, for reasons beyond their control, could not advance beyond living at subsistence level and at times experienced extreme poverty, with even basic food needs going unmet. Low salaries in the cities were blamed on the state, and some participants who had been initially supportive of Evo Morales's government communicated disillusionment with what they saw as the slow pace of economic change (see chapter 6 for further discussion). Lack of infrastructure and employment prospects in rural areas was likewise often blamed on the state, and sometimes the absence of an inclusive welfare system was also mentioned.

To this I would add the worrying facility with which some interviewees had acquired loans that were far beyond their means to pay back; this is perhaps an indication of a lack of financial regulation that may affect most adversely those who are already in insecure situations. Thus, while what could be identified as precarious employment was a central factor contributing to migrants' being positioned on the economic periphery in Bolivia, it was not the whole story. Overall, their citizenship in Bolivia could certainly be classed as "uncertain" from an economic perspective; though not indigent, many experienced a fairly hand-to-mouth existence and lacked the possibility of planning financially for the future. The irony, of course, is the incompatibility between their full *legal* citizenship status in their home country and the realities of their access to this dimension of substantive citizenship.

To speak of migration as a "practice of citizenship" may provide a means of highlighting this irony: by moving to a place where they do not possess full legal citizenship, many migrants act on the dream of becoming economic citizens, either in that country or through remittance sending and saving to enable this in the future in their countries of origin. It is perhaps, therefore, a way of challenging the false binary between forced and voluntary migration and indicating the complex relationship between structure and agency. Migration for economic reasons has often been viewed as "voluntary" migration, and to a degree there is an element of choice involved in this type of migration. Nonetheless, if, as previously discussed, many of the economic factors underlying participants' migration can be understood as structural, the notion of a dichotomy between "forced" and "voluntary" migration is complicated.[8] Referring to migration as a practice of citizenship both indicates the agency of the migrants and reminds us that they are taking this decision because they cannot be full, certain citizens in their country of origin. Furthermore, this approach may underscore the danger of "dependency on migration as a development strategy," which, as Kavita Datta and colleagues suggest, can lead to a situation wherein people are more valued as migrants than as citizens, with national governments encouraging the transition from citizens to migrants rather than facilitating migrants' return home.[9] This also enables states to shirk their responsibilities to undertake structural reform at home.

Thus, referring to migration as a "citizenship practice" also references the wider debate around the potential for remittances to cure development ills. Following a certain degree of hype around the development potential of remittances from the late 1980s to the early 2000s, it has increasingly been realized that the role they play is far more ambiguous than previously thought.[10] They may alleviate "transient poverty" but fail to have an effect on long-term "structural poverty," resulting in uneven development within communities.[11] Moreover, as is gradually being recognized, the effort and sacrifice made on the part of the migrants may lead to detrimental health and social outcomes for them.[12]

On the one hand, then, migration and consequent remittance sending can be understood as an agentic decision taken as part of a family livelihood strategy.[13] To return to Amanda's story, she described the negotiations with her mother in relation to her migrating as follows:

> I said to my mum, "I'm going, I'm going to go . . . I'm going so I can help to get a piece of land. I'm going to send you money, or we'll get a loan and I'll pay little by little." Like that.
>
> My mum said to me, "No, no, you mustn't go like that, *mi hija*."
>
> But no, that was my decision. And my mum couldn't change my mind. She couldn't make me change the decision I took. She couldn't.

Amanda's mother later agreed that migration was the best idea given the circumstances, although there was then a debate over whether Amanda or her mother should be the one to move. On the grounds of age, the fact that Amanda was single, and the emotional fallout for her younger siblings if their mother left, it was decided that Amanda should go. Several other participants in their late teens and early twenties spoke of similar exchanges with their parents over the decision to migrate. While their parents were reluctant to let them go, they conceded that it appeared to be the most viable option for enabling the economic betterment of the family.

On the other hand, even when participants narrated events leading up to their migration in terms of active decision making and negotiation with family, the degree to which it was a decision taken "voluntarily" was a moot point. Phrases such as "obliged to migrate" and "not much other option [other than to migrate]" were used in conjunction with discussion of migration as a choice. Loreta, age twenty-eight, from Santa Cruz, noted that "in reality, no one forces you to leave your country, but the economic situation is not good at all in my country, we're in a terrible, terrible crisis." Furthermore, the economic outcomes of migration were certainly mixed. The "practice of citizenship" represented by migration by no means always led to a more certain economic citizenship.

LIVING THE DREAM? MIXED ECONOMIC OUTCOMES OF MIGRATION

Indicating the context-specific and varied effects of remittances, migrants I spoke to used remittances in a number of ways, from supporting children and elderly parents to financing debt to buying property.[14] Amanda had managed to do the latter, purchasing a plot of land on the outskirts of El Alto, where her family were in the process of building a house. Amanda's long-term plan was for all the family to live on the same plot but in separate apartments. She described what had been built so far for her parents and two youngest siblings:

> Two bedrooms, a living room, and the kitchen. Four rooms. So each one is going to settle in their own space. Soon we're going to start building up . . . because . . . my thinking was, "Yes, I'm going to build an apartment, my sister's going to build an apartment, and there you have it." Yes.[15]

Aside from the ways in which some migrants like Amanda saw tangible improvement in their economic citizenship status transnationally, there were also less quantifiable ways in which greater involvement in the transnational space of economic citizenship might be experienced. The degree to which such involvement was possible was strongly influenced by gender and was often also contingent on participants' positions within the transnational space of legal citizenship.

Specifically, there was an interesting gendered phenomenon whereby male migrants in regular migratory situations who worked in physically demanding employment, such as in construction or as mechanics (but excluding employment in agriculture), commented on a variety of qualitative improvements as a consequence of their employment in Chile. First, their working conditions in Chile were viewed as better than those in Bolivia. Alberto, age thirty, from Sucre, explained why this was so in construction:

> Everything there, the builder does everything by brute force. While here in Chile it's more about tools. . . . [T]he work is lighter here, Bolivians feel that the work is lighter here. And because of that sometimes the Bolivians, when we meet up at lunchtime or in the morning, in the breaks, we comment that maybe we're going to stay here because the work is better here than in Bolivia!

More advanced technology, combined with greater concern for the health and safety of the worker and, in general, respect for an eight- to nine-hour working day, made for employment that was less physically demanding and dangerous than in Bolivia. Moreover, several participants commented on the opportunities that working in Chile had given them to informally learn about new technology and more advanced techniques in construction or mechanics. Finally, this particular group of male migrants felt they had slightly more disposable income in Chile than they had earned in Bolivia for carrying out the same type of work. This led to better quality of life. For Jonathan, age twenty-one, from Sucre, it translated to being able to buy ham and milk, which for him in Bolivia had been luxury items. Alberto commented that now his wages were sufficient to "even buy my wife a little present for her birthday."

These men conveyed the sense that they felt their employment in Chile enabled them to participate economically more fully than they had before. They found their work fulfilling and interesting because they had the opportunity to learn new skills, and the financial rewards were greater than in Bolivia. In contrast to contexts of South-North migration (and some contexts of South-South migration) in which men may end up working in traditionally feminized employment such as cleaning and caring, there was little evidence that this was the case in Chile.[16] One could posit that this is so in part because Chile retains a more strongly *machista* culture than in many countries of the global North, and thus there would be more resistance from Chileans to employing men in cleaning or caring. For migrant men, this meant that in the workplace their gender identities were not challenged to the same degree as in some other contexts of migration. They also experienced less deskilling than women. These two factors may contribute to more job satisfaction than in some other migration contexts or for some migrant women in Chile.

It must be highlighted, however, that the greater economic inclusion experienced by migrant men working in physically demanding employment only applied when they were legally resident. For those migrant men with irregular status undertaking physical, unskilled labor, work and pay conditions could be very precarious. Additionally, of the sixty migrants I interviewed in depth, less than a third managed to remit regularly or made regular savings in Chile. Many simply couldn't manage to send money home and cover their living costs in Chile.

Unfortunately, continuing or increased economic exclusion was a more common outcome of migration to Chile from Bolivia than its converse, as I indicate through discussion of three particularly illustrative employment niches. Moving from the most to the least severe, I explore lived realities within wholesale clothing retail, agriculture, and domestic labor and cleaning. I consider the degree to which migrants in these labor niches could exercise agency and engage in practices to try to move further toward economic inclusion, as well as the role that migrant organizations played in both helping and hindering this.

Wholesale Clothing Retail

The garment industry is notorious for poor, sometimes appalling, labor conditions. In South America, as discussed in chapter 1, Buenos Aires and São Paulo are known for abuses of the migrant workers (frequently Bolivian) who labor in textile factories dotted throughout the cities. In Santiago, it is not so much with regard to the production but rather the wholesale retail of garments—selling clothing in bulk to small-scale vendors for resale—that abuses of labor rights occur. As indicated in chapter 2, I uncovered a case of human trafficking for labor exploitation in wholesale garment retail in Santiago when carrying out interviews in the shopping arcades along La Alameda in the *comuna* of Estación Central and was also made aware of the labor exploitation occurring more broadly within this sector. Cata and Marta, the women involved, became key informants in my research.

Cata, age twenty-five, was from El Alto. She spoke only Aymara as a child and had struggled in her adolescence to become fluent in Spanish. Nevertheless, she progressed to university, attending the Universidad Pública de El Alto (UPEA), where she studied social work. Public universities in Bolivia are free; however, students must pay for their living costs and for study materials. After completing three years of her degree, Cata was unable to continue with her education because her parents could no longer afford to support her, and the part-time work she was doing was insufficient to make ends meet. Furthermore, she was struggling to keep up with the workload because she did not have access to a computer.

Marta, age thirty-five, was from Oruro and married with three children, ages sixteen, thirteen, and ten. She had no schooling and was illiterate. Like Cata, her first language was Aymara. She spoke Spanish, but at times it was hard to understand due to her use of nonstandard grammar and the way in which she expressed time references in Spanish. In Bolivia, Marta worked in a factory iodizing salt, and her husband worked in the garment industry. Their wages were so low that they were struggling to provide for their children so that they could remain in school, which was the parents' primary objective. Marta and her husband decided that she should migrate to improve their financial situation.

Both Cata and Marta responded to commercials that they heard on local radio in Bolivia advertising for workers to come to Chile. They were "interviewed" by Don X (who professed to be the business owner), offered the job, and told that they would make several hundred US dollars a month—far more than they could earn in Bolivia. On separate occasions, they were accompanied across the border by Don X and told to state at the border that they were simply going on holiday to visit relatives. In Marta's case, Don X declared after arriving in Arica, Chile, that he felt unwell and that Marta would have to go alone to Santiago. He bought her a bus ticket, put her on the bus to Santiago, and gave her a phone number to call once she arrived. She was very scared because she did not know where she was going and had no money with her. Upon reaching Santiago in the dark, she was collected in a taxi and taken to the shop where she was to work, with no idea where in the city she was. Cata had believed that the job to which she was going was actually in Arica, but to her dismay she was forced to travel to Santiago upon arrival in Arica, and she was similarly disoriented by the end of her journey. This type of confusing and coercive process is typically used by human traffickers.[17]

Strategies typical of traffickers/exploiters, including sleep deprivation, crowded living conditions, and severe restriction of payment of wages, continued to be utilized once Marta and Cata were in Chile.[18] They were required to work from 6:30 a.m. to 12:00 a.m. six days a week selling clothes in bulk and sorting and folding new deliveries as they arrived. They slept four to a small room in a *bodega* (see chapter 2). They were given no wages and were informed that they would be paid at the end of a full year of work, although they were sometimes given small "advances" of around US$8 and told these would be deducted from their total salary at the end of the year.

Additionally, Cata and Marta were led to believe that the MTRV, which the exploiters paid for, bonded them to one employer for a year. They believed they would enter into irregular migratory situations if they left and could face deportation as a consequence.[19] In addition to leading them to believe that they were bonded to an employer for one year and barely paying them, the exploiters further restricted Cata and Marta's freedom of movement by constantly monitoring them and allowing them only a few hours of "free time" on Sundays. While never subjected to physical abuse, they were kept isolated from Chilean society, and a relationship of almost total dependence on the exploiters was created.

Analyzing their case in relation to the transnational social space of economic citizenship enables understanding of the structural and agentic factors producing the level of exclusion experienced by Cata and Marta, in addition to the role of social identities and power relations. In structural terms, relatively lax enforcement of labor laws in Chile, the difficulty of prosecuting cases of trafficking for labor exploitation, and the lack of information in the public domain in Bolivia and Chile regarding trafficking and labor exploitation worked to the advantage of the traffickers/exploiters. These people, a Bolivian couple, were clearly fully aware of these factors. Furthermore, as a consequence of their own transnational connections, they appear to have been fully cognizant of the vulnerabilities of Cata and Marta due to the intersections of socioeconomic status, class, gender, and race. There is also the question of Cata's and Marta's exercise of agency in affecting their position within the transnational social space of economic citizenship. Deception, coercion, and manipulation were so great as to severely limit their freedom of choice, contributing to the classification of the situation they were in as trafficking and forced labor—falling at the sharp end of Klara Skrivankova's "continuum of labor exploitation."[20]

Cata and Marta's exercise of agency, however, was crucial to the practices they engaged in so as to move from almost total exclusion from economic citizenship to incipient inclusion. I first interviewed them in early October 2013 in the shop where they were working. After my initial interview, I involved the Asociación, after realizing the gravity of the situation. Together we liaised with the human trafficking unit of the Policia de Investigaciones (PDI). The PDI carried out an investigation and were convinced that it was a case of trafficking for labor exploitation. However, they were unable to gather enough evidence to lead to prosecution. The positive outcome was that both Marta and Cata bravely managed to leave the situation of forced labor of their own volition once they realized the magnitude of what had occurred and that possessing an MTRV meant that they were in a regular migratory situation and were not bonded to one employer. Sadly, they did not recoup the wages they were owed due to the lack of prosecution. They both returned to Bolivia for the summer of 2013 to 2014, then came back to Santiago in early 2014, determined to find decent work. With assistance from the Asociación in Marta's case, they were able to find employment in which their labor rights were respected. While the intercession of a migrant organization was crucial in this case, Cata's and Marta's own agentic actions were also fundamental in challenging their exclusion from the transnational space of economic citizenship.

Agriculture

As with the garment industry, agriculture is well known for precarious work and labor exploitation, particularly of migrant workers.[21] Until very recently the conditions of migrant workers in agriculture in Chile had been largely neglected in research on migration. A recent study, however, presents a quantitative analysis of a survey carried out with 220 migrants, 60 of whom were Bolivian, with half working in agriculture.[22] Summarizing the results, Nicolás Rojas Pedemonte and Sebastián Bueno Moya state that "the subsample of Bolivians is that which presents the highest levels of lack of information with regards to legal matters. . . . Moreover, it is the subsample with the highest proportion of low wages (below US$275), and which has the highest levels of both lack of contract, and concentration in unskilled employment."[23] These markers of exploitation measured in the quantitative study—lack of employment contracts, lack of knowledge of legal rights, and payment below minimum wage—were very much reflected in the experiences of those working in agriculture whom I interviewed. My research also indicated other factors that demonstrated abuse of agricultural workers in the North of Chile. All lived in very poor conditions on the *parcelas* (agricultural smallholdings) where they labored (see chapter 2). On average, they worked nine to ten hours a day, six and a half days a week, far exceeding the maximum forty-five hours per week stipulated by Chilean labor laws. As with Cata and Marta, poor living conditions and long working hours contributed to workers' isolation and dependency on their employer and indicate the role of the temporal in precarious employment, to which I add the importance of physical place.[24] In relation to the latter, the work in itself could be categorized as falling within the three Ds definition: dirty, dangerous, and difficult. I conducted interviews beside migrants who were squatting for hours at a time thinning pepper plants in a greenhouse in which temperatures were easily over 30 degrees Celsius. There was no provision of water. Women worked with their babies and toddlers alongside them or on their backs.

In addition to lack of contracts, low pay, long working hours, and difficult and potentially dangerous working conditions, workplace discrimination and a degree of coercion were further elements that contributed to the exploitation that characterized these migrants' working lives. As previously mentioned, the attitude of the predominantly mestizo *patrones* and overseers toward their largely Aymara workers was sometimes racist, and as discussed in chapter 3, they capitalized on the fact that most were working on tourist visas. Luisa, age twenty-five, from rural Oruro, whose story I have followed throughout this book, had this to say:

> Because you're a foreigner they want to treat you, they want to make you work more, without stopping. They say you're not advancing, that you have to hurry. . . . And because you're a foreigner . . . they threaten that they can kick you out [of the country].

Although not as extreme as in the case of Cata and Marta, there was certainly a degree of coercion involved in the relationship between employer and employee, and the threat of dismissal without pay or of being reported to the immigration authorities seemed very real to migrants.

In sum, many of the conditions experienced by participants laboring in agriculture in the North of Chile would suggest that, though not in conditions of forced labor, they were certainly on the very margins of the transnational space of economic citizenship. With regard to the structural factors leading to these conditions, many are similar to those mentioned above. Lax enforcement of labor laws was certainly an important contributing factor. Migrants' position within the labor market hierarchy was entrenched through landowners' often racist attitudes toward their workers on the basis of nationality and indigenous identity. Nonetheless, migrants exercised a certain degree of agency in choosing to remain on the *parcelas*. While options for leaving were limited, there was some potential for finding other work, perhaps in El Agro market in Arica. Among other factors, the flexibility of being able to return to Bolivia at will because of the seasonal nature of agricultural employment was important for some, making other employment a less viable option.

As in the case of Marta and Cata, the support of migrant organizations was very important in fomenting practices that would better migrants' economic situation. In Arica, Rojas Pedemonte and Bueno Moya found that those who had contact with a migrant organization were the most likely to have greater knowledge of their labor rights.[25] The group mentioned in chapter three with whom the Asociación had been in contact regarding labor rights was organizing to improve members' working conditions in addition to trying to acquire MTRVs through their employer. Crucially, they were requesting that their *patrón* give them employment contracts. This would ensure financial security, as they would be guaranteed a monthly wage rather than being paid at the end of each day's shift, and it would place them in a stronger legal position should they encounter any problems with their employer. Furthermore, greater inclusion in spaces of economic and legal citizenship sometimes led to improved social and political incorporation; this group, for example, was also organizing to demand better living conditions and was interested in contacting other migrant agricultural workers.

Domestic Labor and Cleaning

If agricultural labor is the least discussed of migrant employment niches in Chile, then domestic labor and cleaning is certainly the most.[26] This is a reflection of the feminization of migration to Chile and the large numbers of migrants working in these sectors, but also of the tendency within migration research to focus almost exclusively on Santiago, where work in domestic labor is concentrated.[27] Of those I interviewed, ten women in Santiago were working in domestic labor or cleaning. Seven worked as *nanas*, either *puertas adentro* (living in) or *puertas afuera* (living out) (see also chapter 2). Three worked part-time as cleaners for small businesses or institutions. A further two women who were not working at the time of the interviews had previously worked as *nanas* or in cleaning. No male interviewees, or interviewees of either gender in Arica, worked in domestic labor or cleaning. Thus, the Santiago-centric focus of employment in these areas was mirrored in my study, as was its feminization.

All except one of the women who worked or had worked in domestic labor and cleaning, especially the former, experienced violations of their labor rights, although not to such a severe degree as those working in agriculture.[28] They were receiving the minimum wage or above, and in the case of those *puertas adentro* they received food and board in addition. Those *puertas adentro* also, however, worked more than the hours stipulated by Chilean law, were given insufficient breaks, and were generally not permitted to take sick leave. Fernanda, age forty-five, from Santa Cruz, working as a *nana puertas adentro*, detailed a typical day for her: "I work from eight in the morning until ten, eleven at night. If the baby doesn't sleep, well, I don't either. We work more than the hours we should and they don't pay our taxes, they don't pay overtime." Fernanda experienced her employment as a constant struggle to "estar al pie del cañon" (literally, "be at the foot of the cannon," i.e., be ready for action in all circumstances). What she conveyed with her use of the expression was the sense of having to be constantly attentive, alert, and responsive to the demands of her employer, regardless of the hour.

In addition to the labor conditions, a further issue for those *puertas adentro* was obtaining a contract. Aimy, age thirty-four, from Cochabamba, had worked *puertas adentro* for the same family for two years. In all of this time, she had not had a contract. Thus, when she became pregnant, with no document to guarantee her right to maternity leave, she was dismissed without pay. For those working *puertas afuera* and in cleaning, they tended to work fifty to seventy-two hours a week, which was in accordance with the labor law governing domestic work at the time. Nevertheless, like those working *puertas adentro*, some did not have contracts, or if they did, the contracts were not respected.

Psychologically or emotionally challenging working relationships were another difficulty confronted by almost all participants in domestic labor and cleaning.[29] For Javiera, age forty-three, from Santa Cruz, one of the worst things about her job was the requirement to wear a uniform. As Javiera told it, "[W]hen . . . they put me in a uniform, I cried. I felt humiliated. I know that work is dignified, that it does not denigrate, but I felt humiliated." For her, the uniform implied that she was in a servile role and presented a profound challenge to her identity. Her intense feeling of humiliation was partially because of the deskilling implied by working as a *nana*; in Bolivia, she had worked as a nurse. She was struggling to cope with the loss of her professional identity in Chile, a common experience for migrants globally.[30]

While not positioned as marginally as those in agriculture or wholesale clothing retail, participants in domestic work and cleaning were still partially excluded from the transnational space of economic citizenship. A variety of structural factors contribute to the generation of the exploitative and discriminatory conditions they experienced, not least Chile's domestic labor law. It reflects the uncomfortable compromise between servility and labor rights noted by Carolina Stefoni and

Rosario Fernández in relation to contemporary domestic work.[31] The situation has changed somewhat now, but at the time of my fieldwork, although some labor rights such as having a contract were enshrined in law for domestic workers, they could be required to work up to seventy-two hours a week for the minimum monthly wage.[32] For all other workers in Chile, forty-five hours per week was the maximum number that could be worked before overtime had to be paid in addition to the minimum monthly wage. Domestic workers could also be required by their employers to wear a uniform inside the house and in public spaces. The very legislation governing this particular labor niche was therefore discriminatory and contributed to exclusion from economic citizenship.

In addition to such structural factors, agency must again be considered. All of the participants in domestic labor had exercised freedom of choice when engaging in that work. Overall, many of the women in domestic service or cleaning saw the financial benefits as sufficient to act as a trade-off for certain labor rights. Women stated that they would "put up with things" or "swallow their pride" because the salaries were reasonable. They also at times engaged in practices to negotiate improvement in their working conditions.

Aihwa Ong has analyzed the ways in which such practices of resistance can be highly gendered.[33] Others, such as Pun Ngai and Aysen Ustubici, have also examined the ways in which women may use stereotypes of female irrationality and emotion to their advantage and subvert the notion of the woman as dominated by biological functions.[34] I similarly noted a gendered phenomenon when, for example, Javiera drew on the limited resources available to her in order to negotiate with her employer so as not to wear a uniform. Acting on her genuine emotion, but also, one might speculate, utilizing gendered stereotypes of "emotional women," she said that she "cried to the *señora* and I said to her that I didn't want to wear the uniform anymore.[35] I felt humiliated, frustrated as a professional, I said to her . . . and I didn't wear [the uniform] anymore." Similar practices had been employed by other women working as *nanas*.[36]

Migrant organizations also play a role in affecting the practices in which women in domestic work may engage. In this instance, one migrant organization, Asistencia a las Mujeres Migrantes (AMM; a pseudonym), actually acted to effectively curtail migrant women's ability to enter further into the space of economic citizenship. Among other services, AMM provides a refuge and employment program for migrant women, where the vast majority of jobs they have available are domestic work. Potential employers are invited to register with the service and are then given the opportunity to interview various women who may be interested in working for them.

Seven women I interviewed based in Santiago had stayed at the refuge provided by AMM. Five of them had found employment as domestic workers through the organization. Unfortunately, the experiences of all of them had been negative.

Magdalena said that the refuge was overcrowded, and she found it restrictive and paternalistic to have to have lights off by 9:00 p.m., to have to get up at 7:00 a.m., and to have to leave the building by 9:00 a.m. In relation to the employment program, she and several of the others commented that there was a racialized, nationality-based hierarchy operating whereby Colombian, then Peruvian, then women of other nationalities, and finally Bolivian women were selected by employers using the program.[37]

Furthermore, Diana, age twenty-eight, from Santa Cruz, had been disturbed by seeing the way in which one young woman was sent off with her new employer. A taxi was sent to pick up the young woman, who had just arrived from Santa Cruz, and Diana said, "[I]t made me so sad because she barely knew where she was . . . she didn't even have any money." No one was clear about exactly where the young woman was being sent in the taxi, and Diana, who photographed with her cell phone the number plate of the taxi just in case anything should happen, said that the young woman left in floods of tears. After this experience, Diana was determined not to work as a *nana puertas adentro*.

The five participants who did go on to work in jobs found through AMM experienced poor labor conditions; as outlined above, long hours and limited rest were the norm, in addition to other issues. For example, Rosa, age twenty-nine, from Sucre, told me that her employers found through AMM "made me work on public holidays and the *señora* said that I was lazy and she was giving me the money for nothing. That doesn't seem OK to me." Anahis, age thirty-six, also from Sucre, had been unable to persuade her employer to write her a contract, even though this was supposed to be one of the conditions that employers agreed to abide by when using the services of the organization. Loreta had been working *puertas afuera* and had come alone to Chile before bringing her children six months later. When she mentioned to her employer that her children had arrived, she was dismissed because the employer was concerned that an employee with children would start missing work or requesting time off.

There were clear problems with the system used by AMM, some of which were recognized by a staff member from the organization, whom I was eventually able to speak to after repeatedly requesting an interview with the organization for four months. First, there was no formal follow-up process once the women found employment. Second, the process by which potential employers was filtered was deeply problematic. It was only after three negative reports from three different women who had been employed by the same person that an employer would be removed from the books for a six-month period while, as the staff member put it, she "went away and thought about things and changed her attitude." If she then reemployed someone through AMM after the six-month break and the same problem was reported, the employer would be suspended from the service for a year.

Thus, while in some cases migrant organizations acted to support migrants to move from exclusion from spaces of economic citizenship to inclusion, there were unfortunately cases in which they were complicit in migrants' continued exclusion, demonstrating, among other things, the ambiguous nature of (migrant) civil society organizations involved in the pursuit of "development."[38] While AMM certainly had good intentions, it would seem that it may contribute to the poor conditions experienced by many migrant women in domestic labor. Furthermore, the organization's promotion of such work as appropriate for migrant women contributes to the production of a gendered, racialized migrant division of labor. Additionally, for these women, social and political exclusion is made more likely due to the isolation entailed in the long hours and type of work undertaken by a *nana*.

CONCLUSION

As I outlined in the introduction, the incorporation of economic citizenship within the overarching framework of this book builds on feminist scholarship, which has indicated the necessity of considering more fully citizenship's economic dimension, including when researching migration.[39] Thinking in terms of a transnational space of economic citizenship brings together a variety of different aspects of migrants' relationship to "the economic." It not only allows consideration of migrant access to decent work, the gendered and racialized migrant division of labor, and precarious employment, but also takes into account the wider meaning of "the economic" for migrants, including the economic conditions contributing to migration, the forced/voluntary dichotomy as it pertains to the "economic migrant," and the potential for positive economic outcomes of migration. Finally, the agentic practices in which migrants engage to incrementally improve their access to economic citizenship are given due weight, as are the ways in which such practices are encouraged—or constrained—by migrant organizations.

For the majority of migrants I interviewed and worked with, especially those from rural communities, economic marginalization was a defining feature of their lives in Bolivia, and this laid the foundation for their pursuit of *el sueño chileno*. In the context where they possessed legal citizenship, they were precluded from economic citizenship, and through migrating they engaged in a paradoxical "practice of citizenship" in the hope of becoming more fully integrated as economic citizens. Some certainly moved closer to *el sueño chileno*, as they were able to send remittances, collect some savings, and even experience qualitatively better employment. Nonetheless, even when they were able to send remittances or save, their labor rights were frequently violated. Gendered, racialized hierarchies in the labor market operated to confine them to employment niches where this was the norm, and while it was not uncommon for interviewees to engage in practices to try to improve the conditions under which they labored, their success was limited.

Unfortunately, at times this limited success was in part due to the actions of AMM, although in other instances other migrant organizations acted to support migrants in pursuing greater economic inclusion.

For many, then, *el sueño chileno* remained just that: a dream never quite within their grasp. The anxiety of not knowing if they would make ends meet, of struggling to both buy nutritious food in Chile and finance debts or support children in Bolivia, was a daily reality for many. Even when the financial burden was perhaps not quite so heavily felt—such as for those engaged as *nanas*—respect for labor rights and human dignity were rare commodities in their working lives. Thus, again, uncertainty permeated migrants' experiences of this aspect of citizenship. And as so simply and poignantly illustrated by the image at the start of this chapter of the mother saying good-bye to her child as she leaves in search of better opportunities, such uncertain economic citizenship profoundly impacts migrants' social well-being and that of their families. This, and other dimensions of social citizenship, are the topic of the following chapter.

5

Solidaridad

When I asked Constanza, age thirty-two, from Sucre, what she would most like to see improve for migrants in Chile, she said simply, "I wish they [Chileans] would show us more solidarity." This came at the end of a series of reflections on the difficulties she had faced in accessing housing, health care, and education for herself and her young family, and on the isolation that she felt in her daily life as a full-time mother in a downtown Santiago *migrant cité*. Her desire for "more solidarity" from Chileans succinctly summarizes the way in which most migrants I interviewed felt their access to what is here termed "social citizenship" could be advanced.

There was a sense that greater "solidarity" had been expected of Chileans and was not forthcoming; in spite of the geopolitical tensions between the two countries, they were, after all, both South American nations and should therefore share a certain Bolivarian bond. This framing of the issue of differentiated access to social rights, as well as broader social exclusion, is perhaps rather different from how migrants might express this in some other migration contexts, where historical and cultural differences between the "sending" and "receiving" countries are perceived to be greater. As this chapter indicates, a perceived lack of solidarity at the point of access to housing, health care, and education, and in terms of forming wider social networks, was a defining feature of many migrants' lived experiences of social citizenship.

THE CONTOURS OF SOCIAL CITIZENSHIP

Since T. H. Marshall provided his seminal definition of citizenship in 1950, the social has been considered one of its essential elements.[1] It is also perhaps its most contested.[2] There is consensus that social citizenship refers to welfare provision and access, but there are, of course, as many differences in opinion about *how* welfare provision should be defined, *what* welfare support should be provided by the state, and *who* should be able to access it as there are colors in the political spectrum. In this book I do not seek to become too embroiled in this normative debate. Rather, I focus on the lived reality of migrants' differentiated access to the welfare provisions that are (nominally) available to legal citizens in their sending country, in this case Bolivia, and especially in their receiving country, in this case Chile.

I have been led by the stories of migrants themselves, and guided by feminist scholar Ruth Lister's use of Len Doyal and Ian Gough's conceptualization of human need, to focus my attention on four categories of welfare provision, or social rights, understanding these as the core constituents of the space of social citizenship.[3] Doyal and Gough identify two basic human needs that are universal: physical health and autonomy. As Gough puts it, fulfilment of these basic needs enables people to "think and act" and so allows "for the successful and, if necessary, critical participation in a social form of life."[4] The fulfillment of these basic needs is ensured by the satisfaction of eleven "intermediate needs":[5]

- nutritious food and water
- protective housing
- a nonhazardous work environment
- a nonhazardous physical environment
- appropriate health care
- security in childhood
- significant primary relationships
- physical security
- economic security
- appropriate education
- safe birth control and child-rearing

Lister clarifies that without the fulfillment of these intermediate needs and therefore our basic needs of physical health and autonomy, we are unable to fully participate in society through exercising our civil and political rights. Therefore, she argues, intermediate needs can be understood as the social rights that constitute social citizenship and enable other forms of citizenship.[6]

In the process of analyzing the social rights most salient in migrants' narratives, I have adapted Doyal and Gough's "intermediate needs" to reflect only the strictly social ones; I explored migrants' working environment and economic security under the rubric of economic citizenship in the previous chapter instead.[7] I have then broadly categorized these social rights into what I consider the four elements of social citizenship: shelter, health care, education, and social support (see table 2).

TABLE 2. Adaptation of Doyal and Gough's (1991) Intermediate Needs to Reflect
Elements of Social Citizenship

Shelter	Health care
Nonhazardous physical environment	Appropriate health care
Physical security	Safe birth control and child-rearing
Protective housing	
Nutritious food and water	
Education	**Social support**
Appropriate education	Significant primary relationships
Security in childhood	Supportive social networks

SOURCE: Megan Ryburn, 2017.

Within the category "social support" I have included not only significant primary relationships, but also supportive social networks more broadly; as already indicated by other research into migrants' daily lived realities and as confirmed in my research, social networks are fundamental to migrants' ability to participate as social citizens.[8]

Considering social citizenship as a space that encompasses four key elements represents a new way of conceptualizing migrant access to social rights. Multiple social rights have certainly been addressed individually in migration research, and there are also studies that consider simultaneously migrant access to a few different social services and how this may be affected by legal status, economic position, and intersectional factors.[9] I endeavor to expand on such approaches to holistically consider not only access to social services, but also family life and social relations. I am also concerned with how inclusions and exclusions from social citizenship interact with other inclusions and exclusions from citizenship. In the following four sections I address each of the four elements of social citizenship and consider the overlaps among them.

Although not necessarily more affected by exclusion, women tended to focus more on the social aspect of citizenship in their narratives, especially with regard to access to health care, education, and family life. This is possibly because of the predominance in Latin America of the expectation that women will largely bear responsibility for the home and childcare, although gender roles are varied, fluid, and mutable in Latin America, as elsewhere.[10] Additionally, it is possible that men felt less able to discuss these issues with me because of my gender. Finally, it was women who were the most likely to have needed health services (mainly due to pregnancy) and were also the most likely to be separated from their immediate family because of migration; thus health care and family life were pertinent topics for them. As a consequence, while men's experiences are considered in this chapter, it is women's voices that are the strongest here.

SHELTER

When you're looking for a room and you have children, well, they don't give it to you . . . and when they know you're a foreigner they distrust you.
—CONSTANZA, AGE THIRTY-TWO, FROM SUCRE

A series of legislative obstacles prevent foreigners from easily renting property in Chile. Prospective renters must present Chilean identification cards—and so must have at least temporary residency in Chile—in addition to a minimum of three months' pay stubs and proof of pension contributions. Their monthly wage should be three to four times the monthly rent. They will also be required to pay a deposit of at least one month's rent. In addition, it is likely that they will be asked to provide a Chilean or permanent resident guarantor, as well as their credit score. There are various housing subsidies to enable access to social housing and other affordable housing available in Chile; however, at the time of my fieldwork it was necessary to have held permanent residency for five years in order to access these.[11] As should be evident from the stories told in this book so far, these requirements would be next to impossible to meet for the vast majority of migrants with whom I had contact.

As a consequence of these stipulations, a burgeoning informal rental market has sprung up in the heart of downtown Santiago. Subletting is permitted under Chilean law as long as there is no clause to the contrary in the contract the landlord draws up with the renter. It has become common for migrants with financial resources and long-standing permanent residency, or those who have naturalized, in addition to some Chileans, to rent entire *migrant cités* (see chapter 2) and then sublet them. The rental value of the property as a whole is unlikely to be more than US$800 per month; a room can be charged at up to US$150 per month, and as there are generally around ten rooms per *migrant cité*, the profit margin for the renter may be around US$700 per month or more.

The advantage of this informal market is that it enables migrants who otherwise would have to pay at least US$7 per night for a bed in a hostel to acquire a cheaper roof over their heads. The disadvantages, however, are many. To begin with, none of the migrants I spoke to who lived in *migrant cités*—who constituted over two-thirds of all those interviewed in Santiago—had written contracts. Chilean law does not require a written contract to be drawn up for either those subletting from renters or those renting directly from landlords.[12] While technically it is possible to bring tenancy disputes before the municipality with only a verbal contract, in reality this would be difficult. Additionally, as indicated to me by Yolanda, a municipal worker in charge of migrant affairs, even if a case were brought, the balance of power would be strongly in favor of the landlord or renter rather than the subletter.

Due to this highly unequal relationship, the renter can raise the monthly cost of the room at will. Furthermore, the renter and landlord generally show a total dis-

regard for carrying out repairs or for the health and safety of the occupants, leading to the conditions described in chapter 2. Finally, the lack of contract gives the
renter or landlord the ability to evict subletters with little or no notice. Fernanda,
age forty-five, from Santa Cruz, told me about her recent experience of eviction:

> We lived in [the *comuna* of] Recoleta, and the thing is that . . . we didn't really know
> who the owner was, and so from one day to the next he asked us to leave. There were
> loads of Bolivians living there, loads of foreigners, and he kicked us out and said,
> "You've got to go this week, get looking already." *Chuta* (Shoot)!
>
> And one asks for time off work, and sometimes they don't give it, so at the week-
> end you have to find whatever you can—whether it's cheap or whether it's expensive.
> You just don't want to end up sleeping on the street.

It appears that in their case, the landlord was unaware that his property was
being sublet, which is not uncommon, and upon learning about it evicted all of the
subletters. In desperation, Fernanda and her husband sublet a room in Renca, a
comuna on the northwestern fringes of Santiago. This entailed a two-hour bus
journey to their respective jobs as a *nana* and in construction in the wealthy
northeastern *comunas*. By contrast, from their room in downtown Recoleta it had
been a one-hour commute.

While finding rooms to sublet is difficult for all migrants with low-paying jobs
and without the paperwork required to rent directly, as Constanza's words at the
beginning of this section indicate, migrants with children are at a particular disadvantage. Loreta, age twenty-eight and from Santa Cruz, had, like Constanza, experienced discrimination when she applied to sublet with children in *migrant cités*:

> The first thing they ask when I go out looking [for a room] is, "How many children
> do you have?" And actually lots of people have insulted me, they've said to me, "This
> isn't a day-care centre." . . . I mean, they don't just say, "No"—simply, "No"—they say
> that to me.

This "lack of solidarity" was also shown to Cristina, age thirty-seven, from
Cochabamba, when she was evicted following the arrival of her children from
Bolivia to live with her in her room. And Constanza explained that even though
she now had a room of around twelve meters square shared with her husband and
children, she was constantly worried about the same happening to her because of
her neighbors' complaints about her three boys, ages seven, four, and two, being
too noisy. From what I saw, they were very well behaved, but as Constanza said,
"[T]hey are little boys . . . and they don't have anywhere to run around and play
chase, so yes, they make a ruckus (*meten bulla*)."

Low-wage migrants, and particularly women like Constanza who have small
children, are locked out of stable and secure access to protective housing in
Santiago, a fundamental element of social citizenship. Restrictive legislation is

propitious to abusive practices in the informal rental market, resulting in migrants occupying overcrowded, unsanitary, and dangerous accommodations. Those I spoke to did their utmost to employ the little freedom of choice they had in finding a place to live, often knocking on doors over a period of several days in search of the best available room. They engaged in the limited home-making practices that they could: sticking free publicity posters on their walls to add a little color; pooling their resources to buy a washing machine, refrigerator, or cooker for the whole *migrant cité*; or donating their unwanted furniture to new arrivals and exchanging items with neighbors. Nevertheless, structural factors dictated that their ability to exercise agency was severely restricted. Furthermore, migrant access to rental accommodations and the conditions of the *migrant cités* in Santiago remain topics yet to be broached by both the state and migrant organizations, as one of the managers at the Asociación indicated to me.

In Arica, a slightly different picture emerged. I spoke to fewer people renting on the private market, as many lived and labored on *parcelas* in the conditions discussed in chapter 2. Those who did desire to rent, however, faced the same difficulties as those in Santiago. Furthermore, migrants who had sufficient savings to put down a deposit on a house or land in cheaper, rural areas near Arica were unable to do so unless they were naturalized as Chileans. This is because such land is classed as "frontier" territory and can only be "settled" by Chileans, evidence of the legacy of the War of the Pacific and more generally of the unease and xenophobia often generated when migrants wish to purchase part of any national *terra*.

One reaction to these factors has been the construction of *campamentos* (informal settlements) on the periphery of Arica on land classed as, or likely soon to be classed as, "urban."[13] There are six in Arica, largely clustered on the southeastern periphery of the city. An estimated 174 families—both Chilean and migrant—live in them.[14] Precise figures regarding the number of migrant families dwelling in these settlements are not available, but data from other *campamentos* in the North and anecdotal evidence from nongovernmental organizations (NGOs) working with settlement occupiers suggest that around one-third of the families are migrants, and the majority are Bolivian.[15] This particular type of *campamento* is known as a *toma* (squatter settlement), where unoccupied land has been laid claim to through the building of makeshift shelters. This practice has a long history in Chile, as elsewhere.[16]

The reaction of the state to this type of irregular settlement has varied—and continues to vary—across time and place, from violent displacement of occupants, to ambivalence, to interest in facilitating access to services and legal tenure. In many countries in the global South, there has been an increasing tendency toward "enabling" occupiers to regularize their settlements. This is often through a combination of assistance provided by NGOs, support from the state, and sometimes funding from private enterprises or microcredit institutions. Such a strategy can have positive outcomes, as it foments an innovative approach to housing already adopted by poor urban dwellers and maintains their established networks while incorporating them more fully into city life and wider society. Nevertheless, there can also be negative consequences, including the potential to absolve the state of responsibility for providing adequate housing.[17] More common than this enabling approach in Chile has been the resettlement of *campamento* dwellers in "identikit" social housing on the very periphery of urban areas, which has generated significant social exclusion.[18] Yet there is now increasing awareness of the segregation this has caused, and new strategies involving more input from *campamento* occupiers are being developed.[19]

In Arica, Julieta, age forty-two, from La Paz, and an occupant of Campamento Esperanza (a pseudonym) on Arica's periphery, lived in hope that she and other occupants would be able to stay there, despite some previous settlers having been moved to social housing elsewhere. It requires great tenacity to remain in such makeshift housing, building everything from scratch and facing the constant threat of eviction. Yet as James Holston argues regarding periphery dwellers in urban Brazil, it is by "legalizing the illegal . . . through appropriation of the very soil of the city itself" that occupants can make visible their claims to citizenship.[20] Those in Campamento Esperanza had occupied the territory for nearly four years when I interviewed Julieta in 2014, so there seemed to be some chance that inhabitants would be granted legal tenure (in Chile, this can happen after a period of five years if the land is state owned). Water was being delivered in tankers on a weekly basis by the municipal government, and there was talk that electricity and a sewage system might be installed soon. Additionally, an NGO had been working closely with *campamento* occupants in Arica to try to address their housing needs and support them in their legal struggles. Nevertheless, in September 2017 Julieta informed me via WhatsApp audio message that, as far as she understood it, legal tenure was not likely to be granted, but instead she was on the waiting list to be moved to social housing, which she was ultimately pleased about. In the meantime, her living conditions continued to be much the same.

Some attention is being paid, then, by NGOs and the state to this particular struggle on the part of migrants to access protective housing in northern Chile, even if the pace of change is slow. Little has yet been done, however, to address poor conditions on the *parcelas* in the region or to tackle the inequalities of access to the rental market across the country, which impacts women and children in particular. Perhaps visibility is the key here. Those in the *campamentos* make a more strident, obvious claim to this aspect of social citizenship and are thus harder to ignore than those migrants hidden away down the dark corridors of the *cités* or in tin shacks on the private land of the *parcelas*. Nevertheless, whether in the *campamentos*, on the *parcelas*, or in the *migrant cités*, almost all the migrants to whom I spoke indicated that housing was one of their primary concerns in

Chile; there was consensus that their living conditions were worse than in Bolivia, and it was one of the issues that they most urgently wanted to tackle. This was not least because the quality and location of accommodation has multiple repercussive effects on the ability to access other social rights, such as health care and education.

HEALTH CARE

The social worker said to me, "If you don't have a Chilean ID card, it's going to cost you a million pesos to give birth in the hospital."
—LUZ MARÍA, AGE NINETEEN, FROM SANTA CRUZ

The health-care system in Chile today features a complicated mixture of private and public provision and is highly segregated.[21] There was an integrated public system, known as FONASA (Fondo Nacional de Salud, National Health Fund), from the 1950s until the dictatorship period. Under Pinochet, however, the sweeping implementation of neoliberal policies led to private health provision becoming the favored option for people with financial resources, as they were encouraged to become members of the new ISAPREs (instituciones de salud previsionales, health insurance institutions). This resulted in severe inequalities in the health service.[22] Currently, both the FONASA and ISAPREs systems remain in operation. There has, however, been a steady decline in membership of ISAPREs. Now, around 14 percent of the national population is enrolled in ISAPREs, compared with 78 percent in FONASA, 3 percent in other health-care schemes (largely those provided by the army), and 4 percent who have no health-care coverage or do not know what health-care provision they have.[23]

Those in FONASA are enrolled in one of four categories. Service users in Category A, around 30 percent, are those living in poverty according to a means test.[24] They are entitled to entirely free health care in public hospitals. All other users are divided among Categories B, C, and D. They all pay a 7 percent contribution of their earnings to FONASA. Those in categories C and D must also pay a 10 or 20 percent "copayment" of costs following treatment in public hospitals. Furthermore, Category B, C, and D users can choose to seek medical attention in certain private institutions, where the copayments vary depending on the establishment.[25]

All migrants with regular legal status nominally have the same access to FONASA and ISAPREs as Chileans. Furthermore, universal coverage programs such as vaccinations are available to everyone regardless of legal status, as is emergency care. Additionally, special measures have been taken to ensure equal access to health care for pregnant women and children irrespective of migratory status:[26]

Pregnant women—Pregnant women with irregular status can visit the public primary care clinic nearest to their homes. Here they will be attended to and will also receive documentation to enable them to apply for a temporary residence visa, which can then be converted into permanent residency.

Children and young people—Those under age eighteen whose parents or guardians have irregular status can go to the public primary care clinic nearest to their homes. They will be given documentation that will enable them to regularize if they are not enrolled in education; if they are enrolled, they will do this through their schools.

Emmanuel Scheppers and others, in a review of migrant and ethnic minority access to health care predominantly in the global North, approach the subject by assessing barriers to access at "system level," "provider level," and "patient level."[27] Migrants' ability to access appropriate health care is strongly influenced by gender, as well as by other aspects of intersectionality, in addition to legal status and length of time spent in the receiving country. Jasmine Gideon asserts that this is as true in the Latin American migration context as it is of South-North migration flows.[28] Taking the same approach here, and drawing on the small body of work carried out in Chile already, it could be said that, in terms of health provision for migrants at the "system level" overall, Chile has a range of policies that meet international standards.[29] Moreover, there have been laudable attempts by the government in recent years to fully incorporate pregnant migrant women and child migrants into the health system and to assist them in regularizing their migratory status. Nonetheless, even for these supposedly protected groups, the everyday reality of migrant access to health care is rather different, due to a variety of factors at the provider and patient level.

According to CASEN data, 9 percent of the adult migrant population, compared with 2.5 percent of the Chilean-born population, reports having no provision of health care, either public or private.[30] One factor contributing to this is likely that many of these migrants have irregular status (CASEN does not gather data on migratory status).[31] In my research, one-third of interviewees in Santiago, and nearly half in Arica, had no health-care provision. While being in, or having previously been in, an irregular status position was the reason given by over half of these migrants for having no health-care provision, it was not the sole reason.

A combination of other factors also contributes to lower health-care coverage for migrants. These include the complexity of the health-care system in Chile, which makes it difficult to understand for migrants, particularly recent arrivals.[32] This was a common complaint made by those I worked with, especially when they did not have employment contracts. While those in regular migratory situations but without employment contracts could have accessed FONASA Category A health care, they were quite often unaware of this. Those with employment contracts were more likely to have assistance from an employer in filling out the necessary paperwork for inscription in the system and therefore were more likely to be enrolled. Among those who *were* enrolled in FONASA, the time needed to attend appointments, and inflexibility in terms of the open hours of primary care clinics, were barriers to access on a provider level. While quality of care in terms of resources and infrastructure was viewed positively by most migrants in comparison with Bolivia, perceived discrimination and poor service compared with that afforded to Chileans was a common complaint.[33]

The complexities of access at the provider and patient level were made clearest in the stories of the six women I interviewed who had been pregnant in Chile in recent years. I am very grateful to them for sharing these deeply personal experiences with me for the purposes of this study. They reflected in depth on their experiences of the Chilean public health service. Four had given birth in Chile, one had returned to Bolivia to have her baby, and one had miscarried. Only one, Aimy, age thirty-four, from Cochabamba, living in Santiago and working as a *nana puertas adentro*, reported an excellent level of service through FONASA during pregnancy and birth. She said that the waiting times were long, but the care was good, and she thought it better than that available in Bolivia.

The three women from Arica who had been pregnant—Julieta, Nina, and Antonia—had all been fearful of the Chilean health service because of their migratory status and because of their distrust of the care that would be provided. Julieta, who at that time had irregular status, said of her fear of being reported to the immigration authorities, "As a migrant, I wanted to escape, I wanted to leave . . . because I didn't have the things, the documents." However, her husband, who is Chilean, insisted that she be seen, advocated for her, and assisted her in applying for the special temporary resident visa available for pregnant women. Julieta thought the care she received was good on the whole, although she was made to wait for longer than the Chilean women at the clinic.

Nina, on the other hand, had a Bolivian partner, Marcos, and very little contact with Chileans, as she lived and worked on a *parcela*. She was age twenty-four and from rural Oruro. She spoke Spanish but was more comfortable speaking Aymara. She was very worried about her irregular status and about the type and quality of antenatal care provided in Chile. As a consequence, she received no medical attention throughout her pregnancy and returned to her rural community in Bolivia to give birth, where she was attended by a traditional Aymara *partera* (midwife). Conversations with other women, and with migrant organization staff, suggest that this may not be uncommon among women migrants in Arica and reflects tendencies in Bolivia, where some Aymara (and other indigenous) women's needs are not met through the public health system.

The infant mortality rate per 1,000 live births in Bolivia is 31, compared with a Latin American and Caribbean average of 15.[34] The maternal mortality rate per 100,000 live births is 206 in Bolivia, compared with a Latin American and Caribbean average of 67.[35] Indigenous women and babies are disproportionately represented in these figures. According to the recent Wawachaña project carried out by Medicos del Mundo and previous work by Barbara Bradby and Jo Murphy-Lawless, one of the reasons for this is the highly medicalized, interventionist approach to birth in many Bolivian hospitals.[36] They indicate that spaces provided for giving birth are cold and clinical; only a limited number of people are permitted to be present; women generally are not allowed to choose the position in which they give birth if it is a vaginal birth, and must lie on their backs; and over 40 percent of births are by caesarean section. These practices may be contradictory to the cultural, social, and emotional needs of some women, particularly some indigenous women.[37] Thus they may avoid contact with public health providers during pregnancy and birth due to their lack of cultural sensitivity. This can unfortunately lead to complications going undetected or to difficulties in resolving them.

In Arica, a survey of 150 migrant women ages eighteen to forty, the majority of whom self-identified as Aymara Bolivian, found that 17 percent had never had contact with a public health provider in Chile in spite of the fact that on average they had been in the country for two years.[38] Furthermore, of those who had, only 15 percent had been for gynecological or obstetric care or checkups (including universally available free Pap smears and mammograms). In general, their contact with public health providers had been through checkups for their children rather than for themselves. As in Bolivia, the approach to pregnancy and birth in the public health service in Chile is highly medicalized and interventionist.[39] While research is lacking on this issue, it is quite possible that this is a factor preventing indigenous Bolivian women in particular from feeling comfortable about engaging with the Chilean public health service in relation to their reproductive health. As has been indicated regarding some Peruvian women migrants, it also seems that there may be a lack of knowledge about reproductive health care among some Bolivian migrants, which could be an additional contributing factor.[40]

Antonia's story is illustrative. She self-identified as Aymara and was from urban La Paz. She was single, living in the *bodega* mentioned in chapter 2 with her sister and others and working in El Agro, Arica's central market, for minimum wage. She had an MTRV and was in the process of applying for permanent residency. She paid FONASA contributions and was a Category B service user. During carnival in February 2014, she told me, she became pregnant. However, early in her first trimester she experienced cramps and heavy bleeding. Frightened, she was accompanied by her sister to the primary care unit where she was enrolled. She was told that they could not attend to her because her application for permanent residency was in process and thus she could not present the relevant documentation (a valid Chilean ID card). This information was inaccurate, for two reasons. First, while prior to 2009 this would have been the case, a law was passed in that year so that migrants whose permanent residency applications were being processed could be seen through FONASA.[41] Second, Antonia was pregnant and so should have been attended regardless of her migratory status.

Antonia's sister, Isabela, explained the factors she thought were behind the problem:

> Maybe because we have that face of "humble people" and we don't know how to express ourselves very well, some specific words that the doctor wants. . . . [W]e go with the words that we learn there in Bolivia, with those words, and they don't understand. They say, "I can't hear you, you speak very fast."

Isabela, who was more confident than Antonia, insisted on her sister being seen and eventually arranged an appointment. At the appointment, Antonia was told that she had miscarried, and the doctor informed her that she would need to have the pregnancy tissue surgically removed from her uterus. The process, however, was not explained in words that Antonia could easily understand. She thought that it was comparable to an abortion, which for her was morally unacceptable, and that it would affect her future fertility.[42]

The point at which I met Antonia was following this first appointment, and she was tearful and afraid. She asked me for advice, so I referred her to Gabriela at the Asociación, who had previously worked on health and gender issues in Bolivia. She was able to advise and explain things to Antonia, offering to accompany her to future medical appointments. Antonia, however, was sufficiently reassured by Gabriela's advice to attend the appointments with Isabela. In further conversations with Gabriela, I learned that such culturally insensitive encounters with health providers were common, sometimes exacerbated by women's lack of understanding of reproductive health. The Asociación in Arica would often advise in these instances, accompanying women to appointments on occasion and assisting them with paperwork for the temporary resident visa for pregnancy if that was relevant.

In Santiago, two women other than Aimy I spoke to had been pregnant and given birth in Chile, Luz María and Rosa. Like the women from Arica, their experiences were colored by lack of understanding by providers of the health care available to migrants, as well as a lack of empathy and cultural sensitivity. Luz María arrived in Chile with her partner Wilson knowing that she was around two months pregnant. She avoided going to her primary care clinic until she was over five months pregnant, as she was frightened because of her irregular migratory status. As indicated by the quote at the start of this section, the social worker whom she saw during her first consultation told her that she would have to pay a million Chilean pesos (US$1,657) to give birth in a hospital without a Chilean ID card. Strictly speaking, it is true that there are a number of problems, including the possibility of having to pay for health care, if a migrant woman does not have her temporary resident visa for pregnancy prior to giving birth. Nonetheless, in Luz María's case there was still time to arrange for this, and the social worker's statement made her extremely anxious. Fortunately she was referred to the Asociación in Santiago by the primary care clinic following this first appointment, and the staff were able to assist with her temporary residency application and paid for her and Wilson's visas through the DAS scheme (see chapter 3).

In spite of the difficulties with the social worker and several weeks of anxiety regarding her visa application, Luz María's general evaluation of the care she received was positive. While she self-identifies as part Quechua and explained to me some of the Quechua beliefs and practices around birth that her aunt and other family members adhere to (such as preferring home births), Luz María felt comfortable with the Chilean public health system and with giving birth in a hospital environment. In particular, she thought that the Chile Crece Contigo (Chile Grows with You) program was very good. All women who have antenatal care and give birth in public hospitals in Chile are incorporated in this program. Information about each month of pregnancy, in the form of a calendar, is given to expectant mothers. It is factual, clearly explained, and well illustrated. Luz María showed me her calendar and explained that she had been unaware of much of the information it contained, despite already having one child; she told me, for example, that she had not known it was OK to still have sex during pregnancy. Furthermore, she was delighted that enrollment in Chile Crece Contigo entitled her to a free bassinette, diapers, and some baby clothes upon the birth of her child.

Rosa, by contrast, had a very poor experience with the Chilean health service, a combination of all of the exclusions discussed thus far. We sat on a bench in the Parque Quinta Normal near the *migrant cité* that she shared with ten other people, Rosa holding her tiny five-week-old daughter in her arms. She began her story:

> Well, first of all, they didn't want to enroll me because my temporary resident visa was expired and my permanent one was in process. I had some difficulties, but because I was pregnant, they had to see me. So, well, another person [from the Asociación in Santiago] helped me to talk, and all that and then I could be enrolled. . . . They don't want to see foreigners, let's say. It's kind of discrimination.

Right from the outset, Rosa experienced problems at the provider level; as in Antonia's case, there was a lack of understanding of the health-care provision she was entitled to. Once Rosa was finally enrolled, the care she received at her primary care clinic was poor:

> I wasn't very well attended. . . . [M]y daughter was very small, she wasn't developing. The midwife . . . you imagine she knows what the situation is. She studied for that. But she didn't say anything to me. And at my last check-up with her . . . she said, "She's very small, but she's ok." Then I saw another doctor, who did a scan to see how she was. He got scared, and he said, "No, she's very small, we have to get her out," and they did an emergency caesarean. She was born at eight months.

Rosa went on to explain that during her pregnancy, it had been discovered that she had Chagas' disease (American trypanosomiasis), which is similar to the more well-known African trypanosomiasis or sleeping sickness caused by the tsetse fly.[43] Bolivia has the highest prevalence of Chagas' disease anywhere in the Americas, with approximately thirty-three of every one hundred people being infected.[44] Accurate statistics are very hard to obtain, and research is severely lacking, but according to Medecins Sans Frontiers, in 2004 Chagas' disease accounted for around 13 percent of deaths in Bolivia.[45] Vector-borne transmission of Chagas' disease occurs through being bitten by the "kissing bug" triatoma infestans, known in Bolivia as *vinchuca*. These bugs are predominantly found in the walls of poor-quality housing in low socioeconomic rural and peri-urban areas.

Chagas' disease can also be transmitted congenitally during pregnancy and birth. Newborns infected with Chagas' disease are likely to be born prematurely, have low birth weight, and may experience respiratory problems and a range of other complications. Mortality rates of infected newborns are around 5 percent.[46] If left untreated, babies are likely to develop chronic Chagas' disease, which can result in cardiac and intestinal problems and may lead to death. If detected and treated within the first year, however, the response to treatment is almost 100 percent.[47] In the case of Rosa, in spite of the diagnosis of Chagas' disease, which should have led to an increased level of monitoring, she felt she had not been properly cared for during pregnancy, leading to a very stressful birth and to her baby's life potentially being in danger. Moreover, her daughter's test results for Chagas' disease had been lost by the hospital. When I interviewed her, she was in the process of having her daughter tested again, potentially delaying the start of treatment if her daughter was infected.

There was also a lack of emotional sensitivity and social support throughout Rosa's experience of the emergency caesarean and then postnatal care that left her upset and exhausted. I asked Rosa if her sister, with whom she lived, could be with her after the birth:

> *Rosa:* Well, she came but she wasn't allowed in. And I didn't have anything with me. . . . They took my bag and I said to the nurses to give my sister the key to go and get my things. . . . But they didn't want to give her the key. . . . And they wouldn't let her come and see me afterward, nothing.
>
> . . .
>
> *Megan:* And afterward I guess you stayed in the hospital for at least a few days?
> *Rosa:* Well, they discharged me but not my daughter. . . . [S]he was there for three weeks. I had to go from here [her *migrant cité*, an hour's bus ride] every day. To breastfeed her and everything. . . . At eleven I visited and I was there until six in the evening. So . . . it was very, very, very complicated.[48]

Rosa's story clearly illustrates the difficulties that some migrants face in accessing sensitive and appropriate care through the Chilean health service. In spite of special provisions for pregnant migrant women at the system level, lack of knowledge of these provisions, lack of cultural sensitivity and empathy, and sometimes discrimination at the provider level make access complicated. Indeed, lack of solidarity could again be thought of as part of the problem. Moreover, migrants are often unaware of their rights to health care and may not always have a sound understanding of health issues, particularly about reproductive health. There are certainly attempts being made—such as the Chile Crece Contigo program—to address this. Additionally, migrant organizations such as the Asociación are playing an important role in supporting migrants to access health care, as well as offering workshops to providers on migrant health. Nevertheless, it is clear that there are still migrants who are facing significant exclusion from this fundamental aspect of social citizenship. Women seem to be the worst affected, particularly during pregnancy, further indicating the impact of gender on access to social rights. Furthermore, this means that, as in the case of Rosa's baby daughter, their children may not be given the best start in life.

EDUCATION

My boy, the littlest one, was being bullied and I had no idea.
—CRISTINA, AGE THIRTY-SEVEN, FROM COCHABAMBA

Indicating how important it is to think transnationally about migrants' access to social rights, in both Bolivia and Chile low-income migrants and their families experienced uneven access to quality education. The lifelong, intergenerational, and cross-border effects of this are significant. While the average level of education of the adult migrant population in Chile is above that of the native-born population (12.6 years and 11 years, respectively), Bolivian migrants on average have fewer years of schooling than Chileans.[49] Data from CASEN indicate that only 54 percent of Bolivian migrants in Chile have more than ten years of schooling, compared with 77 percent of Peruvian migrants. Approximately 15 percent of Bolivians have less than four years' schooling, the highest percentage in this category of any migrant group.[50]

These tendencies were certainly reflected among those I worked with. Moreover, even among those who had completed secondary school, literacy levels were often poor. I would be asked to read information sheets and consent forms to some interviewees who had stated that they had finished secondary school, or they would visibly struggle to read them, despite the forms being designed for an average reading age of twelve. This was the case in both Santiago and Arica and was strongly linked to coming from a low socioeconomic background, but it was particularly apparent in Arica, where many migrants are from rural areas in Bolivia. These observations fitted with conversations with third-sector workers in Bolivia, who highlighted the continuing prevalence of low-quality education in rural communities and marginalized urban areas, although school attendance is now good throughout the country. This is confirmed by a 2011 nationwide study: although the majority of children and young people attend school, only 12 percent of secondary school students in state schools achieve a "high level" of reading comprehension.[51]

I found that women, and particularly women over the age of thirty-five, were disproportionately represented among those migrants who had no schooling, primary schooling only, or incomplete secondary schooling. It was also noticeable that women who spoke Aymara as a first language struggled more with speaking Spanish than their male counterparts, despite Spanish being the main teaching language in Bolivian schools. While today there is gender parity in terms of school attendance and literacy rates in Bolivia, this was not at all the case in the recent past.[52] In 2001 the adult population (age nineteen and over), had on average 7.4 years of schooling. For rural women, however, the average was just 3.1 years, compared to urban men at 10.1 years.[53] Some migrant women I interviewed reflected with deep regret on the lack of educational opportunities that had been available to them. Generally, it was lack of family resources that had prevented them from continuing with their education in Bolivia. For example, Carolina, age thirty-eight, from Cochabamba, had at the age of eight commenced work as a live-in domestic helper in Bolivia following a family crisis that compelled her to find employment at that young age.

While younger women I spoke to all had at least some secondary schooling, several said that their dreams of continuing to higher education had been curtailed by family needs and expectations. This was the case for Agustina, age twenty-one, from La Paz, working in Arica, who had finished secondary school:

> After a while I went out to work, but I wanted to study and my dad didn't want me to, so . . . such a disappointment. And then I met her father [*indicates baby daughter*]. . . . And now because I have my little daughter, I can't study.

Socioeconomic background, the rural/urban divide, gender, and ethnicity all had a significant role to play in the ease of access to, and quality of, education received by migrants in Bolivia. Low levels of education reverberate in negative ways throughout people's migration journeys. These might range from restricted employment opportunities and wage-earning capacity in Bolivia compelling migration to Chile, to being at a disadvantage in the Chilean labor market compared to migrants of other nationalities, to struggling to understand everyday bureaucratic processes for acquiring legal status.

In addition to low educational attainment in Bolivia impacting migrants' lives in Chile, a further problem on the Chilean side of the border is achieving equal access to education for migrant children. Article 28 of the Convention on the Rights of the Child recognizes that every child has the right to education and stipulates that states must provide at a minimum compulsory free primary education to all children. The reality in many of the 192 countries that have ratified the Convention is, however, very different. This is undoubtedly the case for migrant children, whose legal status can significantly impact their ability to access education. In the European context, for example, Luca Bicocchi and Michele LeVoy explain that "undocumented" children often face many barriers to education, which "may be practical, such as lack of identification; institutional, such as discriminatory legislation or broadly societal, such as the fear of being detected."[54] Access to education for migrant children without legal status can likewise be complicated in other parts of the global North.[55]

There is, however, a great paucity of research on migrant access to education in the global South. Moreover, as Lesley Bartlett and Ameena Ghaffar-Kucher explain, "the studies that do exist suggest that the denial of the right of education is a serious issue in many parts of the global South. Further, existing studies suggest that im/migrant populations experience significant harassment and discrimination, as well as low-quality schooling."[56]

Research to date on migrant children and education in Chile reflects these findings. As Iskra Pavez Soto, one of the key figures working on the topic, writes, "The migration experience of girls and boys in Chile is strongly marked by constant situations of discrimination and racism."[57] Indeed, a UNICEF-led study in 2004 indicated that 46 percent of Chilean children thought that Chileans were "superior" to people of other Latin American nationalities. Asked to indicate to which nationalities they believed Chileans were superior, 32 percent stated that they were superior to Peruvians, and 30 percent believed that they were superior to Bolivians; these were the nationalities most discriminated against.[58] In spite of the passage of time since this study was done, these attitudes were certainly reflected in the experiences of the children of migrants I worked with. Five interviewees in Santiago had children who had been bullied—verbally, physically, or both— because of their nationality, skin color, phenotypical features, and/or supposed personality traits linked to their nationality.[59]

The bullying had been severe enough for parents to report it to their children's schools. Teachers, and in some cases educational psychologists, had subsequently intervened. Nevertheless, the bullying had to be significant, and parents had to become involved, before the school reacted. The Asociación in Santiago and another migrant organization that works specifically with migrant children have partnered with a number of schools in Santiago to promote intercultural education and attempt to reduce discrimination. Contact with some of these schools during this research and as a volunteer on an intercultural education program through the Asociación in Santiago for six months from 2010 to 2011 demonstrated to me that these interventions are having a localized effect. Nonetheless, arguably a great deal more still needs to be done at municipal and national levels to combat discrimination and racism in schools.

Bullying was less common in Arica than in Santiago. This is likely attributable to the fact that most of the children in the families with whom I had contact attended schools in the Valle de Azapa, where up to 80 percent of the student body is migrants. Certainly in other schools in northern Chile, migrant children can face significant discrimination.[60] Additionally, some schools in the Valle de Azapa make a concerted effort to engage in intercultural education and to include parents in their children's education. They may even have Aymara language programs, which include teaching written Aymara. This was highlighted by Belén, age twenty-seven, from rural La Paz, who speaks Aymara but cannot write it and was pleased that her children are learning it in written form. Schools in the Valle de Azapa also hold parent-teacher meetings at times convenient to parents who are agricultural workers and have a focus on educating parents and the community as well as the children.

Two schools in particular in the Valle de Azapa, with the support of the Asociación in Arica, had organized drives to regularize the migratory situation of their students. Strictly speaking, state primary and secondary schools in Chile must accept all children regardless of their legal status. Once enrolled, irrespective of their or their parents' migratory situation, children and young people under age eighteen technically can obtain a permanent student visa. Nevertheless, as Sara Joiko and Alba Vásquez indicate, this can involve an "extensive administrative process."[61] If parents have an official certificate from the country of origin that recognizes the child's level of study, then things are relatively straightforward. If they do not have this document, however (which is a common occurrence), a labyrinthine procedure must be followed. Among other things, it involves legalizing documents with the Ministry of Foreign Affairs or the equivalent in the country of origin, legalizing documents in the Chilean consulate in the country of origin, and presenting this document to the Chilean Ministry of Education Exam Unit.

Students frequently get stuck somewhere in this bureaucratic maze and are subsequently issued an ID card with no definitive ID number. They are colloquially known as "niños RUT 100" because the number they are assigned is "100.000.000-0." Possessing this card means that they can go to school, but they are not officially in the educational system. They cannot be credited for the education they have undertaken in Chile and thus cannot move from primary to secondary school, obtain a certificate at the end of their secondary schooling, or access any of the benefits such as lunch vouchers to which children from low-income families are entitled. In 2016 it was calculated that 24,865 migrant children in Chile were niños RUT 100.[62]

In the Valle de Azapa there were many such children. In 2014 I attended meetings with the Asociación in Arica and spoke individually with staff members about students' migration situations at one school, Liceo 14 (a pseudonym) in the Valle de Azapa. Liceo 14 was renowned for accepting many migrant students when other schools would not; nonacceptance of migrant children is common despite the law.[63] Liceo 14 issued all of its students with matriculation certificates as proof of their enrollment, but struggled to persuade parents, the majority of whom had irregular status, to complete the other necessary steps to acquire permanent student visas for their children.

According to the school social worker, this was for three key reasons. First, parents had low literacy levels and so could not understand the complex written instructions for the procedure they needed to follow or the forms that they needed to fill out. This is indicative of the intergenerational impact of exclusion from quality education. Second, the cost of traveling to Bolivia to obtain the legalized documents that they would need to complete the process was high, and in addition they sometimes did not have passports for their children but only the ID cards required to enter Chile; acquiring a passport involves additional cost (see chapter 3). Third, they were fearful of the authorities and were unconvinced that their migratory status would not be brought into question by applying for a visa for their children. In collaboration with the Asociación in Arica, Liceo 14 had already run some successful workshops for parents to assist them in understanding the permanent student visa application process. Further sessions for teachers, parents, students, and the wider community were planned. I helped at a similar workshop at a nursery school in Arica and witnessed the positive impact it had on parents and nursery school staff; following the workshop, parents came to the Asociación in Arica offices on an individual basis for assistance with visa applications for themselves and their children.

The situation in Santiago regarding school access is very similar. Certain schools are known to be "migrant friendly," in that they accept all students regardless of their migratory status. Others, however, create many obstacles for parents, leading them to enroll their children in the migrant-friendly schools that they hear about through their social networks. As Pavez Soto emphasizes, it is concerning that some schools are not fulfilling their legal obligation to accept all children, and the creation of migrant-friendly schools may lead to ghettoization of low-income migrant and second-generation children.[64] Again, at the heart of this issue is a "lack of solidarity" by people working in the public sector, as well as in the wider society. This has prevented significant numbers of migrant children from accessing appropriate education or at the least has limited their choices with regard to the institutions that they attend.[65] Of additional concern is that many migrant children are exposed to racism and bullying even once they are incorporated into

formal education in Chile. The good news is that since September 2016, the Asociación has been running a campaign to end the RUT 100 and ensure equal treatment of all children; this gained significant traction and some positive response
from the government under Michelle Bachelet. There is, however, still a long way
to go before migrant children in Chile, and particularly those from low-income
families, enjoy full and equal access to education.

SOCIAL SUPPORT

*I speak with my daughters two days a week by Skype. Then we can see each
other, we can hear each other. . . . There is nothing, nothing, nothing, nothing
that can stand in the way of those calls.*

—ANAHIS, AGE THIRTY-SIX, FROM SUCRE

The "right to family life" or "primary relationships" is frequently disrupted by
migration, typically when parents migrate in order to try to better provide financially for children whom they leave behind. It is important not to see such families as "broken," and to acknowledge the agency of those migrating.[66] Nevertheless, as the literature on global care chains has amply illustrated, separation from
family, especially from children, certainly has a profound emotional impact on
migrants' lives and on the lives of those "left behind."[67] Furthermore, as has
already been discussed in this book (see chapter 4), the need to migrate, and the
subsequent rupture in family life that this causes, may well be generated by structural factors outside of migrants' control. In addition to the impact on their significant primary relationships, migrants may also find it difficult to form social
relationships in the receiving country, in particular if they have irregular status.[68]
For many with whom I worked, exclusion from both these broader social networks in Chile and everyday, physical primary relationships was a deeply felt
consequence of migration.

As one would expect, separation from family had a far greater impact on those
in Santiago than on those in Arica. Many in Arica traveled often to Bolivia, and
they knew that they could travel back at short notice and for a relatively low cost;
a bus ticket from Arica to La Paz is a little over US$30 round-trip. For those in
Santiago, however, the journey by bus would take over thirty hours to La Paz and
fifty or more to Santa Cruz. The cost for a return ticket would be approximately
US$200. The cost of cheap flights would actually be comparable, but many poorer
migrants had never considered the possibility of flying. The distance and cost of
travel from Santiago to Bolivia meant that it was a trip that could be made about
once a year.

Amanda, age twenty-five, from El Alto, whose migration story was discussed in
chapter 4, spoke to me about how hard it was for her to only see her mother, father,
and siblings once a year:

It's not at all easy to be so far from your family, it's not at all easy. As much as . . . here I try to look for all that is good, but there are always those moments when I think about my family. How are they? My mum, how is she? Because one does not own life. You don't know when they're not going to be beside you anymore, and you think, "Oh no, why have I not made more of the chance to be with them?" It makes me very sad sometimes. It makes me very sad and I think, "I just hope I have more opportunities to be with them and that I achieve my goal [of building a house for her family] as soon as possible to be able to be there."

For those with children who had stayed in Bolivia, the sentiments expressed by Amanda were often compounded by deep anxiety regarding their children's well-being, as well as feelings of guilt.[69] In the majority of cases, their children were in the care of their mothers or mothers-in-law, which appears to be the most common arrangement in global care chains.[70] Parents worried that their children would forget or resent them, a phenomenon that sadly has been well documented in other contexts.[71] Staff at the after-school club at the youth center in Plan 3000 (see chapter 2) told me that challenging emotional dynamics within families following parents' migration were indeed an unhappy reality for many.

Javiera, age forty-three, from Santa Cruz, had two children in Bolivia living with her mother. She recalled a recent conversation with her thirteen-year-old daughter back in Bolivia, from whom she had been separated for two years with one short visit, saying "she wants us to go back, she says she needs her mum, her dad, she doesn't care what we give her, she wants to be with her parents." The tension between her daughter's distress at being apart from her parents and Javiera's awareness that in Bolivia she could not earn enough to fund higher education for her children made her feel that "one leads a very sad life here [in Chile]. Being a migrant is seriously tough."

Parents such as Javiera did, however, develop strategies for transnational parenting in order to sustain their relationships across borders as well as possible.[72] Maintaining a ritual of a Sunday phone call from a call center or over Skype from and to an internet café was common. Anahis, quoted at the beginning of the section, used her conversations with her daughters not only to check on their well-being and catch up with their lives, but also to help them with their homework. Migrants also viewed not bringing their children to Chile as a responsible parenting decision, and some who had brought them were considering sending them back to be with family in Bolivia. There were several reasons for this. First, as explained above, accessing adequate housing with sufficient space for a family was not easy. Second, children restricted parents' ability to work the long hours required to earn a reasonable wage; moreover, Chilean currency went a lot further in Bolivia than in Chile, enabling their children to have a higher standard of living there than in Chile. Third, there were concerns about the standard of education available to their children in Chile and the potential for their children to be bullied.

Additionally, as discovered elsewhere, parents often wished for their children to be educated "at home" so as to maintain the cultural values that they saw as positive.[73] Almost universally, those I interviewed thought that Bolivian children and young people were politer, more respectful toward their elders, and less inclined to drink, take drugs, or be involved in crime than their Chilean counterparts. Chilean young people, particularly adolescent girls, were described as "*despiertos/as*" (awake), which in this context means worldly and implies being sexually aware. Regardless of the accuracy of this problematic descriptor—and I suggest that negative stereotyping of the host culture may in part be a reaction to experiences of discrimination—it had a powerful influence on parents' decisions and was mentioned by all of those with children who had remained in Bolivia as a factor that influenced them in making this decision.[74] Among those who did have children in Chile, Constanza, for example, had become alarmed at what she saw as her eldest son's unacceptably assertive behavior and new habit of "answering back" since beginning school in Chile. She was questioning whether it would be better for him to return to Bolivia.

Thus, the factors that kept migrants from maintaining everyday, physical relationships with family members, and children particularly, were both agentic and structural. There was an element of choice in whether or not migrants brought their children to Chile, influenced by their concerns over the kinds of values their children might learn in the new social milieu. The need to sustain significant primary relationships was, however, also disrupted by structural factors. Poor living conditions, inflexible working hours, and the lack of availability of quality education free from discrimination in Chile were of fundamental importance. There was also a profoundly transnational dimension to this exclusion from social citizenship because, as discussed in chapter 4, it was often their families' economic necessity that had compelled the migration of parents as a survival strategy for the extended family.

Lack of social networks exacerbated the sense of isolation that separation from family could generate. With the exception of a handful of people who had spent fifteen years or more in Chile, all commented that their social networks and friendships in Chile were far reduced from what they had been in Bolivia.[75] This was irrespective of socioeconomic background in Bolivia or employment in Chile. Things were certainly worst, however, for those in precarious employment, and particularly women in domestic work or cleaning. I met with Carolina, who worked as a *nana puertas afuera*, early one morning before she began work in a house in the upper-class *comuna* of Las Condes. We sat on a bench in the Vega Chica market, which was at about the halfway mark on her bus journey of over one hour from home to work. Reflecting on her social life in Chile, she cast her eyes down to our polystyrene cups of Nescafé and powdered milk and told me:

> The truth is I don't have many friends. Look, I've lived in Quilicura [a *comuna* in Santiago] almost four years and I speak to two women, two Chileans, but hardly. I don't have time. I leave early, I arrive late, and I don't have many friends.

Not only did this lack of networks have emotional consequences, but it also had material ones in relation to finding accommodations and jobs.[76] For example, as discussed in chapter 4, lack of social networks was one of the factors that compelled migrants on *parcelas* in Arica to remain there. In Santiago, rooms in *migrant cités* were primarily found through contacts, and so those without contacts were more likely to sublet the worst quality, most expensive rooms. There was a high level of awareness of the impact of social networks on the ability to find work and accommodation, as well as on emotional health. To the extent that it was possible, migrants engaged in a variety of practices to extend, or "bridge," their networks.[77] Most common among those who did not live in the places where they worked was to try to form connections with neighbors. They were generally also migrants, although often of different nationalities. There was some distrust of, and discrimination against, other nationalities, particularly Peruvians.[78] However, this was usually overcome following sustained contact with migrant groups from other countries, as in the case of Luz María and Wilson.

Upon moving to Santiago, through kinship networks they knew one other Bolivian couple, who assisted then with finding a room and Wilson with finding a job in construction. This couple also lent Luz María and Wilson money to pay for a deposit on their accommodation. This was the extent of Luz María and Wilson's social network in Chile for some months. When I first met with Luz María in her room in a *migrant cité*, she informed me in hushed tones that the neighbors, who were mainly Peruvian, were given to drinking and partying and would not always clean the bathroom. Over time, however, she became more open to socializing with people who were not conationals. She formed friendships with the Peruvian hairdresser next door to her *migrant cité* and with the residents of the *cité*.

After six months of living there, Luz María invited my partner and me to the baby shower that her neighbors had organized. Fifteen or so of them had decorated the common space with blue and white ribbons and an enormous banner announcing "Baby Shower." The hairdresser had given Luz María and Wilson free haircuts, and they were both smartly attired in new outfits. We were invited to take a seat and were served soft drinks, beer, and elaborately prepared snacks, which everyone had contributed to buying and making. Everyone had also brought a gift for the baby, which they placed in a basket for the game that followed. The men had to take turns guessing what each gift was before Luz María opened it. If they guessed incorrectly they were "punished," which involved drinking beer from a baby bottle, crawling around, or putting on a large towel as a nappy.

Following the game, which had generated much hilarity, one of the residents— a Peruvian who had lived in Chile for thirteen years—brought out her set of crystal glasses, which she kept for special occasions. The tone became more solemn as sparkling wine was poured for everyone and we toasted the couple and the baby on the way. Then some of the other neighbors served *ají de gallina*, a traditional Peruvian dish, and later the dancing began. It was a touching demonstration of solidarity and care for the young couple for whom this informal social network had become very important, particularly in the physical absence of family. Although, as Louise Ryan and colleagues highlight, it is important not to overstate the value of social networks in mitigating limited access to economic opportunities or welfare, migrants with more extensive networks were able to acquire better employment and accommodation than their counterparts without such networks and thus enter further into the space of social citizenship.[79] It appears, however, that it was the emotional support offered by these networks that was of most importance, and its lack was keenly felt by those without them.

CONCLUSION

Throughout this chapter I have developed an integrated approach to examining a range of social rights that are often considered separately within migration studies. Adaptation of Doyal and Gough's taxonomy of intermediate needs allows for holistic consideration of not only access to shelter, health care, and education, but also significant primary relationships and social networks—all fundamental to migrant incorporation in the transnational space of social citizenship. The impact of migrants' social identities, in addition to their in/exclusion from other spaces of citizenships, on accessing varied social rights is also accounted for using this approach.

In the Chilean-Bolivian context, a pattern regarding these social rights emerges, which again gives weight to the concept of migrants' citizenship as often being grounded in uncertainty. In general, Chilean legislation is on a par with internationally expected standards for migrant access to health care and education and to a lesser extent, to housing. Nevertheless, at the middle level where providers (health-care professionals, educators, landlords, etc.) interact with migrants, there abounds a "lack of solidarity," which impedes access. Moreover, the bureaucratic processes for accessing social rights are often excessively convoluted. For those I worked with, this led to significant exclusions from various dimensions of social citizenship and a pervasive sense of social *in*security. Difficulty accessing social rights was greater for women, people of indigenous descent, and those from lower socioeconomic backgrounds. Furthermore, it could be impacted by the degree to which they had previously experienced exclusion from social rights in Bolivia—the case of education is emblematic here.

Nevertheless, demonstrating the flickering promise contained in uncertainty, there were some limited instances in which, supported by migrant organizations, greater inclusion of migrants was occurring, such as in Liceo 14 in the Valle de Azapa. Furthermore, migrants individually engaged in strategies to enter further into social citizenship, particularly with regard to expanding their informal social networks, which led to greater material, but above all emotional, support. Sometimes the search for social networks also led participants to engage in practices of political citizenship, as I explain in the next and final chapter.

6

"¿De Dónde Somos?" "¡De Bolivia!"

After the break, we started off again, this time with more confidence. We all got swept up by the brass band's music and the adrenaline, and I felt that I started to understand what carnival is about. There was a sense of traditions being lived and remembered, of sharing beauty with others, and of a celebration of the sheer joy of being alive. The procession finished down Avenida Recoleta, and it was fairly incredible to be dancing along one of Santiago's main avenues holding up the traffic. We were joined by some stray dogs towards the end, and the last five minutes were a crazy cacophonous blur with the crowd joining in, confetti everywhere, and cars and buses beeping their horns.

—FIELDNOTES, DECEMBER 1, 2013

These were the reflections I wrote in my field journal over a strong cup of coffee the morning after dancing with Corazón de Tinkus (a pseudonym) in the Fifth Annual Patronato Carnival in Santiago. To the applause and whistles of onlookers, many of whom were Chilean, for a few brief hours the dance fraternity laid claim to public space in the heart of the city. With the call and response—"¿Quiénes somos?" "¡Tinkus somos!" "¿De dónde somos?" "¡De Bolivia!" ("Who are we?" "We are *tinkus*!" "Where're we from?" "From Bolivia!")—strongly declared at regular intervals, this was an affirmation of transnational belonging, a citizenship practice in the realm of the political.

Throughout the course of my fieldwork, I came to understand that dance was a political citizenship practice of fundamental importance for some Bolivian migrants in Chile. To date, the potential political significance of dance and other forms of artistic expression for migrant groups has not received as much attention as it might have in the scholarship that analyzes migration and citizenship. I use this chapter to first explore the degree to which the migrants with whom I worked engaged in the political practices—both formal and informal—more typically acknowledged in this body of research. I then bring into dialogue perspectives from a variety of fields of study in order to finish with a close analysis of dance as an informal political citizenship practice. I understand all these practices as occurring within, and constructing, a transnational space of political citizenship, which overlaps and intertwines with other spaces of citizenship. Those migrants incorporated in this space through the exercise of formal or informal citizenship practices may or may not be within other spaces of citizenship, and their position within other spaces may impact their ability to participate as political citizens.

MIGRATION AND FORMAL AND INFORMAL POLITICAL CITIZENSHIP

As indicated in the introduction, feminist scholars of citizenship have called for an expansion of its political dimension to include not only formal but also informal politics. Classic interpretations have emphasized the right to vote and the right to run for office as political citizenship's key components. This reflects a strong masculine bias, given that throughout history and continuing in the present, women have been excluded from both of these rights, whether by legislation or by structural factors, such as the expectation that women will take primary responsibility for childcare. In addition, a purview that focuses only on formal politics neglects the often substantial contributions that women have made to informal, community politics, where they have had more possibility of participating.

Frequently referencing feminist perspectives, further critiques of a narrow interpretation of political citizenship have come from those studying migration, largely in South-North contexts.[1] It is vital to consider other ways in which migrants, as a population who habitually cannot vote in the receiving country, may be involved in "the political." Marco Martiniello, for example, constructed a typology of the ways in which migrants may engage in politics in both the receiving country and transnationally, from participation in state politics to what he terms "ethnic community mobilisation."[2] Political involvement with the sending country has also been examined in-depth, including, for example, a growing body of work that analyzes extraterritorial voting or involvement in hometown associations.[3] With respect to participation more specifically in the receiving country, there has been interest in migrant participation in unions and "new social movements."[4]

These studies with a particular focus on either the sending or receiving country nonetheless reflect a transnational sensibility. Indeed, it has been shown that there is a connection between greater transnational participation and greater participation in the receiving country.[5] This is also borne out in the work of those such as Robert Smith, who ethnographically explores migrants' political engagement in both sending and receiving countries, focusing on Mexican migration to New York.[6] Furthermore, in line with the feminist perspective that guides much of this research, from the early stages of work on migrant political participation, a gendered and more recently intersectional approach has been taken.[7] Migration scholars have thus embraced a relatively broad definition of the political, including both formal and informal practices, taking into account the impact that social identities have on migrants' participation both in the receiving country and transnationally. This approach partially guided my forays into exploring Bolivian migrants' engagements with political citizenship, and it is reflected in the subsequent discussions of formal political involvement in the form of voting and party politics and of informal involvement in terms of mobilizations, hometown associations, and grassroots community organizing. In both instances, migrants' involvement was characterized by ambivalence and lack of conviction in the efficacy of such politics.

Voting and Party Politics

Around 115 countries make extraterritorial voting possible for their diasporas.[8] Jean-Michel Lafleur suggests three sociopolitical variables that may interact to promote extraterritorial voting.[9] The first is lobbying from migrant groups regarding the external vote; however, Lafleur cautions that this should not be given undue emphasis, as there are other processes at work that are perhaps more powerful. He proposes two other variables: the state's level of economic dependence on migrants, and domestic politics. The economic dependence variable considers the importance of migrants' remittances to the country's economy, but also the potential role of migrants' "capacities to transfer knowledge and to open markets abroad" in order for the state "to better integrate into the global economy."[10] The domestic politics variable takes into consideration the impact of any national regime or institutional changes (which may act as a political opportunity for migrant lobbies to push their cause), as well as the potential benefits of the extraterritorial vote for domestic actors.

In Bolivia, extraterritorial voting has been possible since 2009 in its four largest migrant-receiving countries: Argentina, Brazil, Spain, and the United States. Alfonso Hinojosa Gordonava and colleagues argue that the Bolivian extraterritorial vote became possible due to a combination of the aforementioned variables.[11] Granting extraterritorial voting rights was, in part, recognition of the substantial contribution that migrants make to Bolivia's economy; nevertheless, domestic politics and the migrant lobby played a key role. Primarily, Hinojosa Gordonava and colleagues suggest, a political opportunity was provided for external migrant lobby groups as a consequence of the "context of crisis and changes" in Bolivia, which has been focused on extending democratic participation.[12] Furthermore, the demands of the migrant lobby—particularly strong in Buenos Aires—for greater inclusion in the Bolivian demos fitted well with the MAS (Movimiento al Socialismo, Movement for Socialism) party's stated objective of incorporation of the poor, indigenous, and marginalized in a plurinational state.

Indeed, in São Paulo and Buenos Aires, Evo Morales received an extraordinary 95 and 92 percent of the vote respectively in the 2009 presidential elections. In Spain Morales won 46 percent of the vote. In the United States the opposition party, Convergencia, was the clear winner. In all countries except the United States, the voter turnout was high; over 70 percent of registered voters came out to vote.[13] What is particularly interesting is the profile of those who voted in São Paulo and Buenos Aires, the most relevant points of comparison with Chile. There is consensus that generally it is those with higher levels of education in professional employment who are the most likely to exercise extraterritorial voting rights, and those with irregular migratory status are less likely to vote.[14] Nevertheless, it would appear that in São Paulo and Buenos Aires, voter turnout was high among those with only secondary school education working in low-end jobs, especially textile manufacturing, and that some people with irregular status did vote. It has been postulated that this was due to the type of politics represented by Morales, the areas of the city in which polling stations were set up (migrant barrios in the poorer parts of the cities), and the high levels of migrant involvement in migrant organizations and other forms of transnational politics in these two cities.[15]

Findings from my research, and the results of the 2014 general election and 2016 constitutional referendum, indicate that the situation in Chile is perhaps slightly different from that of Brazil and Argentina. While extraterritorial voting from Chile in the cities of Arica, Antofagasta, Iquique, Calama, and Santiago was possible for the presidential election of October 12, 2014, the majority of migrants I spoke to, of all backgrounds, were unaware of this when I asked them fifteen to six months before the election if they were thinking of voting. None had returned to Bolivia specifically to vote in the past, and none had been involved in lobbying for voting rights for Bolivians living in Chile, although most stated that they would vote from Chile once they realized that this was going to be a possibility. When I tried to engage in further conversation about party politics in Bolivia, reactions were frequently unenthusiastic, and the topic was quickly discarded. Ignacia, age thirty-four, from La Paz, for example, decisively ended my line of questioning on the topic, saying, "[L]ook, the only thing I know is that Evo Morales is the President, nothing else."

Those who did share an opinion with me often told me that they had initially supported Morales and felt that some change with regard to respect for indigenous cultures and improvement in the living conditions of the poor had come about as a consequence of his presidency. Luz María told me that she identified with Morales because she felt that he came from a background similar to hers, and she liked the way he dressed—she commented particularly on his array of sweaters—because to her it represented his humility. Nonetheless, Morales had failed to fully meet her, and others', expectations. Illustrating this, Ana María, age fifty-five, from La Paz, thought that while there was some positive recognition for indigenous peoples, the constitutional changes made under Morales had not signified a real change in society: "[J]ust like in all other Latin America countries, wealth has stayed in the hands of the very few." Indeed, as discussed in chapter 4, many people had migrated during Morales's time in power with a deep sense that the country had not experienced the economic growth they had hoped would improve their standard of living.[16] Aimy, age thirty-four, from Cochabamba, declared that in contradiction to her initial hopes, Morales's government "in general hasn't been good for the country. There are a lot of people who've left because of that, they've had to leave to find work."

Others simply had no faith in party politics or politicians. Amanda, age twenty-five, who self-identified as Aymara, had the following to say:

> *Megan:* Have things changed a bit since Evo Morales came to power?
> *Amanda:* No. I think that all that stuff to do with politics, well, nothing.... They always look out for themselves, not for others. For me, that's what politics will always be about. First they see that they're ok.

Even Gabriela, age twenty-eight, a lawyer for the Asociación in Arica and a migrant herself, was no longer convinced of the efficacy of party politics. This was despite the fact that she had stood as a mayoral candidate in the Bolivian *departamento* of Tarija and had been heavily involved in organizing the youth branches of the opposition in eastern Bolivia.

It is outside the scope of this book to discuss in any great detail the 2014 and 2016 voting patterns of Bolivians in Chile, given that the general election and referendum respectively took place after fieldwork had been completed. There are, however, some points worth mentioning. For example, it is interesting to note that turnout of those who registered to vote in the 2014 election was high; 80 percent of the 14,300 who registered to vote in Chile did so.[17] Nevertheless, given that, as previously established, the Bolivian population in Chile is estimated at around 50,000 (and legal status in the country of residence does not affect the ability to register to vote), unmediated claims of "high voter turnout" need to be approached with caution; this also applies to the other countries where extraterritorial voting is possible. Overall, the MAS party under Evo Morales won the 2014 general election with 61.3 percent of the vote. Of those Bolivians in Chile who did vote, 67 percent were in favor of the MAS, which was lower than the 92 percent in Argentina or 87 percent in Brazil who supported them, but higher than for most other Latin American countries, the United States, and Spain.[18]

The referendum of November 20, 2016, held to establish whether the Bolivian constitution could be altered to allow Morales to run for a further term in office, was a rather different story. Morales narrowly lost the election, with 51.3 percent of the total electorate voting "No" to allow him to run for another term. Extraterritorial voter turnout was low internationally; only 31.3 percent of Bolivians living outside the country and registered to vote did so, with approximately 5,000 Bolivians in Chile turning out to vote.[19] Overall, those participating extraterritorially voted "Sí" by a slim margin; 51.3 percent compared to 48.6 percent for "No." The vast majority of this support for Morales came from Argentina (82 percent voted "Sí") and Brazil (76 percent voted "Sí"). In Chile, 50.2 percent voted "No," and 49.7 percent voted "Sí." This would seem to indicate a shift away from support of Morales by Bolivians in Chile. It is, however, difficult to assess this with any certainty given the much lower turnout than for the 2014 general election and the fact that the issue at stake in the referendum was different from the choices being made during the general election.

These electoral results appear to at least partially corroborate findings from my conversations with Bolivians in Chile. The ambivalence toward formal politics that my interviews revealed seems to also be indicated by many not registering to vote and by low turnout at the referendum. In terms of the political candidate favored, the results indicate support for Morales in 2014, but less fervently so than in Argentina and Brazil, with a decline in support by the time of the 2016 referendum. A possible reason for the difference in results compared with Argentina and Brazil is that Chile is a more recent destination for large flows of Bolivian migrants. One could hypothesize that having directly experienced the somewhat slower pace of change under Morales than initially anticipated by many, these more recent migrants may be less enamored of the MAS and party politics in general.

With regard to engaging in formal politics in Chile, as might be expected given the aforementioned correlation between political participation in sending and receiving countries, migrants I interviewed demonstrated a similarly ambivalent attitude toward the power of politicians and party politics to bring about change. The interviewees who expressed any interest in Chilean politics broadly favored the left-wing Nueva Mayoría (New Majority), led by Michelle Bachelet at that time.[20] They cited reasons similar to their rationale for supporting Morales: Bachelet was seen as an advocate for the poor and as more likely to be supportive of migrants than other candidates. Luz María drew a comparison with the cash benefits available for poor families and pregnant women under Morales and the Chile Crece Contigo (Chile Grows with You; see chapter 5) program started under Bachelet. On migrants' rights, Martina, age fifty-four, from Cochabamba, who had lived on and off in Arica for thirty years, said, "Before, as a foreigner under Pinochet, you couldn't have anything . . . nor with the democratic governments after him. But now it seems that the vision has changed, I think with Bachelet."

With respect to actually exercising the right to vote, migrants are able to vote in Chile after holding permanent residency for five years. All those interviewees in this position, in addition to those who had naturalized in Chile—nine of a total of sixty—had previously voted. Voting is not, however, necessarily indicative of a particular desire to participate in formal politics, as voting was compulsory for those registered in Chile until 2012. Nevertheless, it is interesting that those who were able to vote had registered to do so. In general, there are many migrants in Chile who have held permanent residency for five years or more but are unaware of their right to vote or not interested in registering. This was made clear to me through participation in the "Migrant Vote" campaign run by the Asociación in Santiago. It had come to the Asociación's attention that there were many migrants eligible to vote, the majority thought to be Peruvian and in the *comunas* of Recoleta and Independencia, who were not informed of this. Ahead of the presidential and local elections in November 2013, the Asociación aimed to encourage migrants to register to vote and to explain the Chilean electoral system to them, without expressing any political bias.

A team of six volunteers—all Chilean except for myself—was formed, and we engaged in a range of activities over a two-month period in September and October 2013. We got in touch with the approximately seventy candidates for Congress and the Senate in areas with a high concentration of migrants in Santiago, Arica, and Antofagasta to make them aware of certain migrants' eligibility to vote and presented them with a document highlighting key issues for migrants and policy recommendations. Most were not particularly receptive, with the exception being younger candidates who had been involved in the 2011 student movement in Chile. We also contacted all grassroots migrant organizations known to the Asociación in Santiago to give them campaign materials that we had prepared. Finally, in an endeavor to engage in direct contact with migrants, we handed out flyers in the Plaza de Armas, where many migrants congregate on the weekend; ran three workshops for migrants in the *comunas* of Recoleta and Independencia; and held a stall at the Recoleta Fería de Ciudadanía Migrante (Migrant Citizenship Fair).

Few of the eligible migrants we spoke to, however, showed great interest in registering to vote, or indeed in the formal political process in Chile. Our experience at the Recoleta Fería de Ciudadanía Migrante was illustrative. The Fería was held on a Saturday at one of the schools known in the *comuna* to accept high numbers of migrant children (see chapter 5). There were around eight groups present at the Fería. In general, the organizations there were offering services to migrants to help them with visas, situations of irregularity, health care, and other legal and social work services. We were the only stand doing something slightly different. We did manage to distribute some information, but the majority of migrants attending were not very interested. They had come to sort out legal and other problems that they were facing. In fact, quite a few came to us for this type of advice, so our role mainly ended up being handing out information about the free services offered by the Asociación.

It appeared that many migrants with whom we came into contact during the "Migrant Vote" campaign—none of whom were Bolivian—were experiencing multiple exclusions from transnational spaces of citizenship that had a more immediate impact on their daily lives than (not) exercising the right to vote.[21] Returning to the experiences of interviewees, those who were eligible and had registered to vote were all well established in Chile, with a Chilean partner or spouse in most cases, and were not experiencing such significant exclusions from other spaces of citizenship. This finding relates to the adaptation of Len Doyal and Ian Gough's theorization of intermediate need that I developed in the previous chapter.[22] Where migrants' social rights, such as access to shelter, were not being met so as to enable health and autonomy, their participation as political citizens via formal political channels appeared to be limited. They expressed ambivalence and disillusionment regarding formal politics, contributing further to a sense of uncertainty. This was also true with respect to some informal practices of political citizenship.

Mobilizations and Community Organizations

Much research on migrants' informal political participation has focused on involvement in political mobilizations, trade unions, engagement in new social movements, and the formation of hometown associations.[23] The focus has been on South-North migration, with interest in the topic beginning in the United States and gradually moving toward Europe.[24] Davide Però and John Solomos provide a brief historical overview of migrants' political mobilization in Western Europe.[25] They trace the move away in the 1980s from mobilization focused on "redistributive justice" to a more depoliticized involvement in NGOs focused on ethnic recognition in a multicultural framework. This shift was driven by the rollback of the state and consequent contracting out of previously state-run services to NGOs and other civil society organizations.

Summarizing the impact of this change on migrants' political involvement, Però and Solomos state that "during this period, migrants and minorities were encouraged to organize around ethnicity, forming associations and NGOs in exchange for resources and recognition from the state (national and local) that saw them as governmental tools for social cohesion and status quo maintenance."[26] Nevertheless, in recent years, as migrants' access to social rights and legal status has become ever more restricted, xenophobia toward and criminalization of migrants has become increasingly commonplace in public discourse, and frequent abuses of their labor rights have gradually come to light, the focus of political engagement has changed. Slowly, "openly political and democratically 'conflictive' mobilizations and protests for basic rights and/or for dignified working and living conditions" have emerged, and arguably (hopefully) look set to continue in this era of Donald Trump and Brexit.[27]

The context in Chile is clearly different from that of the United States and Western Europe, but I suggest that there are some similarities, as well as various fundamental differences. First, it is important to acknowledge the crucial importance of transnational political engagement by Chilean exiles during the dictatorship period. Throughout the 1970s and 1980s, the hundreds of thousands of people exiled from Chile were extremely politically engaged in transnational politics and in the politics of their receiving countries, which numbered over forty.[28] Following the return to democracy, Chile experienced several decades of limited political mobilization, and a progressive "NGO-ization" characteristic of neoliberalism, as was the case during the same period in Western Europe.[29] During this period some returned exiles—with their memories and experiences of intense political participation—became involved in NGOs established to promote migrants' rights in Chile, as well as in a plethora of other civil society organizations and left-wing political parties that were now within the mainstream political arena. In spite of the socialist beliefs of many founders and members of these organizations and parties, most seemed reluctant to rock the boat—so to speak—with regard to making politicized claims for redistributive justice.[30]

In 2011, however, there was a dramatic change in political practices in Chile and perhaps something of a return to past activism. For a host of reasons, this year saw massive student mobilizations, widely supported by much of society. The Asociación in Santiago and some other migrant organizations participated in the demonstrations. I was volunteering with the Asociación at the time and went on multiple protest marches with staff and volunteers between July and September 2011. Those who led us in joining the demonstrations had either been in exile or were veterans of the Left who had remained in Chile during the dictatorship; they were completely unfazed by tear gas, water cannons, and burning tires. We marched under banners promoting diversity, respect for indigenous cultures, and support for the student cause rather than any issue related explicitly to migrant rights. This was partly due to the focus of the demonstrations on injustices in the educational system, although a multitude of issues other than the right to education were represented in the largest demonstration, which was on the day of a general strike. Additionally, however, the conspicuous absence of migrant participation in the demonstrations meant that they did not seem the right forum for addressing issues specific to migrants.

During my fieldwork period from 2013 to 2014, there was likewise little evidence of migrant participation in the various political mobilizations that occurred. This even included the march for indigenous rights on October 12, 2013, which is a public holiday to celebrate/commemorate (depending on your perspective) the arrival of Europeans in the Americas.[31] On this day, as illustrated in figures 9 and 10, demonstrators employed Mapuche and Rapa Nui symbols, as well as the *wiphala* (flag representing indigenous peoples of the Andes, and Bolivia's co-official flag); however, there was little evidence of any migrant presence. I had thought that some Bolivian migrants might become involved with such demonstrations,

FIGURE 9. Indigenous flags at demonstration, October 12, 2013. Photo by author.

given the power of social movements and political mobilizations around such topics in Bolivia over the decades, but this did not seem to be the case.

Indeed, interviews revealed that no participants had been involved in mobilizations in Bolivia, in spite of the fact that several came from El Alto and had been
living there during the protests of the early 2000s. Amanda described what she
witnessed during the demonstrations of 2003 that resulted in the overthrow of
President Gonzalo Sánchez de Lozada:

> I didn't participate. But I saw it, I saw it. In my *zona* they went out to set fire to things,
> it was terrible. I thought that at any moment we were going to end up in a war.
> Because it was like that, with people dead, I don't know, it was awful. That was the
> time when they were fighting to get rid of Goni [President Gonzalo Sánchez de
> Lozada]. We didn't have, there was no food, everything was so expensive. My mum
> always stored *chuño* [freeze-dried potato] so at least there was that, but there were
> people with more children whose parents couldn't work. How was it for them?

The fear Amanda had felt during the mobilizations was palpable, and while she
concluded that the overthrow of Sánchez de Lozada had been positive, the whole
experience seemed to have contributed strongly to her political ambivalence.
Other interviewees similarly mentioned past and present violence by police and

FIGURE 10. Flyposting during demonstration, October 12, 2013. Photo by author.

demonstrators in Bolivia and Chile as factors that would prevent them from participating (riot police in Chile are certainly intimidating; for a mild example see figure 11). There was also a sense of weariness with regard to political protests, and sometimes people questioned whether it was an appropriate form of action. For Jonathan, age twenty-one, from Sucre, it seemed that "every day people are going out there to march, there are *bloqueos* of the highways with trucks," and he wondered how effective this was. Certainly, as James Dunkerley reminds us, in Bolivia "from 2000 onwards it is the *bloqueo* . . . that is the principal mechanism of 'disorder'. Notwithstanding the massacre of October 2003, it is the masses, not the armed forces, who are the principal authors."[32]

In sum, in addition to the specific Bolivian context that appears to have made participants wary of political mobilization, I suggest that the lack of migrant social

FIGURE 11. Riot police move in on demonstration, October 12, 2013. Photo by author.

movements in Chile more broadly can be put down to a number of factors. First, migration on a grander scale is still a recent phenomenon in Chile. Consequently, grassroots organizations with significant migrant participation are largely still in a fledgling state; it is from these organizations rather than larger NGOs such as the Asociación, with their focus on legal advice, social work, and other forms of advocacy, that a social movement would need to spring. The lack of such organizations means that there is arguably not yet a coherent enough collective identity to form what Charles Tilly and Sidney Tarrow would deem a "social movement base" to mobilize around issues of migrants' rights.[33] This lack of grassroots networks also impedes the mobilization of resources, another crucial factor in forming a successful social movement.[34] Finally, the "political opportunity" that might give rise to a migrant social movement does not yet seem to have occurred; perhaps if exploitation of migrant workers becomes more openly discussed, as in Western Europe, or now that the proposed new legislation to reform Chile's antiquated migration law has finally been sent to Congress (see chapter 3 and conclusion), we may see the occurrence of a social movement focused on these topics. And even then, perhaps many migrants who are struggling on a daily basis simply to make ends meet may not feel inclined to also go and struggle on the streets.

Thus, with regard to this particular kind of informal political citizenship practice, there was little involvement by those I worked with or migrants more generally.

With respect to the other kinds of informal political engagement mentioned in the South-North migration literature, I similarly found little participation. Although there is some evidence of an increasing proliferation of hometown associations in Bolivia, according to a 2005 survey of twenty-eight hundred Latin American migrants from twelve countries living in the United States, Bolivians had the lowest participation in hometown associations of all migrant groups.[35] Only 1.6 percent belonged to this kind of organization, compared with a mean of 5.5 percent. Of those I worked with, none were involved in what could properly be deemed a hometown association or in sustained community activism as it is typically understood in the South-North migration scholarship. This could, of course, in part be related to the networks and groups to which I was able to gain access. Although I made a concerted effort to make the net of my enquiry as widespread as possible, there are clearly limitations to what an individual researcher is able to achieve, which are also contingent on positionality (see chapter 1).

I did, however, speak to one particularly active member of the Club Social de Bolivia (a pseudonym) in Santiago. Sonia, age sixty-five, was originally from an upper-middle-class background in La Paz and had moved to Santiago when she was in her thirties. The Club Social is indeed chiefly a social club that organizes occasional events, but it also sends money on an irregular basis to small NGOs in Bolivia. It has its roots in an earlier, small-scale Bolivian migration of intellectuals and professionals during the 1940s and appears to have modeled itself on the European social clubs that were once common throughout Latin America. These days, membership is small—there are around 180 people in its Facebook group— and its ability to bring large groups together is limited. Sonia implied that this was because of the changing nature of Bolivian migration to Chile. As she put it:

> Before it was professionals who came here, more than anything. Lots of professionals, many doctors, many people who . . . with a different type of education. Now that's not the case. People come in search of opportunities.

Consequently, she thought that a new type of organizing was required and was trying to find ways to go about this. Above all, she was particularly concerned for the most marginalized migrants, and she led a group, which I accompanied on one occasion, that visits migrants in Santiago Men's Prison 1. This was not, however, a group specifically for or organized by Bolivians, although there were Bolivian men in the prison who participated in the group, which was mainly a forum for discussion.

The only other activity of which I was aware was the infrequent organization— every eight weeks or so—of Sunday lunches at the Bolivian consulate. A group of women who worked as *nanas puertas adentro* during the week cooked and sold traditional Bolivian dishes from the premises of the consulate, with the profit divided among them or given to a family in particular need.[36] The organization of these events was rather haphazard, and on two occasions during my fieldwork the lunches were canceled at the last minute. No notice was given through the mailing list or the Facebook page, resulting in various people (myself included) turning up at the consulate only to find the gates firmly closed. Nevertheless, the occasion on which I was able to attend was fairly well attended, with around thirty people.

Likewise, in Arica the Vecinos Bolivianos (a pseudonym) held similar, infrequent events, although they were more directly involved in addressing poverty in the region. One of their most popular events was a Christmas gift giving for migrant children, mainly children of agricultural workers from *parcelas* in the Valle de Azapa. Kevin, age forty-five, from La Paz, who was heavily involved in the association, said of this event:

> It's wonderful to see the kids' smiles.... [I]t's lovely because, for example, here in Arica the neighbourhood associations worry about the [Chilean] children in *campamentos* ... but who remembers about the migrant children? In the Valle de Azapa ... the reality is that there are children without shoes, there's no drinking water, no sewerage system.

In spite of the preoccupation of a few small groups and individuals such as Sonia and Kevin, there was overall little evidence that I could find of informal political participation as it is generally understood in the literature on South-North migration. This was partly, perhaps, as Sonia's comment implied, because the new flows of Bolivian migrants have other priorities and may be significantly marginalized economically, socially, and in terms of legal status. It is probable that such exclusion from other spaces of citizenship contributed to their lack of engagement with informal politics as it is typically understood; uncertainty across these dimensions of their citizenship translates to uncertainty and ambiguity in relation to the political as well. I suggest that it is also, however, because of how "political practices" are defined within the migration literature, which is predominantly produced in the global North. To more accurately reflect the ways in which migrants I worked with were engaging politically, I looked beyond this field of study to broaden further the definition of migrants' informal political practices.

CLAIMING CITIZENSHIP THROUGH DANCE

As Marco Martiniello and Jean-Michel Lafleur indicate, popular culture and arts can be important political outlets for migrants and ethnic minorities because of constraints felt by these groups in relation to engaging in "a conventional and direct participation in politics."[37] The authors highlight, however, that popular culture and arts are underacknowledged in the literature on contemporary migrants' political participation. Focusing on dance specifically, the small body of work to date on contemporary migrant use of dance is largely framed in the language of belonging, identity, and memory, but does not draw out its potentially more explicitly political meanings.[38] Writing on Chilean exiles' performance of *cueca* (the Chilean national dance) in Sweden, for example, Jan Knudsen states, "Dancing *cueca* in the diaspora creates links in time and space, reviving personal as well as collective memories; it is a symbolic compensation for the loss of country and history."[39] I suggest that by claiming belonging in the home country, transnationally, and in the receiving country, migrant dance can often be understood as profoundly political. This is particularly the case when dance is performed in public space (as opposed to private theaters or church halls, for example), as work drawn from fields other than migration studies indicates.

Performances in public space can be political tools used to both uphold and counter hegemony.[40] Presidential inaugurations and royal coronations are examples of the former. Carnival—of central importance to discussion here—has been understood as an example of the latter. In his seminal discussion of medieval carnival and the carnivalesque in Europe, Mikhail Bakhtin indicates that carnival "marked the suspension of all hierarchical rank, privileges, norms, and prohibitions."[41] During this demarcated time, the world was inverted and subverted. Setha Low, writing on the politics of public space in Latin America, similarly concludes that the popular fiesta or parade (including carnival) in a Latin American context can be understood as a "symbolic protest" that expresses "unresolved social relations."[42] Participants, who are generally not from the elite, demand to be seen and included, and the dances and acts they perform often also provide some sort of social commentary.

Nevertheless, there is some debate about the ability of present-day carnivals to offer a space for the subversion of the normal order of things, given their frequent commercialization and the restrictions imposed by the state on their organization.[43] In the Bolivian context, where carnival is a highly significant annual event, national governments, not to mention Bolivian big businesses, have consistently realized the value—economic and symbolic—that particular interpretations of carnival can have. As Sian Lazar puts it: "Contemporary Bolivian media tends to present the famous Entradas as tourist attractions, something exotic and colourful—folkloric remnants of an indigenous past. The Bolivian government encourages such an interpretation, for example in its campaign to get the Oruro Carnival declared a "Masterpiece of the Oral and Intangible Heritage of Humanity" by UNESCO."[44] This vision of "carnival-for-export" should not, however, detract from the fact that, as Lazar continues, for many in Bolivia such celebrations are "much more than an exhibition of dance and costume; [they are] a central part of the annual cycle of modern Bolivian communities."[45]

This was made abundantly apparent to me during the 2014 Oruro Carnival, which I was fortunate enough to attend with the linguist and anthropologist Xavier Albó, SJ. Although in his eighties, Padre Albó accompanied the dancers and musi-

FIGURE 12. The Anata Andina, Oruro carnival, 2014. Photo by author.

cians on their pilgrimage to the Virgen del Socavón, both on the Friday, the day of the Anata Andina, and on the Saturday, the day of the Entrada. The Anata Andina is the procession of indigenous rural communities from the *departamento* of Oruro, whereas the Entrada is the procession of groups from throughout Bolivia (see figures 12 and 13). Padre Albó meandered in and out of the dancers, chatting to them in Quechua and Spanish and explaining the significance of different dances and moments to me, as well as guiding me on a very informative tour of the Church of the Virgen del Socavón.[46] Although the commercial element was apparent (for example, one of the largest fraternities is sponsored by the Ferrari Ghezzi biscuit company) and acknowledged by participants and residents of Oruro, carnival holds far deeper meaning than simply representing an opportunity to eat, drink, dress up, and be seen. While carnivals in Oruro and elsewhere in Bolivia have different significance for different people, they are a moment to express both pluri/national identity—indigenous, mestizo, rural, urban, regional, national—and, in doing so, make a claim to recognition by the nation-state.[47]

In contexts more marginal than Oruro, carnival, or other public fiestas and parades, may serve additional politically symbolic purposes. In his analysis of a community on the urban periphery of Cochabamba, whose residents are predominantly

FIGURE 13. The Entrada, Oruro carnival, 2014. Photo by author.

internal migrants from the *departamento* of Oruro, Daniel Goldstein understands carnival as a form of spectacle. He highlights the potential for carnival to provide "migrants and other groups, displaced and powerless to control ordinary forms of social inclusion, with a mechanism for transforming their condition and making claims on the nation," although he also indicates that "discord, ambiguity, and conflict may be any spectacle's eventual result."[48]

Writing about the Peruvian Andean context, Karsten Paerregaard analyzes the meanings with which village community public fiestas become imbued when villagers who have migrated transnationally return to participate. Building on previous research on the role of internal rural-urban migrants in such fiestas, he argues that through their participation, migrants make claims to recognition of both their place in the village community and of the success that they have had in the places to which they have migrated. Like Goldstein, Paerregaard highlights the potentially conflicted and conflictive nature of these claims, indicating that there is a division between villagers and returning migrants. This "clearly shapes the fiesta, during which migrants and villagers negotiate and contest the shared values and symbols associated with Cabanaconde's [the village where research was conducted] ritual life."[49]

When carried out away from the national territory, dance and music can acquire an additional set of shifting, and potentially contested, political meanings, and are used to express ever-more-complex multiple identities. The following two sections bear this out empirically through examination of the origins, foundation, and structure of the largest Bolivian dance fraternity in Chile, Corazón de Tinkus—with whom I was fortunate enough to rehearse and perform for three months in 2013—and the claims to belonging and citizenship being made through their use of dance as a political practice.

Corazón de Tinkus: Origins, Foundation, and Structure

Tinku means "encounter" in Quechua and in its original sense refers to a type of ritual fighting once widespread throughout the Andes but in the present day largely limited to northern Potosí.[50] The *tinku* is a battle between equals—in age, sex, weight, and height—from different *ayllus* (loosely, clan) in which, according to Olivia Harris, "[b]lood must flow on both sides as a sacrifice to the earth in order to produce a bountiful harvest."[51] She describes the encounter thus:

> The men wear bull-hide helmets modelled on those of the conquistadores, known as *muntira*, and also use wide woven belts, and often there is a stone, or lump of lead, in the palm of their hand to give extra force to their blows.
>
> . . .
>
> Men are drunk when they fight, and they stamp their feet on the ground bellowing *soy toro carajo* (I am a bull carajo . . .). They wait for an opponent to step forward swinging his arms and also bellowing like a bull.[52]

Although now officially outlawed, stone throwing, whips, and slingshots used to also sometimes be used in the conflict. Young single women may also fight, although they do not aim to draw blood but rather pull each other's hair and clothing.[53]

Over time, and due to repeated intervention by local authorities, *tinku* fighting in northern Potosí has become less dangerous, and in other parts of the Andes, as Henry Stobart explains, it has been "transformed into a dance."[54] As a dance performed at carnivals and other open-air processions and celebrations, *tinkus* retains certain elements of its origins in the ritual battle. My impressions after my first rehearsal with Corazón de Tinkus reflected this. From the edge of the large church hall where the dancers were rehearsing, the roots of the *tinku* combat were apparent in the movements of the dance. I noted that men and women both dance very energetically and forcefully. The steps are done flat footed, always leading with the right foot, and follow the repetitive beating of a drum, which pervades the music. There are arm movements, but the focus is largely on the footwork. The arms are always moved with strength, often in a swinging motion, and with closed fists in a punching gesture. Dancers move their heads to follow the movements of their arms. For much of the dance, they remain bent at the waist, straightening only to jump and turn. All of the dancers have a *honda* (slingshot), which they tie around their waists. Movements with the *honda* form part of the dance sometimes, and sometimes the dancers shout all together in time with the music.

The dance of *tinkus* has become a standard feature of carnival processions and other festivities in Bolivia. It is probably the most popular of the *danzas autóctonas* (indigenous dances), which also include those such as the *llamerada* and *tobas* and contrast with the *danzas estilizadas* (stylized dances) such as the *caporal, diablada*, and *morenada*. Alejandro Grimson provides an explanation of the distinction between these categories: "This classification covers at least three elements: type of dance, clothing, and musical instruments. The indigenous dances are those that, although highly modified, refer to pre-Conquest rituals. The dancers wear outfits of many different textiles whose colours come from herbs and plants. The band that accompanies them plays indigenous instruments. By contrast, the stylized dances . . . use shiny costumes that employ cardboard and plastic, and their bands have Western instruments like the saxophone, trumpet, trombone, cymbals, side drum, and kettle drum."[55] Nevertheless, as Grimson indicates with reference to Bolivian dance fraternities in Buenos Aires, there is significant overlap between these two groupings. Many *tinkus* dance fraternities use synthetic fabrics and bright colors in their costumes, and their bands tend to incorporate Western instruments in addition to the indigenous ones.

This was the case for Corazón de Tinkus, founded in 2010 by Antony, age twenty-eight, from Bolivia, and Marcia, age twenty-two, from Chile, a couple who live in Santiago with a young daughter. Antony had previously been involved in dancing *tinkus* in Bolivia, and Marcia was also interested in dance. The group initially was formed by Antony, Marcia, and a few cousins of Marcia's. They performed a range of Bolivian dances, not just *tinkus*, at small-scale cultural events around Santiago. Gradually, however, the group grew in popularity among both Bolivian migrants and Chileans and split into the core group, referred to as the *elenco*, and a larger group, known as the *bloque*. The *elenco*, with around ten members, has continued to practice many different types of Bolivian dance and has been invited to perform at prestigious music and culture festivals in Chile.

The *bloque*, of which all members of the *elenco* are also a part, only dances *tinkus*. When I danced with them, there were approximately thirty members between sixteen and thirty years old, with slightly more women than men. Just over half the members were Chilean, and the rest were Bolivian and Peruvian. There is a strict hierarchy within the *bloque* based on length of membership but also skill. Members are assigned a position within the four lines that form the *bloque* according to how long they have been in the group and how well they know the *pasos* (dance sequences). As in all carnival dance fraternities, each line has a *guía* (guide). The *guías* coordinate with one another to decide which steps will be done at which moment and raise their right hands in a series of signals to indicate this to their lines.

There are also certain special roles within the *bloque*. The role of *ñusta* is particularly important. *Ñusta* is a Quechua word referring originally to an Inca princess, but in the context of modern-day Andean carnival it finds its translation as something paralleling a May or homecoming queen. This title is awarded both as an internal prize within dance fraternities, and as a "Queen of the Carnival" prize ahead of different carnivals following competition among all the various dance fraternities' *ñustas*. The elections for *ñusta* in Corazón de Tinkus are taken very seriously. Each candidate prepares a portfolio of photos and a personal statement, which is available through the group's Facebook page, and then presents two dances and appears in evening wear during an event open to the public, after which there are elections. The *ñusta* is chosen not only for her dancing but also for her personal characteristics and—above all—appearance.[56]

The dance itself consists of *avances* and *pasos*. *Avances* are the basic steps that the *bloque* uses to move forward in procession. The *pasos* are the more complex dance sequences in which the *bloque* remains more or less in one place, and each lasts for around two minutes. Corazón de Tinkus had five *pasos* and several different types of steps that could be used as *avances*. These were learned through intensive rehearsals twice a week, in addition to frequent weekend performances. At rehearsals, we would dance for two hours with a water break in the middle, and then have *once* (supper/afternoon tea) and a meeting. Rehearsals took place in a church hall or in public plazas in downtown Santiago and were well attended and punctual; there was a fine for being late or nonattendance without prior agreement.

As Lazar has commented in the Bolivian context, belonging to a *bloque* is an expensive exercise, and this is no less true in Santiago than in El Alto.[57] Corazón de Tinkus charges a joining fee of US$11, which includes a teaching DVD of the *pasos*, and a monthly subscription fee of US$3. Additionally, each member must pay to rent a dance costume for the year, which costs over US$60, and buy her own rehearsal uniform for around US$15.[58] Women need to purchase hair extensions, false eyelashes, and specific makeup, at a cost of approximately US$15. There are also fund-raising and social events that members are expected to contribute to. For example, there is a roster for the provision of cake and soft drink for *once* at each rehearsal, which is funded by two members at each rehearsal, who sell slices of the cake and cups of drink to members (for US$2) and pass on all the money to the group. Finally, the band and photographer for each event must be paid, and the average cost per member for this is US$20.

The astonishing thing about Corazón de Tinkus was that, in spite of the high cost of membership and the significant time commitment that it entailed, membership truly cut across socioeconomic background, age, and gender. Moreover, outside of Corazón de Tinkus, a significant minority of interviewees of different backgrounds had danced in carnival previously in Bolivia, a few were part of a *bloque* that danced in Arica, and around a third of all interviewees returned to Bolivia during carnival to see family but also to join in the festivities. This reflects Lazar's comment that "[d]ance is central to Bolivianness for Bolivians of all social classes" and indicates that this continues to be true when they leave the national territory.[59]

Among the Bolivian members of Corazón de Tinkus were young professionals, university and secondary school students, a professional football player, technicians, manual laborers, and cleaners. They were from the *departamentos* of La Paz, Cochabamba, Oruro, and Santa Cruz. Likewise, the members from Chile were from diverse backgrounds and came originally not only from Santiago but also from regions in the north of the country. Although, as discussed previously, the ways in which people experience dance and festivals are polysemous, there was also a collective understanding in Corazón de Tinkus of what dancing meant in terms of belonging and citizenship.[60]

Belonging, Citizenship, and Place-Claiming through the Practice of Dance

Here I attempt in three parts to unravel the tangle of meanings that dance held as a political practice for members of Corazón de Tinkus, focusing on the experiences of Bolivian participants. First, being part of Corazón de Tinkus enabled them to feel that they belonged to a community. Second, this community had an explicitly stated purpose, with which members were strongly in agreement: to "reclaim" the dance of *tinkus* and present a positive image of Bolivian identity in Chile in order to make claims to recognition. How was this Bolivian identity defined and constituted, however? I address this final, fundamental question in the third part of this section.

"You Could Call it a Kind of Therapy": Providing a Sense of Belonging. Loneliness and solitude often characterize the migrant experience, and as detailed in chapter 5, these were feelings frequently expressed by those I spoke to. Thus, the sense of being part of a collectivity that dancing can produce was of tantamount importance to migrant members of Corazón de Tinkus.[61] That's not to say that the fraternity was without conflict; in fact, there would often be arguments in the meetings after rehearsals. The standards expected were high, and there was little sympathy for other demands on members' time such as work and studies. Nevertheless, when the music was playing and all else that could be heard was the rhythmic stamping of the *avances* and *pasos*, there was an overwhelming feeling of cohesion and often exhilaration. We would grin at each other as we neared the end of a *paso* that had been near-perfectly executed, *hondas* twirling satisfyingly in time as we

flicked them out and caught them again. The fraternity offered sanctuary and a place of belonging, where legal status, employment conditions, and social insecurity could be forgotten.

Paloma, age twenty-nine, from Cochabamba, had been desperately lonely during her first months in Chile, trying to negotiate the visa application process, struggling to find work, and as she put it, "shut away" in her room with limited possibilities for going out and meeting people given her lack of financial resources. She was a naturally sociable person, was an accomplished dancer, and had been *ñusta* of a fraternity dancing *caporales* in Bolivia; the alteration of her daily life that moving to Chile entailed was significant. Thus, when she eventually discovered and joined Corazón de Tinkus it really did transform her life in Chile, and being elected as *ñusta* in her first year as a member meant a great deal to her.

The same degree of transformation was true for Diana, age twenty-eight, from Santa Cruz, who was introduced in chapter 2. To recapitulate, Diana came from a poor background in Santa Cruz and had had a difficult childhood and adolescence. At the age of twenty she moved to Buenos Aires, where she lived in overcrowded and dangerous conditions in the *villas miserias* and worked in a sweatshop. After living there for almost ten years, she moved to Santiago. She lived in a room in a *migrant cité*, at one point sharing it with seven other people. She worked for the minimum wage in a café. She was very unhappy, traumatized by her experiences in Argentina and upset by her continued poor standard of living in Chile. At various times, she told me, she had turned to alcohol which, in her words, she used as a means "to forget."

After being in Chile for nearly a year, she saw Corazón de Tinkus dance in the annual carnival for Bolivian Independence Day that takes place in the Plaza de Armas in Santiago. She had danced *tinkus* as a child and was completely taken by the display of something that to her was so representative of Bolivia occurring in the heart of Santiago. She got in touch with Antony following the event, and we began rehearsing on the same day and danced next to each other in the *bloque*. Diana told me in an interview what her involvement in *tinkus* meant to her:

> I love it. I love it because, with all that I carry with me from Argentina—I don't forget the things that happened there—I would come home from work, shut myself in my room, and every day my husband would find me crying, I mean every day. . . . But [*tinkus*] fortunately, you could call it a kind of therapy. I don't remember anything, I forget, and I concentrate. You see how I concentrate when I dance, I don't know, I *want* to dance, I want to do this, and I forget completely.

Diana felt as though she was a part of something that mattered, and she eagerly anticipated our rehearsals. She expressed how beautiful she thought the dance was and how proud it made her of her country. She said that she had not valued it when she lived there, but now wanted to learn about Bolivia's dances and show them to others, something also stated by other members of Corazón de Tinkus whom I interviewed.[62] For Diana, then, dancing *tinkus* had helped to begin to heal some of the damage done by her experiences of marginalization and uncertainty. It was a form of rapprochement with Bolivia. She could begin to rescue the positive from a country that she felt had largely let her down and forced her to leave. And she could also use it as a means to demonstrate an aspect of Bolivia that is internationally praised and thus combat some of the discrimination that she faced as a migrant and a Bolivian.

Reclaiming Tinkus *and Bolivian Identity.*   Indeed, for the Bolivian participants in the group, presenting a positive image of Bolivia was certainly one of the key motives for participation. Frequently discriminated against in their daily lives, often excluded from other spaces of citizenship, here they had a chance to challenge the negative image of Bolivians, and migrants, in Chilean media and public discourse.[63] In fact, the raison d'être for the founding of the fraternity was precisely to present what was viewed by Antony as an accurate image of Bolivian culture in the face of its perceived co-optation by Chileans.

As explained by Francisca Fernández Droguett and Roberto Fernández Droguett, in Santiago *tinkus* has been adopted by Chilean young people, predominantly university students, and incorporated into protest marches on a range of issues, but particularly relating to support for the rights of Chile's indigenous peoples.[64] The process began in the late 1990s, when *tinkus* began to be performed in the carnivals of the North of Chile, such as la Virgen de La Tirana. From there it gradually spread to Santiago and started to be used as a dance of protest intending to represent "all social struggles against neoliberalism, patriarchy, and colonialism," to quote Fernández Droguett and Fernández Droguett.[65]

Corazón de Tinkus was founded in response to the use of the dance of *tinkus* by such political groups in Santiago. Antony claimed that these groups were unaware of the origins and meaning of *tinkus*, and that many believed it to be, or were trying to pass it off as, a Chilean dance from the north of the country. And indeed, it does seem that there is a tendency to refer to *tinkus* as an "Andean" dance by such groups. Although true strictly speaking, this has the effect of glossing over the fact that it is undoubtedly Bolivian in origin and suggests a historic connection with Chile that, in the case of this particular dance, does not exist. That Chileans are "stealing" Bolivian culture through these types of acts, as they "do not have a culture of their own," was a common complaint made by migrants I spoke to who were both members and nonmembers of Corazón de Tinkus. This sense of injustice was often linked to the sea access dispute and to the discrimination that participants experienced from Chileans.

Antony's reaction to what he saw as an appropriation of Bolivian culture for particular political ends was to found a group that represented what was to him authentic *tinkus*. The focus was to be on doing the dance properly (he thought the other groups were sloppy in their performance) and shouting loud and clear—literally—that it comes from Bolivia. Moreover, group members would have to possess a well-rounded understanding of what it means to dance in carnival in Bolivia and of the rituals and traditions behind *tinkus* and other dances. Chileans and people of all nationalities would be more than welcome to participate, but it was fundamental that they understood the purpose of the group. To that end, the registration form, which had to be signed and returned to Antony, contained a sentence stating that Corazón de Tinkus is an organization with no political motive or bias. I suggest, however, that Corazón de Tinkus was in fact extremely political in its objective of reclaiming *tinkus* as Bolivian and severing it from its association in Chile with radical left-wing politics, which had arisen because of its use in political demonstrations (even though, ironically, most in the group were left of center in their personal political beliefs).

Moreover, Antony was well aware of the discrimination, invisibilization, and hardship faced by many of his compatriots in Chile and saw dancing in public space as a way to challenge this. Corazón de Tinkus was committed to making a strong, positive statement about Bolivian identity and Bolivian migrant identity. Nevertheless, this was also an identity that could be learned and expressed by Chileans, and the Bolivians expressing it also wished to belong to the Chilean demos. This was therefore explicitly not an attempt at developing a differentiated "cultural citizenship" in the vein of Renato Rosaldo, but rather a demonstration of a claim to transnational belonging, identity, and citizenship.[66] What precisely, however, conformed this identity? How was it expressed and experienced? The final part examines these questions through the lens of the Fifth Annual Patronato Carnival, with which this chapter began.

The Fifth Annual Patronato Carnival: Dancing Gendered Pluri/National/Transnational Citizenship. The Fifth Annual Patronato Carnival was held in the *barrio* of Patronato in the *comuna* of Recoleta. It is a *barrio* known for its lively, colorful clothes market, full of reproductions of the latest fashion at bargain prices. It is also one of the areas where there are concentrations of migrant populations—chiefly Peruvian, but also of other Latin American nationalities, including Bolivian, as well as Chinese, Korean, and Palestinian. The carnival is organized by the *junta de vecinos* (neighborhood association), which invites groups from throughout Santiago (many of them migrant groups) to participate. In 2013, when I danced, it occurred on a Sunday and involved several hundred people in a procession that snaked through all the main streets of Patronato to the municipal school, which is known as one of the schools that is welcoming to migrants (see chapter 5).

The elaborate process of getting ready for the carnival illustrated perhaps better than anything else the gender and ethnic identities being performed by Corazón de Tinkus. Several Bolivian women got me ready to dance, amused by my ignorance of how to make myself up and arrange my hair according to their cultural script. They delighted in my transformation into their vision of Bolivian femininity, which began as we sat on the steps of the school where we were to get ready. Mónica, a Bolivian migrant member of the fraternity, and her friend Lula, who had come to help, offered to braid my hair for me. Unbraiding my poor attempt, I handed over the tangled mess I had made of my newly acquired hair extensions. Mónica and Lula sat one on each side of me, pulling my hair so tight it made my eyes water. Their speed and dexterity was amazing, a skill learned in childhood, when schoolgirls often wear their hair in two neat French braids, and which when worn in adulthood particularly is strongly associated with identifying as Quechua or Aymara.

Hair was followed by makeup application, which in my case was achieved by four women. I borrowed products from a variety of people, as the eyeshadow I had brought with me was nowhere near bright enough, and the fake eyelashes I had purchased were judged disappointing in length and dramatic effect. When I was eventually judged ready, all the women exclaimed over how beautiful I looked with my hair up and all the makeup on, laughing at how they had made me a *bolivianita* (little Bolivian/Bolivian señorita). I was then presented with my costume for the first time. I had only seen the costumes from a distance before and had been impressed then, but up close the intricate embroidery was incredible. I felt awed to be allowed to wear one. It was another battle to put my dress and hat on and then to attach the *chakana* to my hat, which was a battery-powered device representing the Inca Cross in flashing LED lights, to be switched on when we danced after dark. It took the whole fraternity nearly three hours to get ready, and at around 7:00 p.m. we finally set out.

The elaborate preparations for the carnival contained elements reminiscent of Arnold van Gennep's and Victor Turner's conceptualizations of ritual.[67] I was viewed as a novice and initiated into how to "perform" a particular hyperfeminized gender identity through routine acts of hairstyling and makeup application.[68] The gender identity learned in adolescence that I perform on a daily basis through my version of these acts was deemed inadequate, and I was only declared "beautiful" once in my new role. The heavy makeup, false eyelashes, and intricate hairstyle seemed to draw on the beauty pageant tradition so valued in Bolivia, where those chosen to represent their region or country are, in the words of Andrew Canessa, "invariably tall, white women."[69] Discussing child beauty pageants in the United States, Kerry Robinson and Cristyn Davies describe them as sites "in which young girls are produced as the ultimate, heterosexual, gendered citizen subjects."[70]

Arguably, in the precarnival rituals of preparation, we were similarly transforming ourselves into idealized, gendered citizens, although the gendered message was not clear-cut. On the one hand, a highly feminized appearance was crucial. On the other hand, our costumes covered all of our bodies, unlike the more revealing, sexualized costumes of the *morenada*, *diablada*, *tobas*, and other dances, and the movements that we performed in the dance were bold and warrior-like, the leaders exhorting us to demonstrate *fuerza* (strength) when we danced. These were the attributes, then, of the ideal female Bolivian citizen as portrayed through the bodies and movements of women in Corazón de Tinkus: exhibiting stereotypical feminine beauty through hairstyle and makeup; modesty through dress; but also strength, stamina, discipline, and control through the movements of the dance.

Of course it was not only gender but also ethnic identity that was being performed. As with the Bolivian beauty queens, we were enacting an indigenous identity that is not ours; none of the Bolivian members of Corazón de Tinkus were Quechua from Potosí, although Antony identified as Quechua and spoke the language, and some other members of the group (Bolivian, Peruvian, and Chilean) identified as indigenous or part indigenous.[71] They were not in the majority, however. From a critical perspective, then, perhaps like the beauty queens, we were playing to the idea of an exoticized Other, one that would intrigue and attract the predominantly Chilean onlookers.[72] Nevertheless, I cannot simply reduce the pride—almost reverence—in the beauty of the costumes and respect for the traditions from which they originate to such an interpretation. Rather, as Lazar writes of the community where she worked "by dancing dances that come from specific regions of Bolivia, vecinos [neighbors] of Rosas Pampas were emphasizing their belonging not only to Rosas Pampas but also to Bolivia. . . . Dancing each dance enacts a Bolivianness that is composed of multiple regional and ethnic identities, and dancing cross-culturally, as the urban Aymara do when they mimic indigenous peoples from the eastern lowlands or tinku fighters from northern Potosí, simultaneously reinforces and breaks down those identifications."[73]

Corazón de Tinkus, I argue, was not claiming a particular indigenous identity, but rather using the body to demonstrate its interpretation of the nonbinary nature of the "plurinational" at the core of modern Bolivianness. Not only that, a positive transnational migrant identity was being claimed. In the Fifth Annual Patronato Carnival (see figure 14), just as Bakhtin suggests, the normal order of things was inverted, and power relations were flipped upside down as we temporarily claimed space and place with our movements.[74] Instead of police officers detaining migrants, they were detaining the traffic to let the migrants pass. So often ignored, discriminated against, and invisibilized, migrants—side by side with supportive Chileans—were shouting about their identity in public spaces. A dance so integral to plurinational Bolivian culture was inviting smiles and cheers from the crowd in place of the insults and negative press attention Andean migrants too frequently receive in Chile. This act of place claiming was an enactment of a right to be within the bounds of transnational spaces of citizenship.

FIGURE 14. Performing in the Fifth Annual Patronato Carnival, 2013. Photo by Pablo Torres.

CONCLUSION

The importance of "theorizing back" from the South is revealed particularly through this chapter.[75] The political practices of South-South migrants have not been widely researched, and the spectrum of practices considered political by migration scholars has largely been developed by researchers in the North. Those with whom I worked were not particularly engaged in the types of practices generally considered by scholars of South-North migration as political. Party politics and voting and involvement with social movements and hometown associations were viewed with ambivalence, and only a handful took part in these activities. In this sense, migrants were excluded to a certain degree from the transnational space of political citizenship.

While this was partially due to agentic choices made by individual migrants, there were other contributing factors as well. There was a degree of alienation from formal political processes, founded in part on frustration at the perceived slow pace of change under Evo Morales in Bolivia, and there was likewise a weariness with regard to the power of social movements to act as a force for political change. Multiple exclusions from other dimensions of citizenship, and the effort required to mitigate these exclusions, did not necessarily leave time and resources for engagement in groups such as hometown associations. The exclusionary elements of uncertainty were therefore present in migrants' experiences of this facet of citizenship as well.

Dance, however, was one political practice used by some to push back against exclusion.[76] I suggest that it is the therapeutic sense of collectivity, the transformative beauty of dance, and the sense of cultural self-recognition offered by being part of a fraternity like Corazón de Tinkus that made this rather than the other informal political practices I discuss in this chapter appealing to some Bolivian migrants. It offered migrants who were facing hardship and isolation a public means of reclaiming personal dignity and inclusion, in a manner that being part of something like a hometown association perhaps could not. Furthermore, it allowed them to present an embodied vision of pluri/national/transnational citizenship, claiming a place for themselves through performing in public spaces, thus making a more direct and open statement than engaging in formal politics would perhaps allow. Nevertheless, while carnival and similar performances in public space certainly offer the possibility of making claims to recognition, they do so in a way that is less likely to invite censure (or even arrest) than, say, participating in a social movement, which is an important consideration for marginalized migrants.

Taking dance seriously as a political citizenship practice enables recognition, then, of a crucial way in which some migrant groups may express their hope of experiencing more certain citizenship. That is not to say, however, that it is not important to encourage and enable marginalized migrants to participate politically in other ways. Moreover, it is crucial that this kind of dance not be stripped of its political meaning and simply packaged as part of a neat display within a framework of neoliberal multiculturalism. It is offered as a challenge to discrimination and invisibilization, as a subversion of the usual uncertain order of things—if only for a brief moment in time and space—and should be read as such.

Conclusion

From Luz María and Wilson working irregularly and eating just enough to get by as they tried to support their young family, to Diana sleeping seven to a room as she worked to save for a little house in Santa Cruz. From Marcos on the *parcela* organizing to petition for MTRVs and better living conditions, to Cata and Marta eventually leaving the situation of trafficking in which they became embroiled. From Constanza bringing up her young boys in a *migrant cité* to Javiera working as a *nana puertas adentro* to ensure her children's education back in Bolivia. These and the other migrant journeys traced throughout this book have been characterized by tenacity and motivated by possibility. Leaving Bolivia was a leap into the unknown often compelled by economic marginalization and lack of opportunities. Many were driven by the hope of a better future for their children, younger siblings, or ailing parents.

Once in Chile, they frequently faced a multitude of challenges in different arenas—difficulties acquiring regular legal status, exploitative labor conditions, poor housing conditions, problems accessing health care and education, social isolation and discrimination, and a sense of ambivalence toward and exclusion from certain forms of political participation. In the face of significant adversity across these multifarious dimensions, they drew on different resources, sometimes including migrant organizations, to attempt to incrementally improve their situations. Reflecting upon these diverse lived experiences of migration and citizenship—which nonetheless have common threads running through them—in these concluding remarks, I draw together the contributions made in this book and then outline the possibilities they might suggest.

LIVING UNCERTAINTY ACROSS TRANSNATIONAL
SPACES OF CITIZENSHIP

This book has responded to calls for far greater engagement with the phenomenon of South-South migration, given its global importance and increase in recent decades. Furthermore, it has sought to specifically address a South-South migration flow about which very little has been known, but which had previously been identified as potentially involving groups facing particularly high levels of exclusion. These conjectures were certainly substantiated through the fieldwork I undertook, which endeavored to explore *multiple* aspects of the transnational lived experiences of citizenship of low-wage Bolivian migrants in Chile. Examining multiple aspects—legal, economic, social, and political—together represents a holistic approach that has not always been present in research to date.

In relation to legal citizenship, those I worked with transitioned through many and varied (ir)regular statuses, and there was often not a clear linear progression from status to status. There was also no universal goal of naturalization as Chilean. This strongly corroborates other research in a South-North context that challenges binary understandings of migratory statuses and emphasizes instead their dynamism and state of constant flux. Nevertheless, there were specificities to the Bolivian-Chilean case, stemming from the perpetuation of migration legislation adopted under the Pinochet dictatorship. While migrants' agentic practices did impact their legal status, they were significantly constrained and influenced by this legislation and its differentiated enforcement by border agents and other public officials, lack of clear and appropriate information regarding the visa application process, and the practices of employers. I stress that both at a legislative level and at the level of enforcement by officials, the visa acquisition process was markedly discriminatory. Those who were worst affected tended to be from lower socioeconomic backgrounds and were often of Aymara descent. The support of migrant organizations in acquiring the MTRV or permanent residency was often fundamental for those who found themselves in irregular status positions.

As established in previous research on South-North migration, there was a clear relationship between having irregular legal status and experiencing labor exploitation. Nevertheless, many migrants with regular legal status were also exposed to exploitative and precarious employment conditions, which can be understood as occurring on a spectrum, rather than in straightforward, black-and-white terms. There was a definitively gendered and racialized hierarchy in the labor market, most adversely affecting women and, again, those from low socioeconomic backgrounds and those who identified as indigenous. While there was evidence that the practices of some migrant organizations were enabling migrants to access qualitatively better employment, unfortunately other organizations were in fact reinforcing the gendering and racialization of certain labor niches. In particular, through its employment program AMM was encouraging women to work as *nanas puertas adentro* in conditions that were often exploitative and discriminatory. Employment in Chile is not the only aspect of economic citizenship addressed in this book, however. It has also been concerned with the economic marginalization that obliged many I worked with to leave Bolivia, engaging in a paradoxical "practice of citizenship" whereby they left their country of legal citizenship in the hope of achieving greater inclusion as economic citizens elsewhere.

I have addressed the social dimension of citizenship through the lens of an adaptation of Doyal and Gough's[1] theorization of intermediate needs. This integrated approach enables analysis of migrants' experiences of housing, health care, and education, but also the level of social support they receive, interrogating how access to these social rights is impacted by their social identities. In relation to the more tangible social rights identified, access to decent quality housing was particularly problematic, and the assistance offered by migrant organizations in relation to this was limited. Exclusion from health care was also not uncommon, and discrimination in the educational system in Santiago in particular appeared to be prevalent. The key issue was the negative attitude of the Chilean gatekeepers of these social provisions, or their "lack of solidarity," as Constanza characterized it, framing the issue in a different way from how it would perhaps be framed in South-North contexts. While migrant organizations are aware of these issues and are working with health care and education providers to tackle them, there remains a great deal to be done. Social support is considered in this book in terms of both maintenance of significant primary relationships and forging social networks in Chile. As in other contexts, for parents with children in Bolivia, maintaining significant primary relationships was extremely challenging and provoked complex emotional reactions. Likewise comparable to other contexts, experiences of forming social networks in Chile were mixed, with some migrants feeling a strong sense of isolation, but others connecting with neighbors, colleagues and conationals in such a way as to alleviate some of their negative experiences.

For those who were part of Corazón de Tinkus, involvement with this group also helped to alleviate feelings of isolation and exclusion. More than this, however, it provided an important forum for constructing and presenting a gendered pluri/national/transnational vision of "Bolivianness" that was used to claim space and place and to make a political statement about identity and belonging. Other informal and formal political practices more frequently studied by scholars working on South-North migration, such as participation in hometown associations and social movements, voting, and engagement with party politics, were often viewed with ambivalence, and participants' involvement was limited. Thus, this was one way in which theorizing back from the South proved crucial in this book. The importance of dance, and especially carnival dance, for Bolivians both in Bolivia and abroad should not be underestimated and is an important medium for political participation. I suggest that dance could be fruitfully added to the repertoire of practices that are more commonly considered within the realm of the political by migration scholars.

Across legal, economic, social, and political dimensions of citizenship, then, I found that Bolivian migrants in Chile experienced a wide array of shifting transnational inclusions and exclusions, impacted by their social identities and sometimes influenced by contact with migrant organizations. Moreover, these inclusions and exclusions were forged through diverse interrelations between structural processes and agentic practices and through specific histories of discrimination and oppression. Existing theorizations of migration and citizenship could not comprehensively encompass, and allow for holistic analysis of, these intricate relationships with citizenship as they are lived on a daily basis. Thus, building on work that has encouraged a focus on migrants' lived practices rather than the development of normative models of citizenship, and on that which has offered spatially and intersectionally aware approaches to migration and citizenship, this book has proposed the twin concepts of *transnational spaces of citizenship* and *uncertain citizenship*.

Thinking about citizenship as overlapping and intertwined transnational social spaces, I have argued, enables cognizance of the ways in which migrants are often simultaneously incorporated in and marginalized from various of its dimensions across nation-state boundaries. It also encourages thinking about both the structural factors and agentic practices that construct these spaces and migrants' positions within them, accounting for the ways in which social identities affect possibilities of inclusion. Additionally, it allows for the important role of migrant organizations within these spaces, considering the ways in which they both encourage and inhibit migrants' practices of citizenship. Finally, this conceptualization allows for complexity and messiness in a way that previous binary and triadic theorizations of spaces of citizenship had not.

Above all, therefore, it is an approach that responds to the ways in which migrants actually practice and live citizenship. So, while the legal element of citizenship is addressed in-depth because it is certainly central to migrants' inclusions/exclusions from citizenship, the other substantive elements of citizenship are also afforded due weight, reflecting how crucial they too are in migrants' lives. Economic citizenship is analyzed as a separate, but overlapping, transnational space given its fundamental importance for migrants, who are often moving because of economic marginalization and who frequently experience poor labor conditions. Social citizenship is considered in relation to access to tangible social rights vital to the material quality of everyday life, but also in terms of the more intangible maintenance and forging of primary relationships and social networks that also contribute significantly to a sense of inclusion and belonging. Finally, political citizenship is understood in a way that is sensitive to non-northern understandings of the political in order to account for the different means migrants may have of "being political."

Assessing migrants' relationships to citizenship through the lens of uncertainty further enables recognition of complexity and lived experience. It accounts for the ambiguous positions of migrants within multiple spaces of citizenship, acknowledging that they can be at once included and excluded across diverse dimensions. It also expresses the emotionality of migrants' lived citizenship, which frequently invokes insecurity and sometimes fear, but also hope, often felt simultaneously in relation to different aspects of citizenship. It thus eschews a reading of lived citizenship as either exclusion or inclusion or as a straightforward in-between state across all its dimensions. Rather, viewing citizenship from the stance of uncertainty promotes an analysis that is sensitive and nuanced; it is aware of migrants' many physical and emotional journeys through, across, and outside of its transnational spaces.

FUTURE POSSIBILITIES OUT OF UNCERTAINTY

As has been suggested throughout this book, a sliver of possibility is encompassed within the subtleties of uncertainty. Through suggestions about how the contributions from this book may illuminate future possibilities, it is with this fraction of hope that I would like to end. I have wondered whether this is naïve. Although I am wary of sweeping pronouncements declaring worldwide epochal moments, evidence does suggest that we are entering a (sadly not unprecedented) era of exacerbated racism and xenophobia. In the global North, the rise of Trump and the victory of Brexit have been preceded and followed by an increase in discrimination toward migrants and minorities and a stunning lack of compassion toward refugees. In other northern countries, such as Australia and France, asylum seekers, migrants, and established minorities have also been facing increased racism. But in often neglected contexts of the global South, migrants and minorities are similarly subject to abuse; the Rohingya in Myanmar, Bangladesh, Malaysia, Thailand, and Indonesia, and Indian and Nepali migrant workers in Qatar are recent examples. In Chile, too, the end of 2016 saw prominent politicians make incendiary statements linking recent arrivals to crime and delinquency, and such comments have continued to pervade public debate.[2]

Faced with this bleak international scenario, and reflecting on the multiple exclusions faced by those whose stories I have shared in this book, is it ingenuous, then, to speak of possibility and hope? My response to this has been heartened by recent exchanges with fellow scholars and migrants' rights advocates. I think that it is, in fact, imperative to take up this discourse and try to put it into practice even, and especially, when the odds seem stacked against diversity and recognition of common humanity. Not to do so risks enabling the triumph of fear and hatred.

Moreover, to draw on Joel Robbins, not to do so also risks ignoring the "aspirational and idealizing aspects of the lives of others" that are present in the narratives of those, such as the migrants in this book, who strive and hope and aspire in the face of significant adversity.[3]

In this time of deep uncertainty for many migrants across space and place, it is necessary to seize on the germ of possibility that uncertainty contains and present an alternative politics based on inclusive citizenship. What might this look like? Of course this book can't provide anything nearing a complete answer, and first and foremost what is required is collaboration: between scholars and activists, policy makers and the general public. But I also suggest that engaging in studies like this one that aim to document and analyze migrants' lived citizenship is one small step.

There needs to be scope within such studies for considering the many complicated overlaps and disparities in patterns of migrant inclusion and exclusion from citizenship across borders. Thinking in terms of *transnational spaces of citizenship* viewed through the lens of uncertainty offers one approach, as this book has proposed. Furthermore, it is vital that this kind of work be carried out in contexts of South-South migration—in addition to those of South-North migration—in order to broaden the purview of migration studies and the consequent knowledge bases on which to found action. Greater dialogue between those scholars who are working on South-South migration is likewise essential so as to draw attention to the heterogeneity of these migration flows, but also to find the points of comparison, particularly in terms of the pressing issues of exploitation and human rights abuses. Additionally, greater dialogue would facilitate a more coherent international research agenda and subsequently more strategic use of the limited resources available for such projects. From such studies, it is possible to identify incremental, context-specific strategies for challenging migrants' multiple exclusions from citizenship, which also speak to a wider political agenda.[4] In addition to pushing for structural changes, the practices in which migrants are already engaging to seek greater inclusion in transnational spaces of citizenship can be amplified with the support of scholars and activists.

To provide an indication of how this might be done, I conclude with some suggestions about what such strategies might look like in the Bolivian-Chilean context. Taking first the legal, as a matter of urgency the legislation governing migrants' entry into and legal status within Chile must be addressed, as it is outdated and exclusionary, and does not reflect the present reality of migration to and from the country. At the time of going to press, in May 2018, a bill is currently before Congress to bring about significant reform to the 1975 migration legislation. There is, however, concern among Chilean academics and migrant organizations that it continues to be restrictive and discriminatory.[5] It is sincerely to be hoped that such concerns are given due consideration before the bill passes into law.

There is much to be praised in terms of the legislation pertaining to access to health and education for migrants. Nevertheless, what exists on paper is often not being put into practice, with lack of knowledge of migrant rights and discriminatory attitudes rife among public officials, health workers, and educators. Some excellent training by the Asociación and other organizations is already under way for these essential gatekeepers; however, I suggest that the pursuit of solidarity be increased with support from the state.

It is also important that labor regulations be better enforced, that employers similarly be made aware of migrant rights, and that the discriminatory attitudes of some be challenged. Moreover, it is crucial that migrant organizations do not support employers who fail to respect the rights of their workers, and that they also attempt not to perpetuate a racialized and gendered division of labor but instead encourage migrants to seek out diverse and fulfilling employment. Also in relation to labor, the fledgling work of migrant organizations and law enforcement agencies with respect to human trafficking must continue and grow, and incorporate greater awareness of the issue of trafficking for labor exploitation in addition to that of trafficking for sexual exploitation.

Finally, recognizing the work done already by migrant organizations, it is still imperative to foment advocacy and awareness campaigns around migrant rights and discrimination. There is a wealth of evidence to indicate that migrants, including many children, face high levels of discrimination on a daily basis. Prominent public campaigns with state backing may go some way to challenging such attitudes. It is also vital to support instances of genuine communication and exchange between migrants and Chileans through groups such as Corazón de Tinkus and to ensure that such groups have access to public space. They can play an important role in presenting positive depictions of migrants and confronting some of the stigma and stereotypes surrounding migration.

Identified through close analysis of the multiple ways in which migrants are marginalized from and incorporated within the bounds of citizenship transnationally, these incremental, multilevel strategies could, when combined, offer a route to greater inclusion. Thus, through mapping uncertain citizenship across borders, the interstitial possibilities contained within it can be identified. Claiming and expanding on these possibilities may offer pathways to a more just, more certain citizenship.

INTRODUCTION

1. Pertinent examples include Joanna Dreby, *Everyday Illegal: When Policies Undermine Immigrant Families* (Berkeley: University of California Press, 2015); Seth Holmes, *Fresh Fruit, Broken Bodies: Migrant Farmworkers in the United States* (Berkeley: University of California Press, 2013); and Pierrette Hondagneu-Sotelo, *Doméstica: Immigrant Workers Cleaning and Caring in the Shadows of Affluence*, 2nd ed. (Berkeley: University of California Press, 2007).

2. See Verónica Cano, Magdalena Soffia, and Jorge Martínez Pizarro, "Conocer para legislar y hacer política: Los desafíos de Chile ante un nuevo escenario migratorio," CEPAL, February 2009, https://www.cepal.org/es/publicaciones/7228-conocer-legislar-hacer-politica-desa fios-chile-un-nuevo-escenario-migratorio.

3. Mike Crang and Ian Cook, *Doing Ethnographies* (London: SAGE, 2007).

4. Conducting research in multiple sites was not new per se, but Marcus was the first to develop a more profound rationale for the use of this approach than had previously been expressed. See George Marcus, "Ethnography in/of the World System: The Emergence of Multi-Sited Ethnography," *Annual Review of Anthropology* 24 (1995): 105.

5. Marcus, "Ethnography in/of the World System."

6. Anna Amelina and Thomas Faist, "De-Naturalizing the National in Research Methodologies: Key Concepts of Transnational Studies in Migration," *Ethnic and Racial Studies* 35, no. 10 (2012): 1707–24.

7. Following Patricia Richards and Nancy Postero, and influenced by Peter Wade, I deliberately use the term "race" instead of "ethnicity" because I want to draw unambiguous attention to the ways in which racism operates to exclude and oppress certain groups on the basis of skin color and phenotypical features and/or cultural identifiers such as dress. Ethnicity has been associated more as a place-based marker of origin and therefore has different

connotations from what I mean when I talk about race, racism, and racialization. In addition, there has often been considerable slippage between "race" and "ethnicity," with the latter sometimes standing in as a more "acceptable" term for the former. See Patricia Richards, *Race and the Chilean Miracle: Neoliberalism, Democracy and Indigenous Rights* (Pittsburgh, PA: University of Pittsburgh Press, 2013); Nancy Postero, *Now We Are Citizens: Indigenous Politics in Postmulticultural Bolivia* (Stanford, CA: Stanford University Press, 2007); and Peter Wade, *Race and Ethnicity in Latin America* (London: Pluto Press, 1997).

8. Very similar experiences in the South of Chile in her research with *colonos* and local elites are analyzed by Richards, *Race and the Chilean Miracle*, 28–32.

9. Elements of an earlier, less-developed version of this chapter appear in Megan Ryburn, "Living the Chilean Dream? Bolivian Migrants' Incorporation in the Space of Economic Citizenship," *Geoforum* 76 (2016): 48–58.

1. CITIZENSHIP, MIGRATION, AND UNCERTAINTY

1. Thomas Humphrey Marshall, *Citizenship and Social Class, and Other Essays* (Cambridge, UK: Cambridge University Press, 1950), 28.

2. Engin Isin, *Being Political: Genealogies of Citizenship* (Minneapolis: University of Minnesota Press, 2002), x.

3. This is well established. See, for example, Stephen Castles and Alastair Davidson, *Citizenship and Migration: Globalization and the Politics of Belonging* (New York: Routledge, 2000); Sian Lazar, *The Anthropology of Citizenship: A Reader* (Oxford: Wiley-Blackwell, 2013); and Ruth Lister, *Citizenship: Feminist Perspectives*, 2nd ed. (New York: New York University Press, 2003).

4. Marshall, *Citizenship and Social Class*.

5. Lister, *Citizenship*.

6. Castles and Davidson, *Citizenship and Migration*, 27.

7. Lister, *Citizenship*, 42. See also Alison Assiter, "Citizenship Revisited," in *Women, Citizenship and Difference*, ed. Nira Yuval-Davis and Prina Werbner (London: Zed Books, 1999), 41–53.

8. Michael Sandel, "The Procedural Republic and the Unencumbered Self," *Political Theory* 12, no. 1 (1984): 81–96.

9. Assiter, "Citizenship Revisited," 43.

10. Some critiques have been taken on board by modern liberals. See, for example, Will Kymlicka, *Multicultural Citizenship: A Liberal Theory of Minority Rights* (Oxford: Clarendon Press, 1996).

11. Lister, *Citizenship*, 68.

12. Carole Pateman, *The Sexual Contract* (Stanford, CA: Stanford University Press, 1988).

13. For more extensive discussion see, for example, Assiter, "Citizenship Revisited"; and Susan Moller Okin, *Justice, Gender, and the Family* (New York: Basic Books, 2008).

14. Iris Marion Young, "The Ideal of Community and the Politics of Difference," *Social Theory and Practice* 12, no. 1 (1986): 1–26.

15. Ruth Lister, "Citizenship: Towards a Feminist Synthesis," *Feminist Review*, no. 57 (1997): 28–48; and Lister, *Citizenship*.

16. Lister, "Citizenship: Towards a Feminist Synthesis," 35.

17. Luin Goldring, "The Gender and Geography of Citizenship in Mexico-U.S. Transnational Spaces," *Identities* 7, no. 4 (2001): 501–37. See also Saskia Sassen, "The Repositioning of Citizenship: Emergent Subjects and Spaces for Politics," *CR: The New Centennial Review* 3, no. 2 (2003): 41–66.

18. Bryan Roberts, *The Making of Citizens: Cities of Peasants Revisited* (London: Arnold, 1995), 184.

19. Roberts, *The Making of Citizens*, 188.

20. For further, comparable discussion of the development of citizenship in Latin America, see Elizabeth Jelin, "Women, Gender, and Human Rights," in *Constructing Democracy: Human Rights, Citizenship, and Society in Latin America*, ed. Elizabeth Jelin and Eric Hershberg (Boulder, CO: Westview Press, 1996), 177–224.

21. Of a total Bolivian population of two million people, sixty-five thousand soldiers were killed, deserted, or died in captivity in the Chaco War. See Herbert Klein, *A Concise History of Bolivia* (Cambridge, UK: University of Cambridge Press, 2011), 183.

22. See, for example, Klein, *A Concise History of Bolivia*; James Dunkerley, "The Bolivian Revolution at 60: Politics and Historiography," *Journal of Latin American Studies* 45, no.2 (2013): 325–50; and Forrest Hylton and Sinclair Thomson, *Revolutionary Horizons: Past and Present in Bolivian Politics* (London: Verso, 2007).

23. Simon Collier and William Sater, *A History of Chile, 1808–1994* (Cambridge, UK: Cambridge University Press, 1996).

24. Collier and Sater, *A History of Chile*; and Patricio Meller, *The Unidad Popular and the Pinochet Dictatorship: A Political Economy Analysis*, trans. Tim Ennis (London: Palgrave Macmillan, 2000).

25. For a wide-ranging analysis of the consequences of the Pinochet dictatorship, see Peter Stern's trilogy, published as *The Memory Box of Pinochet's Chile* (Durham, NC: Duke University Press, 2010).

26. Chilean National Commission on Truth and Reconciliation, "Report for the Chilean National Commission on Truth and Reconciliation," trans. Center of Civil and Human Rights of the Notre Dame Law School (Notre Dame, IN: University of Notre Dame Press, 1993), http://www.usip.org/files/resources/collections/truth_commissions/Chile90-Report /Chile90-Report.pdf; and Comisión Nacional sobre Prisión Política y Tortura, *Nómina de personas reconocidas como víctimas en etapa de reconsideración* (Santiago, Chile: Comisión Nacional sobre Prisión Política y Tortura, 2005), http://www.archivochile.com/Derechos_ humanos/com_valech/Informe_complementario.pdf.

27. Thomas Wright and Rody Oñate Zúñiga, "Chilean Political Exile," *Latin American Perspectives* 34, no. 4 (2007): 31–49.

28. See, for example, Peter Winn ed., *Victims of the Chilean Miracle: Workers and Neoliberalism in the Pinochet Era* (Durham, NC: Duke University Press, 2004).

29. Jeffrey Webber, *From Rebellion to Reform in Bolivia: Class Struggle, Indigenous Liberation, and the Politics of Evo Morales* (Chicago: Haymarket Books, 2011); and James Dunkerley, *Bolivia: Revolution and the Power of History in the Present* (London: Institute for the Study of the Americas, 2007).

30. Roberts, *The Making of Citizens*, 200.

31. For discussion of some of these groups, see Julia Paley, *Marketing Democracy: Power and Social Movements in Post-Dictatorship Chile* (Berkeley: University of California Press,

2001); Patricia Richards, *Pobladoras, Indígenas and the State: Conflicts over Women's Rights in Chile* (New Brunswick, NJ: Rutgers University Press, 2004); and Verónica Schild, "Engendering the New Social Citizenship in Chile: NGOs and Social Provisioning under Neoliberalism," in *Gender, Justice, Development and Rights: Substantiating Rights in a Disabling Environment*, ed. Shahra Ravazi and Maxine Molyneux (Oxford: Oxford University Press, 2002), 170–203.

32. Richards, *Race and the Chilean Miracle*, 9. See also Evelina Dagnino, "Citizenship in Latin America: An Introduction," *Latin American Perspectives* 30, no. 2 (2003): 170–203.

33. Richards, *Race and the Chilean Miracle*, 10. See also Schild, "Engendering the New Social Citizenship".

34. By, for example, Charles Hale, "Does Multiculturalism Menace? Governance, Cultural Rights and the Politics of Identity in Guatemala," *Journal of Latin American Studies* 34, no. 3 (2002): 485–524; and Robert Andolina, Nina Laurie, and Sarah Radcliffe, *Indigenous Development in the Andes: Culture, Power, and Transnationalism* (Durham, NC: Duke University Press, 2009).

35. Richards, *Race and the Chilean Miracle*, 13.

36. CASEN, "Pueblos indígenas: Sintesis de resultados," Observatorio del Ministerio de Desarrollo Social, 2015, http://observatorio.ministeriodesarrollosocial.gob.cl/documentos/Casen2013_Pueblos_Indigenas_13mar15_publicacion.pdf.

37. See, for example, Richards, *Race and the Chilean Miracle*; Nicolás Rojas Pedemonte and Omar Miranda, "Dínamica sociopolítica del conflicto y la violencia en territorio mapuche: Particularidades históricas de un nuevo ciclo en las relaciones contenciosas," *Revista de Sociología* 30 (2015): 56–100.

38. By, for example, Nancy Postero, *Now We Are Citizens: Indigenous Politics in Postmulticultural Bolivia* (Stanford, CA: Stanford University Press, 2007).

39. Postero, *Now We Are Citizens*.

40. Nancy Postero, *The Indigenous State: Race, Politics, and Performance in Plurinational Bolivia* (Berkeley: University of California Press, 2017).

41. The 2001 and 2012 census results with respect to self-identification as indigenous can be found at CEDIB, "Indígenas: Quién gana, quién pierde," 2013, http://www.cedib.org/wp-content/uploads/2013/08/Tabla-Poblacion-Indigena1.pdf. The discrepancy of approximately 20 percent between those who identified as indigenous in 2001 (around 60 percent) and those who did in 2012 (around 40 percent) has been widely discussed. See, for example, Leonardo Tamburini, "Bolivia Censo 2012: Algunas claves para entender la variable indígena," SERVINDI, 2013, https://www.servindi.org/actualidad/94399.

42. Postero, *The Indigenous State*, 11.

43. Postero, *The Indigenous State*. See also Andrew Canessa, "Conflict, Claim and Contradiction in the New 'Indigenous' State of Bolivia," *Critique of Anthropology* 34, no. 2 (2014): 153–73; Linda Farthing and Benjamin Kohl, *Evo's Bolivia: Continuity and Change* (Austin: University of Texas Press, 2014); and Webber, *From Rebellion to Reform in Bolivia*.

44. See, respectively, Teresa Caldeira, *City of Walls: Crime, Segregation and Citizenship in Sao Paulo* (Berkeley: University of California Press, 2001); Daniel Goldstein, *The Spectacular City: Violence and Performance in Urban Bolivia* (Durham, NC: Duke University Press, 2004); James Holston, *Insurgent Citizenship: Disjunctions of Democracy and Modernity in Brazil* (Princeton, NJ: Princeton University Press, 2008); Sian Lazar, *El Alto, Rebel*

City: Self and Citizenship in Andean Bolivia (Durham, NC: Duke University Press, 2008); Richards, *Pobladoras, Indígenas and the State*; and Richards, *Race and the Chilean Miracle*.

45. Étienne Balibar, *Nous, citoyens d'Europe? Les frontières, l'État, le peuple* (Paris: La Découverte, 2001).

46. Lazar, *The Anthropology of Citizenship*, 10.

47. Linda Basch, Nina Glick-Schiller, and Cristina Szanton-Blanc, *Nations Unbound: Transnational Projects, Postcolonial Predicaments, and Deterritorialized Nation-States* (London: Routledge, 1994), 7.

48. Richard Alba and Victor Nee, "Rethinking Assimilation Theory for a New Era of Immigration," *International Migration Review* 31, no. 4 (1997): 826–74.

49. Nathan Glazer and Daniel Moynihan, *Beyond the Melting Pot: The Negroes, Puerto Ricans, Jews, Italians, and Irish of New York City*, 2nd ed. (Cambridge, MA: The MIT Press, 1970).

50. Nina Glick-Schiller, Linda Basch, and Cristina Szanton-Blanc, "From Immigrant to Transmigrant: Theorizing Transnational Migration," *Anthropological Quarterly* 68, no. 1 (1995): 48–63.

51. Glick-Schiller, Basch, and Szanton-Blanc, "From Immigrant to Transmigrant"; and Steven Vertovec, "Migrant Transnationalism and Modes of Transformation," *International Migration Review* 38, no. 3 (2004): 48–63.

52. Peggy Levitt and Rafael de la Dehesa, "Transnational Migration and the Redefinition of the State: Variations and Explanations," *Ethnic and Racial Studies* 26, no. 4 (2003): 587–611.

53. Alejandro Portes, Luis Guarnizo, and Patricia Landolt, "The Study of Transnationalism: Pitfalls and Promise of an Emergent Research Field," *Ethnic and Racial Studies* 22, no. 2 (1999): 217–37; and Roger Waldinger and David Fitzgerald, "Transnationalism in Question," *American Journal of Sociology* 109, no. 5 (2004): 1177–95.

54. Luis Guarnizo, Alejandro Portes, and William Haller, "Assimilation and Transnationalism: Determinants of Transnational Political Action among Contemporary Migrants," *American Journal of Sociology* 108, no. 6 (2003): 1211–48.

55. Cathy McIlwaine, "Constructing Transnational Social Spaces among Latin American Migrants in Europe: Perspectives from the UK," *Cambridge Journal of Regions, Economy and Society* 5, no. 2 (2012): 289–304.

56. For some examples, see Thomas Faist, "Transnational Social Spaces out of International Migration: Evolution, Significance, and Future Prospects," *European Journal of Sociology* 39, no. 2 (1998): 213–47; Peter Jackson, Philip Crang, and Claire Dwyer, *Transnational Spaces* (London: Routledge, 2004); Ludger Pries, "Configurations of Geographic and Societal Spaces: A Sociological Proposal between 'Methodological Nationalism' and the 'Spaces of Flows,'" *Global Networks* 5, no. 2 (2005): 167–90; and Michael Smith, "Transnational Urbanism Revisited," *Journal of Ethnic and Migration Studies* 31, no. 2 (2005): 235–44.

57. Peggy Levitt and B. Nadya Jaworsky, "Transnational Migration Studies: Past Developments and Future Trends," *Annual Review of Sociology* 33, no. 1 (2007): 131–32.

58. Levitt and Jaworsky, "Transnational Migration Studies," 132.

59. Andreas Wimmer and Nina Glick Schiller, "Methodological Nationalism and Beyond: Nation-State Building, Migration and the Social Sciences," *Global Networks* 2, no. 4 (2002): 301–34.

60. This understanding of space draws particularly on Henri Lefebvre, *The Production of Space*, trans. Donald Nicholson-Smith (Oxford: Wiley-Blackwell, 1991); and Doreen Massey, *For Space* (London: SAGE, 2005).

61. Levitt and Jaworsky, "Transnational Migration Studies."

62. As indicated by Jackson, Crang, and Dwyer, *Transnational Spaces*.

63. On the importance of considering the impacts of gender on migrants' relationships to transnational social spaces, see Sarah Mahler and Patricia Pessar, "Gendered Geographies of Power: Analyzing Gender across Transnational Spaces," *Identities* 7, no. 4 (2001): 441–59. For an intersectional perspective, see McIlwaine, "Constructing Transnational Social Spaces among Latin American Migrants in Europe"; and Floya Anthias, "Transnational Mobilities, Migration Research and Intersectionality," *Nordic Journal of Migration Research* 2, no. 2 (2012): 102–10.

64. Katja Hujo and Nicola Piper, "South–South Migration: Challenges for Development and Social Policy," *Development* 50, no. 4 (2007): 6.

65. Jonathan Crush and Sujata Ramachandran, "Xenophobia, International Migration and Development," *Journal of Human Development and Capabilities* 11, no. 2 (2010): 209–28.

66. Susanne Melde et al., "Introduction: The South-South Migration and Development Nexus," in *A New Perspective on Human Mobility in the South*, ed. Rudolf Anich et al. (New York: Springer, 2014), 14.

67. Mohamed Berriane and Hein de Haas, *African Migrations Research* (London: Africa World Press, 2012), 2.

68. Dilip Ratha and William Shaw, "South-South Migration and Remittances" (World Bank Working Papers, 2007), https://elibrary.worldbank.org/doi/abs/10.1596/978-0-8213-7072-8.

69. Melde et al., "Introduction," 5.

70. Hujo and Piper, "South-South Migration".

71. Melde et al., "Introduction"; and Sylvia Chant and Cathy McIlwaine, *Geographies of Development in the 21st Century: An Introduction to the Global South* (Cheltenham, UK: Edward Elgar, 2009).

72. The most comprehensive recent figures remain those presented in René Pereira Morató, "Perfíl migratorio de Bolivia," Organización Internacional de Migraciones, 2011, 9, http://publications.iom.int/system/files/pdf/perfil_migratorio_de_bolivia.pdf. The larger estimate comes from Bolivia Cultural, "Las parcelas de la explotación: la migración de Bolivia en São Paulo," 2013, http://www.boliviacultural.com.br/ver_noticias.php?id=364. It is very difficult to accurately estimate the size of the Bolivian population currently residing outside the country, as there is no comprehensive, electronic database for recording the exits and entrances of migrants in Bolivia. Moreover, many enter or remain in destination countries without documentation, thus making accurate statistics even more difficult to obtain.

73. Lesley Gill, *Precarious Dependencies: Gender, Class, and Domestic Service in Bolivia* (New York: Columbia University Press, 1994). See also Charlotta Widmark, *To Make Do in the City: Social Identities and Cultural Transformations among Aymara Speakers in La Paz* (Uppsala, Sweden: Uppsala University Press, 2003).

74. Xavier Albó, Tomás Greaves, and Godofredo Sandóval, *Chukiyawu: La cara aymara de La Paz*, vol. 1, *El paso a la ciudad* (La Paz, Bolivia: Centro de Investigación y Promoción del Campesinado, 1981).

75. Instituto Nacional de Estadísticas Bolivia, "Intituto Nacional de Estadística Bolivia: nota de prensa," 2012, http://censosbolivia.ine.gob.bo/webine/sites/default/files/archivos _adjuntos/N%204%20Area%20urbanas%20y%20rurales_1.pdf.

76. Klein, *A Concise History of Bolivia*, 246.

77. Webber, *From Rebellion to Reform*, 21–26.

78. This is the aspect of Latin American intraregional Bolivian emigration that is best documented; see, for example, Tanja Bastia, "From Mining to Garment Workshops: Bolivian Migrants in Buenos Aires," *Journal of Ethnic and Migration Studies* 33, no. 4 (2007): 655–69; Alejandro Grimson, *Relatos de la diferencia y la igualdad: los bolivianos en Buenos Aires* (Buenos Aires, Argentina: Eudeba, 1999); Alfonso Hinojosa Gordonava, "La visibilización de las migraciones transnacionales en Bolivia," *Tinkazos* 11, no. 25 (2008): 89–106; Jorge Mondaca Plaza, "Migración laboral y los flujos migratorios," in *Mirada sobre la migración boliviana: aportes para el informe sobre las migraciones*, ed. Jorge Evangelista (La Paz: Capítulo Boliviano de Derechos Humanos, Democracia y Desarrollo, 2007), 23–36.

79. Tanja Bastia's extensive work on Bolivian migrants in the garment manufacturing industry in Buenos Aires is particularly illuminating. See, for example, Bastia, "From Mining to Garment Workshops"; and Tanja Bastia and Siobhan McGarth, "Temporality, Migration, and Unfree Labour: Migrant Garment Workers" (Manchester Papers in Political Economy, Working Paper no. 6, University of Manchester, 2011).

80. Tanja Bastia, "'I Am Going, with or without You': Autonomy in Bolivian Transnational Migrations," *Gender, Place & Culture* 20, no. 2 (2013): 160–77; and Tanja Bastia, "Should I Stay or Should I Go? Return Migration in Times of Crisis," *Journal of International Development* 23 (2011): 583–95. For the 2011 figure, see Pereira Morató, "Perfíl Migratorio de Bolivia," 36.

81. In 2009 it was recorded that there were 222,497 Bolivians residing in Spain, according to Pereira Morató, "Perfíl migratorio de Bolivia," 36.

82. Klein, *A Concise History of Bolivia*, 283; see also chapter 4.

83. Pereira Morató, "Perfíl migratorio de Bolivia," 50.

84. World Bank, "Country Profile: Bolivia," *World Bank Databank*, 2017, http://data bank.worldbank.org/data/Views/Reports/ReportWidgetCustom.aspx?Report_Name=Cou ntryProfile&Id=b450fd57&tbar=y&dd=y&inf=n&zm=n&country=BOL.

85. See Simone Buechler, "Sweating It in the Brazilian Garment Industry: Korean and Bolivian Immigrants and Global Economic Forces in São Paulo," *Latin American Perspectives* 136, no. 3 (2004): 99–119; Bolivia Cultural, "Las parcelas de la explotación"; and Leticia Satie Bermudes, "Two Little Bolivias: The Reality of Bolivian Immigrants in the Cities of Buenos Aires and São Paulo" (master's thesis, University of Columbia, 2012), http:// academiccommons.columbia.edu/catalog/ac:145491.

86. Antônio Tadeu de Oliveira, "O perfil geral dos imigrantes no Brasil a partir dos censos demográficos 2000 e 2010," *Caderna Obmigra—Revista Migrações Internacionais* 1, no. 2 (2015), http://periodicos.unb.br/index.php/obmigra/article/view/14895/10661.

87. Pereira Morató, "Perfíl migratorio de Bolivia," 38–39.

88. All data are from the Banco Central de Bolivia but have been accessed using different sources. For 2007, the information is taken from Pereira Morató, "Perfíl migratorio de Bolivia," 38–39. For 2013, see Gabriela Imaña, "Las remesas crecieron en 8% en 2013," *La Razón* (La Paz), February 11, 2014, http://www.la-razon.com/index.php?_url=/economia

/remesas-crecieron_0_1996600357.html. For 2017, see Banco Central de Bolivia, "Nivel de remesas de trabajadores—mes de febrero de 2017," 2017, https://www.bcb.gob.bo/web docs/10_notas_prensa/NP_20_REMESAS-FEBRERO.pdf.

89. Bastia, "Should I Stay or Should I Go?"; and Jorge Martínez Pizarro, *Migración internacional en América Latina y el Caribe: Nuevas tendencias y nuevos enfoques* (Santiago, Chile: CEPAL, 2011).

90. These population estimates are according to CEPAL, "CEPALSTAT: Base de datos y publicaciones estadísticas," 2015, http://interwp.cepal.org/cepalstat/WEB_cepalstat/Perfil _nacional_social.asp?pais=CHL&idioma=e.

91. CASEN, "Inmigrantes: Principales resultados (versión extendida)," Observatorio del Ministerio de Desarrollo Social, 2015, http://observatorio.ministeriodesarrollosocial .gob.cl/casen-multidimensional/casen/docs/CASEN_2015_INMIGRANTES_21122016 _EXTENDIDA_publicada.pdf. For the 2009 figure, see Martínez Pizarro, *Migración internacional en América Latina y el Caribe*.

92. All data are from the Banco Central de Bolivia. For 2007, see Pereira Morató, "Perfil migratorio de Bolivia," 38–39. For 2013, see Imaña, "Las remesas crecieron en 8% en 2013." For 2017, see Banco Central de Bolivia, "Nivel de remesas de trabajadores—mes de febrero de 2017."

93. Departamento de Extranjería y Migración, "Migración en Chile 2005–2014," 2016, 144, http://www.extranjeria.gob.cl/media/2016/02/Anuario-Estad%C3%ADstico-Nacional-Migraci%C3%B3n-en-Chile-2005-2014.pdf

94. World Bank, "Country Profile: Bolivia".

95. For a comprehensive discussion of this tendency and of the factors influencing migration patterns more broadly, see Hein de Haas, "Migration and Development: A Theoretical Perspective" (University of Oxford International Migration Institute Working Papers no. 9, Oxford, 2008).

96. de Haas, "Migration and Development," 19.

97. Martínez Pizarro, *Migración internacional en América Latina y el Caribe*.

98. CASEN, "Inmigrantes: Principales resultados." According to these estimates, 30 percent of the migrant population in Chile is Peruvian, 13.1 percent is Colombian, 11.9 percent is Argentinean, and 10.1 percent is Bolivian. These CASEN data from 2015 are the most recent estimates available, although they are not as reliable as census data (CASEN data are an extrapolation from a representative sample of the population, as opposed to a survey of the entire population). The 2012 Chilean census was declared unreliable by the Chilean Instituto Nacional de Estadísticas (National Institute of Statistics), and all data from it are currently under review and unavailable. Moreover, in general quantitative data on migrants are notoriously unreliable, as they often fail to fully account for the number of migrants with irregular legal status.

99. Jasmine Gideon, *Gender, Globalization, and Health in a Latin American Context* (London: Palgrave Macmillan, 2014); and Carolina Stefoni, "Perfil migratorio de Chile," Organización Internacional de Migraciones, 2011, http://priem.cl/wp-content/uploads/2015 /04/Stefoni_Perfil-Migratorio-de-Chile.pdf.

100. Hein de Haas, "Migration and Development."

101. OECD, "Society at a Glance 2014: OECD Social Indicators," OECD Publishing, 2014, http://dx.doi.org-10.1787/soc_glance-2014-en.

102. OECD, "Statistics/OECD Factbook/2013/Income Inequality," OECD iLibrary, 2013, http://www.oecd-ilibrary.org/sites/factbook-2013-en/03/02/01/index.html?itemId=/content/chapter/factbook-2013-25-en.

103. OECD, "Society at a Glance 2016: OECD Social Indicators," OECD Publishing, 2016, http://dx.doi.org/10.1787/9789264261488-en

104. Cano et al., "Conocer para legislar y hacer política."

105. For work within migration studies that is concerned with analysis of migrants' citizenship in practice, see, for example, Elaine Ho, "Citizenship, Migration and Transnationalism: A Review and Critical Interventions," *Geography Compass* 2, no. 5 (2008): 1286–1300; Aihwa Ong, *Flexible Citizenship: The Cultural Logics of Transnationality* (Durham, NC: Duke University Press, 1999); Deborah Reed-Danahay and Caroline Brettell, *Citizenship, Political Engagement, and Belonging: Immigrants in Europe and the United States* (New Brunswick, NJ: Rutgers University Press, 2008); and Lynn Staeheli et al., "Dreaming the Ordinary: Daily Life and the Complex Geographies of Citizenship," *Progress in Human Geography* 36, no. 5 (2012): 628–44.

106. Staeheli et al., "Dreaming the Ordinary," 641. For examples of other scholarship adopting a spatial approach to the analysis of citizenship and migration, see Susan Bibler Coutin, "Illegality, Borderlands, and the Space of Non-Existence," in *Globalization under Construction: Governmentality, Law, and Identity*, ed. Richard Warren Perry and Bill Maurer (Minneapolis: Minnesota University Press, 2003): 171–203; Luin Goldring and Patricia Landolt, *Producing and Negotiating Non-Citizenship: Precarious Legal Status in Canada*, 3rd ed. (Toronto: University of Toronto Press, 2013); Engin Isin and Kim Rygiel, "Abject Spaces, Frontiers, Zones, Camps," in *The Logics of Biopower and the War on Terror: Living, Dying, Surviving*, ed. Elizabeth Dauphinee and Cristina Masters (London: Palgrave Macmillan, 2007): 181–203; Charles Lee, "Bare Life, Interstices, and the Third Space of Citizenship," *WSQ: Women's Studies Quarterly* 38, no. 1 (2010): 57–81; and Cecilia Menjívar, "Liminal Legality: Salvadoran and Guatemalan Immigrants' Lives in the United States," *American Journal of Sociology* 111, no. 4 (2006): 99–1037.

107. For binary approaches see Bibler Coutin, "Illegality, Borderlands, and the Space of Non-Existence"; and Isin and Rygiel, "Abject Spaces." Triadic approaches are offered in Lee, "Bare Life, Interstices, and the Third Space of Citizenship"; and Menjívar, "Liminal Legality."

108. For example, see Goldring and Landolt, *Producing and Negotiating Non-Citizenship*.

109. Marshall, *Citizenship and Social Class*.

110. See, respectively, Alice Kessler-Harris, "In Pursuit of Economic Citizenship," *Social Politics: International Studies in Gender, State and Society* 10, no. 2 (2003): 157–75; Carole Pateman, *The Disorder of Women: Democracy, Feminism, and Political Theory* (Stanford, CA: Stanford University Press, 1990); and Yvonne Riaño, "Drawing New Boundaries of Participation: Experiences and Strategies of Economic Citizenship among Skilled Migrant Women in Switzerland," *Environment and Planning A* 43, no. 7 (2011): 1530–46.

111. Kessler-Harris, "In Pursuit of Economic Citizenship"; and Pateman, *The Disorder of Women*.

112. Riaño, "Drawing New Boundaries of Participation."

113. See Elizabeth Cooper and David Patten, eds., *Ethnographies of Uncertainty in Africa* (London: Palgrave Macmillan, 2015); Clara Han, *Life in Debt: Times of Care and Violence in Neoliberal Chile* (Berkeley: University of California Press, 2012); Tatiana Adeline Thieme,

"The Hustle Economy: Informality, Uncertainty and the Geographies of Getting By," *Progress in Human Geography* (2017), http://journals.sagepub.com/doi/pdf/10.1177/0309132517 690039; Henrik Vigh, "Motion Squared: A Second Look at the Concept of Social Navigation," *Anthropological Theory* 9, no. 4 (2009): 419–38; and Austin Zeiderman et al., "Uncertainty and Urban Life," *Public Culture* 72, no. 2 (2015): 281–304.

114. Zeiderman et al., "Uncertainty and Urban Life," 285.

115. Cooper and Patten, *Ethnographies of Uncertainty in Africa*, 3.

116. Susan Whyte, "Uncertain Undertakings: Practicing Health Care in the Subjunctive Mood," in *Managing Uncertainty: Ethnographic Studies of Illness, Risk, and the Struggle for Control*, ed. Richard Jenkins, Hanne Jessen, and Vibeke Steffen (Copenhagen: Museum Tusculanum Press, 2005), 250–51, quoted in Cooper and Patten, *Ethnographies of Uncertainty in Africa*, 3. For a different, but related, use of the concept of the subjunctive mood, see Austin Zeiderman, *Endangered City: The Politics of Security and Risk in Bogotá* (Durham, NC: Duke University Press, 2016), 170–71.

2. PLACES OF UNCERTAIN CITIZENSHIP

1. Doreen Massey, *For Space* (London: SAGE, 2005), 131.

2. Phil Hubbard, Rob Kitchin, and Gill Valentine, eds., *Key Thinkers on Space and Place* (London: SAGE, 2004), 6.

3. Nigel Thrift, "Space: The Fundamental Stuff of Geography," in *Key Concepts in Geography*, ed. Sarah Holloway, Stephen Rice, and Gill Valentine (London: SAGE, 2003), 103–4; and Liz Bondi, Joyce Davidson, and Mick Smith, "Introduction: Geography's 'Emotional Turn,'" in *Emotional Geographies*, ed. Joyce Davidson, Mick Smith, and Liz Bondi (Aldershot, UK: Ashgate, 2007), 6.

4. Such a process is coherent with George Marcus's concept of "following" as the basis for multi-sited ethnography. See Marcus, "Ethnography in/of the World System: The Emergence of Multi-Sited Ethnography," *Annual Review of Anthropology* 24 (1995): 95–117.

5. Rob Shields, *Places on the Margin: Alternative Geographies of Modernity* (London: Psychology Press, 1992).

6. Victor Turner, *The Forest of Symbols: Aspects of Ndembu Ritual* (Ithaca, NY: Cornell University Press, 1967), 97.

7. A detailed account of the War of the Pacific from a relatively nonpartisan, revisionist perspective is given in Bruce Farcau, *The Ten Cents War: Chile, Peru, and Bolivia in the War of the Pacific, 1879–1884* (Westport, CT: Praeger, 2000).

8. William Skuban, *Lines in the Sand: Nationalism and Identity on the Peruvian-Chilean Frontier* (Albuquerque: University of New Mexico Press, 2007), 106.

9. On "Chileanization" and violence at the border, see Skuban, *Lines in the Sand*; Cordelia Freeman, "Violence on the Chile-Peru Border, Arica 1925–2015" (PhD thesis, University of Nottingham, 2016), http://eprints.nottingham.ac.uk/33556/; and Sergio González Miranda, "Patrioteros, marzorqueros, nativos y cowboys en el conflict peruano-chileno por Tacna y Arica," *Si Somos Americanos* 6, no. 5 (2004): 33–69.

10. Paulo Drinot, "Website of Memory: The War of the Pacific (1879–84) in the Global Age of YouTube," *Memory Studies* 4, no. 4 (2011): 370–85; and Freeman, "Violence on the Chile-Peru Border."

11. See, respectively, Fernando Molina, "El himno al mar que canta Bolivia e irrita a Chile," *El País*, February 23, 2015, https://elpais.com/internacional/2015/02/23/actuali dad/1424727376_935994.html; "Canciller de Bolivia: El gobierno de Bachelet es peor que el de Pinochet," *CNN Español*, March 28, 2017, http://cnnespanol.cnn.com/2017/03/28/cancil ler-de-bolivia-el-gobierno-de-bachelet-es-peor-que-el-de-pinochet/; and "La pelea entre Piñera y Morales que nos recordó el '¿Por qué no te callas?' de Hugo Chávez," *CNN Español*, June 26, 2017, http://cnnespanol.cnn.com/2017/06/26/la-pelea-entre-pinera-y-morales -que-nos-recordo-el-por-que-no-te-callas-a-hugo-chavez/.

12. MERCOSUR is an economic and political bloc created in 1991. It is described on the institutional website as "a process of regional integration" (MERCOSUR, "En pocas palabras," n.d., http://www.mercosur.int/innovaportal/v/3862/2/innova.front/en-pocas-palabras). Full member countries are Argentina, Brazil, Paraguay, and Uruguay. Chile, Colombia, Ecuador, Guyana, Peru, and Suriname are associate members. Bolivia is currently in the process of becoming a full member, and Venezuela's membership has been suspended since December 2016. The bloc's goal is to promote freedom of movement as well as free trade, and a variety of agreements with respect to migration exist among the different full and associate members. In the Chilean case, since 2009 Argentine, Bolivian, Brazilian, Paraguayan, and Uruguayan citizens (but not those from the other associate member countries, i.e., Colombia, Ecuador, Guyana, Peru, and Suriname) have been able to enter Chile as tourists and then apply for an MTRV before their tourist visas expire (see chapter 3).

13. Gabi Villalba, "Fragmentos de Ciudad: El Cité," *Plataforma Urbana*, September 22, 2006, www.plataformaurbana.cl/archive/2006/09/22/fragmentos-de-ciudad-el-cite/.

14. Villalba, "Fragmentos de Ciudad."

15. According to data from 2013, 10.7 percent of the migrant population in Santiago but only 1.8 percent of the Chilean-born population lives in seriously overcrowded conditions, with five or more people sharing a room. Some 12.4 percent of the migrant population and 2.5 percent of the Chilean-born population live in conditions considered to have "moderately high" levels of overcrowding, with 3.5 to 4.9 people sharing a room. See Nicolás Rojas Pedemonte and Claudia Silva Dittborn, "La migración en Chile: Breve reporte y caracterización," Observatorio Iberoamericano sobre Movilidad Humana, Migraciones y Desarrollo, 2016, www.extranjeria.gob.cl/media/2016/08/informe_julio_agosto_2016.pdf.

16. Glenn, "Caring and Inequality," 48. For two additional examples of scholarship on migrant domestic workers in the United States, see Pierrette Hondagneu-Sotelo, *Doméstica: Immigrant Workers Cleaning and Caring in the Shadows of Affluence*, 2nd ed. (Berkeley: University of California Press, 2007); and Charles Lee, "Bare Life, Interstices, and the Third Space of Citizenship," *WSQ: Women's Studies Quarterly* 38, no. 1 (2010): 57–81.

17. In Bolivia the terms *mitanaje* and *ponguaje* were used to refer to systems of feudal servitude put in place in the colonial era. Indigenous people were forced to work without any form of compensation for the European and criollo landed upper classes on haciendas, on plantations, in mines, and in their private homes. This practice was only outlawed in 1952.

18. For discussion of contexts other than Chile and Bolivia, see, for example, Séverine Durin, María Eugenia de la O, and Santiago Bastos, eds., *Trabajadoras en la sombra: Dimensiones del servicio doméstico latinoamericano* (Monterrey, Mexico: CIESAS, 2014); and Erynn Masi de Casanova, "Embodied Inequality: The Experience of Domestic Work in Urban Ecuador," *Gender and Society* 27, no. 4 (2013): 561–85.

19. Lesley Gill, *Precarious Dependencies: Gender, Class, and Domestic Service in Bolivia* (New York: Columbia University Press, 1994), 141–42.

20. Elizabeth Peredo Beltrán, *Trabajadoras asalariadas del hogar en Bolivia: Aprendizajes de una larga lucha* (La Paz, Bolivia: Red de Mujeres Transformanda la Economía, 2015), 17.

21. Carolina Stefoni and Rosario Fernández, "Mujeres migrantes en el trabajo dómestico: Entre el servilismo y los derechos," in *Mujeres inmigrantes en Chile: ¿Mano de obra o trabajadoras con derechos?*, ed. Carolina Stefoni (Santiago, Chile: Universidad Alberto Hurtado, 2013).

22. CASEN, "Inmigrantes: Principales resultados (versión extendida)," Observatorio del Ministerio de Desarrollo Social, 2015, http://observatorio.ministeriodesarrollosocial .gob.cl/casen-multidimensional/casen/docs/CASEN_2015_INMIGRANTES_21122016 _EXTENDIDA_publicada.pdf.

23. A similar comparison is made in the Bolivian context by Gill, *Precarious Dependencies*, 73.

24. María Emilia Tijoux Merino, *Racismo en Chile: La piel como marca de la inmigración* (Santiago, Chile: Ediciones Universitaria, 2016).

25. On sexuality and racialization in the Americas more broadly, see, for example, Mara Viveros Vigoya, "Sexuality and Desire in Racialised Contexts," in *Understanding Global Sexualities: New Frontiers*, ed. Peter Aggleton (Oxford: Routledge, 2012), 218–31. On the sexualized racialization of Colombian migrants in Chile specifically, see Jorge Pavez Ojeda, "Affecciones afrocolombianas: Transnacionalización y racialización del mercado del sexo en las ciudades mineras del norte de Chile," *Latin American Research Review* 51, no. 2 (2016): 24–45.

26. Viviana Briones Valentín, "Arica colonial: Libertos y esclavos negros entre El Lumbanga y Las Maytas," *Chungará* (Arica) 36 (2004): 814 (author's translation). The source cited by Briones Valentín is Rolando Mellafe, *La esclavitud en Hispanoamérica* (Buenos Aires, Argentina: Editorial Universitaria de Buenos Aires, 1964).

27. I recognize that to separate "human" and "natural" disasters essentially produces a false dichotomy; for instance, the structural conditions that lead to some people living in poverty also make them more likely to suffer far more the effects of disasters such as earthquakes and floods than their richer counterparts do.

28. On "counting" people and the difference between "population" and "citizenship," see Partha Chatterjee, *The Politics of the Governed: Reflections on Popular Politics in Most of the World* (New York: Columbia University Press, 2006); in addition, on citizenship and the identification of at-risk populations, see Austin Zeiderman, *Endangered City: The Politics of Security and Risk in Bogotá* (Durham, NC: Duke University Press, 2016).

29. On political contestation in El Alto, see Sian Lazar, *El Alto, Rebel City: Self and Citizenship in Andean Bolivia* (Durham, NC: Duke University Press, 2008); and for comparison with Plan 3000, see "Weaving the Rebellion: Plan 3000, Center of Resistance in Eastern Bolivia," *Socialism and Democracy Online*, April 10, 2011, http://sdonline.org/51/weaving -the-rebellion-plan-3000-center-of-resistance-in-eastern-bolivia/.

3. PAPELEO

1. To be born *hijo de transeunte* meant the child could not apply for Chilean citizenship until the age of fourteen (with parental consent) or eighteen (without parental consent),

leading to statelessness in cases where the parents' country of origin did not recognize the child as a citizen because of their citizenship laws. Moreover, even if not technically "stateless," children in this category residing in Chile were barred from accessing a whole range of rights that their counterparts with Chilean nationality could access, such as leaving and entering the country. The gravity of a child being born *hijo de transeunte* has gradually been recognized by the Chilean state following successful lobbying by the Asociación and other organizations, and steps are now being taken to address this issue, with the aim to eradicate this category entirely by 2024. At the time of my research, however, having a child born *hijo de transeunte* was a serious concern for some migrant parents. As of 2016, when the law changed to eliminate the category of *hijo de transeunte*, there were thought to be around twenty-five hundred children born in Chile categorized as such.

2. Deborah Reed-Danahay and Caroline Brettell, *Citizenship, Political Engagement, and Belonging: Immigrants in Europe and the United States* (New Brunswick, NJ: Rutgers University Press, 2008).

3. Bridget Anderson and Martin Ruhs, "Researching Illegality and Labour Migration," *Population, Space and Place* 16, no. 3 (2010): 175–79.

4. Bridget Anderson, *Us and Them? The Dangerous Politics of Immigration Control* (Oxford: Oxford University Press, 2013).

5. On the criminalization of the subject implied by *illegal*, see, for example, Cathy McIlwaine and Anastasia Bermúdez, "Ambivalent Citizenship and Extraterritorial Voting among Colombians in London and Madrid," *Global Networks* 15, no. 4 (2015): 495. For an excellent discussion of the "No One is Illegal" movement, see Peter Nyers, "No One Is Illegal: Between City and Nation," *Studies in Social Justice* 4, no. 2 (2011): 123–38.

6. Those who prefer *undocumented* include, for example, Nicholas De Genova, "Migrant 'Illegality' and Deportability in Everyday Life," *Annual Review of Anthropology* 31, no. 1 (2002): 419–47. Scholars who prefer *non-status* include Peter Nyers, "Community without Status: Non-Status Migrants and Cities of Refuge," in *Renegotiating Community: Interdisciplinary Perspectives, Global Contexts*, ed. Diana Brydon and William Coleman (Vancouver: University of British Columbia Press, 2008): 123–38.

7. On the ambiguity of *undocumented* because "undocumented" migrants may possess some documents, see, for example, Cathy McIlwaine, "Legal Latins: Creating Webs and Practices of Immigration Status among Latin American Migrants in London," *Journal of Ethnic and Migration Studies* 41, no. 3 (2015): 495. Regarding the authenticity of documents, see, for example, Anderson and Ruhs, "Researching Illegality and Labour Migration," 176.

8. Nyers, "Community without Status: Non-Status Migrants and Cities of Refuge," 126.

9. Khalid Koser, "Irregular Migration, State Security and Human Security: A Paper Prepared for the Policy Analysis and Research Programme of the Global Commission on International Migration" (Global Commission on International Migration, September 2005), 5, https://www.iom.int/jahia/webdav/site/myjahiasite/shared/shared/mainsite/policy_and _research/gcim/tp/TP5.pdf.

10. De Genova, "Migrant 'Illegality' and Deportability in Everyday Life."

11. For an excellent example of a study that does just this, see Joanna Dreby, *Everyday Illegal: When Policies Undermine Immigrant Families* (Berkeley: University of California Press, 2015).

12. De Genova, "Migrant 'Illegality' and Deportability in Everyday Life."

13. For some examples, see Richard Black et al., "Routes to Illegal Residence: A Case Study of Immigration Detainees in the United Kingdom," *Geoforum* 37, no. 4 (2006): 552–64; Alice Bloch, Nando Sigona, and Roger Zetter, "Migration Routes and Strategies of Young Undocumented Migrants in England: A Qualitative Perspective," *Ethnic and Racial Studies* 34, no. 8 (2011): 1286–1302; Luin Goldring and Patricia Landolt, *Producing and Negotiating Non-Citizenship: Precarious Legal Status in Canada*, 3rd ed. (Toronto: University of Toronto Press, 2013); Khalid Koser, "Dimensions and Dynamics of Irregular Migration," *Population, Space and Place* 16, no. 3 (2010): 181–93; and McIlwaine, "Legal Latins."

14. A tripartite model is premised on the idea of citizenship, noncitizenship, or belonging to a third category; see, for example, Cecilia Menjívar, "Liminal Legality: Salvadoran and Guatemalan Immigrants' Lives in the United States," *American Journal of Sociology* 111, no. 4 (2006): 99–1037. This represented a very important advancement from previous binary (citizen/noncitizen) models but can be expanded on further. See also chapter 1.

15. Goldring and Landolt, *Producing and Negotiating Non-Citizenship*, 16.

16. McIlwaine, "Legal Latins," 494.

17. McIlwaine, "Legal Latins"; and Goldring and Landolt, *Producing and Negotiating Non-Citizenship*.

18. Lorena Núñez Carrasco, "Living on the Margins: Illness and Healthcare among Peruvian Migrants in Chile" (PhD thesis, Leiden University, 2008), https://openaccess.leidenuniv.nl/handle/1887/13105.

19. Ministerio de Relaciones Exteriores de Chile, "Recomendaciones para ingresar a Chile," 2014, http://www.minrel.gob.cl/minrel/site/artic/20080619/pags/20080619154047.html.

20. Departamento de Extranjería y Migración, "Tipos de residencia temporaria," 2014, http://www.extranjeria.gob.cl/residencia-temporaria/tipos-de-residencia-temporaria/.

21. These contributions, along with other taxes, are automatically deducted from employees' salary before it reaches their bank accounts if they are dependent workers. Employees must be enrolled in the health and pension systems and be paid through the correct channels in order for this to happen.

22. Departamento de Extranjería y Migración, "Tipos de permanencia definitiva," 2014, http://www.extranjeria.gob.cl/permanencia-definitiva/permiso-de-permanencia-definitiva/tipos-de-permanencia-definitiva/.

23. On hierarchy in the creation of citizenship statuses, see Stephen Castles, "Nation and Empire: Hierarchies of Citizenship in the New Global Order," *International Politics* 42, no. 2 (2005): 203–24.

24. Internet Live Stats, "Internet Users by Country (2016)," http://www.internetlivestats.com/internet-users-by-country/.

25. The increase in smartphone use since I completed fieldwork may have an impact on internet accessibility, although this still does not resolve the issue of the convoluted presentation and language used on the DEM website. Very few of the participants in my research had smartphones at the time of fieldwork, but this appears to be changing; one participant with low literacy skills, for example, now contacts me using the WhatsApp audio message function.

26. James Ferguson and Akhil Gupta, "Spatializing States: Toward an Ethnography of Neoliberal Governmentality," *American Ethnologist* 29, no. 4 (2002): 984.

27. If Bolivians in Santiago apply for their passports through the Bolivian consulate, they are entry stamped at this time.

28. Alejandro Portes, "Introduction: Toward a Structural Analysis of Illegal (Undocumented) Immigration," *International Migration Review* 12, no. 4 (1978): 469–84; De Genova, "Migrant 'Illegality' and Deportability in Everyday Life"; Bridget Anderson, "Battles in Time: The Relation Between Global and Labour Mobilities," Oxford Centre on Migration, Policy and Society, 2007, https://www.compas.ox.ac.uk/fileadmin/files/Publications/working_papers/WP_2007/WP0755%20Bridget%20Anderson.pdf; and Alice Bloch and Milena Chimienti, "Irregular Migration in a Globalizing World," *Ethnic and Racial Studies* 34, no. 8 (2011): 1271–85.

29. The fine refers to the amount payable upon leaving the country for overstaying a tourist visa. It is set at the discretion of the border agent.

30. De Genova, "Migrant 'Illegality' and Deportability in Everyday Life."

31. Anderson and Ruhs, "Researching Illegality and Labour Migration," 177. See also Bloch and Chimienti, "Irregular Migration in a Globalizing World."

32. See, for example, James Holston, *Insurgent Citizenship: Disjunctions of Democracy and Modernity in Brazil* (Princeton, NJ: Princeton University Press, 2008); Sian Lazar, *El Alto, Rebel City: Self and Citizenship in Andean Bolivia* (Durham, NC: Duke University Press, 2008); Aihwa Ong, "Cultural Citizenship as Subject-Making," *Current Anthropology* 37, no. 5 (1996): 737–62; and Reed-Danahay and Brettell, *Citizenship, Political Engagement, and Belonging.*

33. McIlwaine, "Legal Latins"; and Goldring and Landolt, *Producing and Negotiating Non-Citizenship.*

34. Franck Duvell and Bill Jordan, *Irregular Migration: The Dilemmas of Transnational Mobility* (Cheltenham, UK: Edward Elgar, 2003).

35. It is important to note that I did not address irregular situations resulting from clandestine entry into Chile. In Chile, clandestine entry *does* occur, but it largely involves people of other nationalities subject to even more restrictive entry and visa requirements—in particular Colombians and to an extent Peruvians—who may enter the country at unauthorized points, mainly in the Atacama Desert. As is inevitably the case with clandestine practices, it is difficult to find reliable statistics on the number of people entering Chile in this manner. From January to May 2014, however, there were ninety-one arrests of people trying to enter Chile on foot through the Atacama Desert. Of these, fifty-four were Colombians and thirty were Peruvians (see Soy Arica, "Colombianos lideran lista de extranjeros que ingresan ilegalmente a Chile," December 5, 2014, http://www.soychile.cl/Arica/Sociedad/2014/05/12/248540/Colombianos-lideran-la-lista-de-extranjeros-que-ingresan-ilegalmente-a-Chile-a-traves-de-Arica.aspx). This corresponds with my experience with the Associacón in Arica, which occurred approximately during this period. During my time there, lawyers and social workers worked on several cases—mainly involving Colombians but also some Peruvians and an Ecuadorian—of people who had entered the country on foot through the desert following the old railway tracks connecting Peru and Chile. This is extremely dangerous due to potential dehydration, adverse weather conditions, and the still-present land mines. There *are* some cases of Bolivians entering clandestinely. In general, however, those entering in such a way are likely to be involved in illegal activities rather than entering to work. The limited evidence available suggests that they tend to be women

being used as drug mules or being trafficked for sexual exploitation. It was outside the scope of the present project to investigate this particular type of irregularity.

36. Bloch and Chimienti, "Irregular Migration in a Globalizing World," 1278.

37. McIlwaine, "Legal Latins," 506.

38. For more extensive discussion of indigenous perspectives on the "triple frontera" of Chile, Bolivia, and Peru, see, for example, Isabel Berganza Setién and Mauricio Cerna Rivera, *Dinámicas Migratorias en la Frontera Perú-Chile. Arica, Tacna e Iquique* (Lima: Universidad Antonio Ruiz de Montoya, 2011), http://centroderecursos.alboan.org/ebooks /0000/0783/11_BER_DIN.pdf.

39. Carol Hardy-Fanta, *Latina Politics, Latino Politics: Gender, Culture, and Political Participation in Boston* (Philadelphia, PA: Temple University Press, 1993); Michael Jones-Correa, "Different Paths: Gender, Immigration and Political Participation," *International Migration Review* 32, no. 2 (1998): 326–49; Cathy McIlwaine and Anastasia Bermúdez, "The Gendering of Political and Civic Participation among Colombian Migrants in London," *Environment and Planning A* 43, no. 7 (2011): 1499–1513; and Lisa Montoya, Carol Hardy-Fanta, and Sonia Garcia, "Latina Politics: Gender, Participation, and Leadership," *PS: Political Science and Politics* 33, no. 3 (September 2000): 555–61.

40. Cf. De Genova, "Migrant 'Illegality' and Deportability in Everyday Life," 422.

41. Austin Zeiderman, *Endangered City: The Politics of Security and Risk in Bogotá* (Durham, NC: Duke University Press, 2016), 145.

42. For an interesting point of comparison, see Clara Han, *Life in Debt: Times of Care and Violence in Neoliberal Chile* (Berkeley: University of California Press, 2012), 55–56. She discusses how women in the poor urban neighborhood of La Pincoya, Santiago, would have to present themselves to social workers in a particular way in order to be considered as living in sufficient poverty to qualify for municipal subsidies.

43. Elaine Ho, "Constituting Citizenship through the Emotions: Singaporean Transmigrants in London," *Annals of the Association of American Geographers* 99, no. 4 (September 17, 2009): 789.

4. ¿EL SUEÑO CHILENO?

1. For discussion of the concept of the migrant division of labor, see, for example, Jane Wills et al., "London's Migrant Division of Labour," *European Urban and Regional Studies* 16, no. 3 (2009): 43–67. On global care chains, see Arlie Hochschild, "Global Care Chains and Emotional Surplus Value," in *On the Edge: Globalization and the New Millennium*, ed. Anthony Giddens and Will Hutton (London: SAGE, 2000), 130–46; and Rhacel Salazar Parreñas, "Migrant Filipina Domestic Workers and the International Division of Reproductive Labor," *Gender & Society* 14, no. 4 (2000): 560–80.

2. See, for example Yvonne Riaño, "Drawing New Boundaries of Participation: Experiences and Strategies of Economic Citizenship among Skilled Migrant Women in Switzerland," *Environment and Planning A* 43, no. 7 (2011): 1530–46.

3. *Chicha de maní* is a traditional Bolivian drink made of peanuts, wheat germ, and quinoa, which is extremely labor-intensive to prepare.

4. Victor Oviedor Treiber, *Rural Poverty, Vulnerability and Food Insecurity: The Case of Bolivia* (Potsdam: Universitätsverlag Potsdam, 2012); Rodrigo Valenzuela Fernández,

"Inequidad, ciudadanía y pueblos indígenas en Bolivia," CELADE/CEPAL, 2004, http://repositorio.cepal.org/bitstream/handle/11362/6070/S043147_es.pdf?sequence=1.

5. Oviedor Treiber, *Rural Poverty, Vulnerability and Food Insecurity.*

6. See, for example, Gillian Creese and Brandy Wiebe, "'Survival Employment': Gender and Deskilling among African Immigrants in Canada," *International Migration* 50, no. 5 (2012): 404–32; Linda McDowell, "Thinking through Work: Complex Inequalities, Constructions of Difference and Trans-National Migrants," *Progress in Human Geography* 32, no. 4 (2008): 491–507; Ilana Redstone Akresh, "Occupational Mobility among Legal Immigrants to the United States," *International Migration Review* 40, no. 4 (2006): 854–84; and Riaño, "Drawing New Boundaries of Participation."

7. A point of comparison regarding debt precipitating migration is offered in Kavita Datta, "Money Matters: Exploring Financial Exclusion among Low-Paid Migrant Workers in London," Queen Mary University of London, 2007, http://citeseerx.ist.psu.edu/viewdoc/download?doi=10.1.1.462.3580&rep=rep1&type=pdf, 24.

8. Cf. Richard Black, "Breaking the Convention: Researching the 'Illegal' Migration of Refugees to Europe," *Antipode* 35, no. 1 (2003): 34–54; Rutvica Andrijasevic, *Migration, Agency and Citizenship in Sex Trafficking* (London: Palgrave Macmillan, 2010).

9. Kavita Datta et al., "The New Development Finance or Exploiting Migrant Labour? Remittance Sending among Low-Paid Migrant Workers in London," *International Development Planning Review* 29, no. 1 (2007): 47.

10. See Hein de Haas, "Remittances, Migration and Social Development: A Conceptual Review of the Literature" (Social Policy and Development Programme Paper, UNRISD, 2007), http://www.unrisd.org/80256B3C005BCCF9/%28httpAuxPages%29/8B7D005E37FFC77EC12573A600439846/$file/deHaaspaper.pdf.

11. For a discussion of the alleviation of "transient" compared with long-term "structural" poverty through remittance sending, see Devesh Kapur, "Remittances: The New Development Mantra?" (G-24 Discussion Paper Series, United Nations, 2003), http://www.cities-localgovernments.org/committees/fccd/Upload/library/gdsmdpbg2420045_en_en.pdf. For a discussion of uneven development in communities as a consequence of remittance sending, see Roger Ballard, "Remittances and Economic Development in India and Pakistan," in *Remittances: Development Impact and Future Prospects*, ed. Samuel Munzele Maimbo and Dilip Ratha (Washington, DC: World Bank Publications, 2005), 103–18.

12. See, for example, Datta et al., "The New Development Finance or Exploiting Migrant Labour?"

13. For classic texts on family livelihoods, remittances, and the new economics of labor migration approach that reflect this perspective, see Oded Stark and Edward Taylor, "Relative Deprivation and International Migration," *Demography* 26, no. 1 (1989): 1–14; and Edward Taylor, "The New Economics of Labour Migration and the Role of Remittances in the Migration Process," *International Migration* 37, no. 1 (1999): 63–88.

14. Datta et al., "The New Development Finance or Exploiting Migrant Labour?"

15. "Building up" is a typical incremental building strategy in Bolivia and Latin America more widely. It is common to see houses that are very much lived in but have metal struts extending above the top story awaiting further construction.

16. Cathy McIlwaine, "Migrant Machismos: Exploring Gender Ideologies and Practices among Latin American Migrants in London from a Multi-Scalar Perspective," *Gender, Place*

& *Culture* 17, no. 3 (2010): 281–300; Raffaella Sarti and Francesca Scrinzi, "Introduction to the Special Issue: Men in a Woman's Job, Male Domestic Workers, International Migration and the Globalization of Care," *Men and Masculinities* 13, no. 1 (2010): 4–15.

17. Elizabeth Hopper and José Hidalgo, "Invisible Chains: Psychological Coercion of Human Trafficking Victims," *Intercultural Human Rights Law Review* 1 (2006): 185–209.

18. See Hopper and Hidalgo, "Invisible Chains."

19. Threats of reporting workers for immigration law violations are common in situations of trafficking and exploitation. See, for example, Klara Skrivankova, "Between Decent Work and Forced Labour: Examining the Continuum of Exploitation" (JF Programme Paper: Forced Labour, Joseph Rowntree Foundation, 2010), http://www.prostitutionresearch.info/pdfs_all/trafficking%20all/forced-labour-exploitation-full.pdf.

20. Skrivankova, "Between Decent Work and Forced Labour"; see also Hannah Lewis et al., "Hyper-Precarious Lives: Migrants, Work and Forced Labour in the Global North," *Progress in Human Geography*, September 17 (2014): 137–48; Megan Ryburn, "Living the Chilean Dream? Bolivian Migrants' Incorporation in the Space of Economic Citizenship," *Geoforum* 76 (2016): 48–58; and Kendra Strauss, "Coerced, Forced and Unfree Labour: Geographies of Exploitation in Contemporary Labour Markets," *Geography Compass* 6, no. 3 (2012): 137–48. The "continuum of labor exploitation" has been developed in order to move beyond the binary of forced labor/decent work to consider the many blurred, gray areas in between. It offers a typology of forms of labor exploitation ranging from the most severe, in which migrants are the subjects of forced labor and may have been trafficked, through less severe cases, in which some labor rights have been infringed. It is useful because it provides a specific tool with which to identify (and potentially prosecute) cases of labor exploitation.

21. On the US case, see, for example Seth Holmes, *Fresh Fruit, Broken Bodies: Migrant Farmworkers in the United States* (Berkeley: University of California Press, 2013). For a point of comparison in a Mexican context, see Christian Zloniski, "Economic Globalization and Changing Capital-Labor Relations in Baja California's Fresh-Produce Industry," in *The Anthropology of Labor Unions*, ed. E. Paul Durrenberger and Karaleah Reichart (Boulder: University Press of Colorado, 2010), 157–88.

22. Nicolás Rojas Pedemonte and Sebastián Bueno Moya, "Redes de inclusión: Estudio estadístico de las condiciones socio-laborales de migrantes en Arica," in *Migración y trabajo: estudio y propuestas para la inclusión sociolaboral de migrantes en Arica*, ed. José Tomás Vicuña Undurraga SJ and Nicolás Rojas Pedemonte (Santiago, Chile: Ciudadano Global and Organización Internacional para las Migraciones, 2014), http://creas.uahurtado.cl/2014/11/libro-migracion-y-trabajo-es-editado.html.

23. Rojas Pedemonte and Bueno Moya, "Redes de inclusión," 86 (author's translation).

24. Bridget Anderson, "Migration, Immigration Controls and the Fashioning of Precarious Workers," *Work, Employment & Society* 24, no. 2 (2010): 300–317.

25. Rojas Pedemonte and Bueno Moya, "Redes de inclusión."

26. For some recent examples, see Elaine Acosta, *Ciudados en crisis: Mujeres migrantes hacia España y Chile* (Santiago, Chile: Universidad Alberto Hurtado, 2015); Irma Arriagada and Marcela Moreno, "La constitución de cadenas globales de ciudado y las condiciones laborales de las trabajadoras peruanas en Chile," in *Mujeres inmigrantes en Chile: ¿Mano de obra o trabajadoras con derechos?*, ed. Carolina Stefoni, Kindle ed. (Santiago, Chile: Universidad Alberto Hurtado, 2013); and Carolina Stefoni and Rosario Fernández, "Mujeres

migrantes en el trabajo dómestico: Entre el servilismo y los derechos," in *Mujeres inmigrantes en Chile: ¿Mano de obra o trabajadoras con derechos?*, ed. Carolina Stefoni, Kindle ed. (Santiago, Chile: Universidad Alberto Hurtado, 2013).

There is also a burgeoning field addressing domestic work in Latin America more widely. As indicated in chapter 2, key works include Lesley Gill, *Precarious Dependencies: Gender, Class, and Domestic Service in Bolivia* (New York: Columbia University Press, 1994); Séverine Durin, María Eugenia de la O, and Santiago Bastos, eds., *Trabajadoras en la sombra: Dimensiones del servicio doméstico latinoamericano* (Monterrey, Mexico: CIESAS, 2014); and Erynn Masi de Casanova, "Embodied Inequality."

27. For evidence of the feminization of migration to Chile, see Rojas Pedemonte and Silva Dittborn, "La migración en Chile: Breve reporte y caracterización," Observatorio Iberoamericano sobre Movilidad Humana, Migraciones y Desarrollo, 2016. The Santiago-centric focus of Chilean migration research is discussed by Menara Lube-Guizardi and Alejandro Garcés, "Circuitos migrantes: Itinerarios y formación de redes migratorias entre Perú, Bolivia, Chile y Argentina en el norte grande chileno," *Papeles de Población* 19, no. 78 (2013): 65–110.

28. The exception was one participant who worked part-time as a cleaner in the school her children attended.

29. Cf. Arriagada and Moreno, "La constitución de cadenas globales de ciudado"; and Pierrette Hondagneu-Sotelo, *Doméstica: Immigrant Workers Cleaning and Caring in the Shadows of Affluence*, 2nd ed. (Berkeley: University of California Press, 2007).

30. Cf. Riaño, "Drawing New Boundaries of Participation."

31. Stefoni and Fernández, "Mujeres migrantes en el trabajo dómestico."

32. Biblioteca del Congreso Nacional de Chile, "Trajadoras y trabajadores de casa particiular (nueva ley)," BCN, 2015, http://www.bcn.cl/leyfacil/recurso/trabajadoras-y-trabajadores-de-casa-particular-(nueva-ley).

33. Aihwa Ong, *Spirits of Resistance and Capitalist Discipline*, 2nd ed. (New York: State University of New York Press, 2010).

34. Pun Ngai, *Made in China: Women Factory Workers in a Global Workplace* (Durham, NC: Duke University Press, 2005); and Aysen Ustubici, *Export-Processing Zones and Gendering the Resistance: "Women's Strike" in Antalya Free Zone in Turkey* (London: London School of Economics, Gender Institute, 2009).

35. *Señora* is the term commonly used by women working as *nanas* to refer to their employers. Note the gender implications regarding who is in charge of domestic arrangements in the home. On this point see Arriagada and Moreno, "La constitución de cadenas globales de ciudado."

36. Negotiations and emotions about wearing uniforms are also discussed by Masi de Casanova, "Embodied Inequalities," in which she presents an incisive examination of the ways in which women domestic workers in Ecuador experience the devaluation of their bodies in a material and symbolic sense and engage in practices to resist this.

37. For an interesting comparison, see Bridget Anderson, "Battles in Time: The Relation Between Global and Labour Mobilities," Oxford Centre on Migration, Policy and Society, 2007, https://www.compas.ox.ac.uk/fileadmin/files/Publications/working_papers/WP_2007/WP0755%20Bridget%20Anderson.pdf.

38. Much has been written about the ambiguity of civil society organizations involved in "development" in general. For an insightful overview of key debates, in addition to more

specific discussion of diasporic migrant civil society and development, see Cathy McIl-waine, "From Local to Global to Transnational Civil Society: Re-Framing Development Perspectives on the Non-State Sector," *Geography Compass*, no. 6 (2007): 1252–81. On diasporic civil society, see also Claire Mercer, Ben Page, and Martin Evans, *Development and the African Diaspora: Place and the Politics of Home* (London: Zed Books, 2008); and Giles Mohan and A. B. Zack Williams, "Globalisation from Below: Conceptualising the Role of the African Diasporas in Africa's Development," *Review of African Political Economy* 29, no. 92 (2002): 211–36.

39. Alice Kessler-Harris, "In Pursuit of Economic Citizenship," *Social Politics: International Studies in Gender, State and Society* 10, no. 2 (2003): 157–75; and Riaño, "Drawing New Boundaries of Participation."

5. *SOLIDARIDAD*

1. Thomas Humphrey Marshall, *Citizenship and Social Class, and Other Essays* (Cambridge, UK: Cambridge University Press, 1950). The following scholars, for example, discuss the centrality of social rights to contemporary understanding of citizenship: Fred Twine, *Citizenship and Social Rights: The Interdependence of Self and Society* (London: SAGE, 1994); and Peter Dwyer, *Understanding Social Citizenship: Themes and Perspectives for Policy and Practice* (Bristol, UK: Policy Press, 2010).

2. Dwyer, *Understanding Social Citizenship*; Ruth Lister, *Citizenship: Feminist Perspectives*, 2nd ed. (New York: New York University Press, 2003).

3. Lister, *Citizenship*; see also Dwyer, *Understanding Social Citizenship*; and Len Doyal and Ian Gough, *A Theory of Human Need* (London: Palgrave Macmillan, 1991).

4. Ian Gough, "What Are Human Needs?," in *Social Policy and Social Justice: The IPPR Reader*, ed. Jane Franklin (Oxford: Polity Press, 1998), 53.

5. Doyal and Gough, *A Theory of Human Need*, 157–58.

6. Lister, *Citizenship*.

7. Doyal and Gough's intermediate needs include "economic security" and a "non-hazardous work environment." This is a reflection of the tendency, discussed in the introduction, from T. H. Marshall onward to conflate the social and economic under social citizenship. As argued previously, however, it was found in this research and by others working from a gender or intersectional perspective that varied inclusions and exclusions with respect to the economic sphere were so significant in migrants' lives and consequent ability to participate in other spheres that they warrant separate consideration. Nonetheless, that is not to deny economic citizenship's clear overlap with social citizenship,—and the idea of interlocking transnational spaces of citizenship developed in this book aims to acknowledge this.

8. For a few examples, see Michael Aguilera and Douglas Massey, "Social Capital and the Wages of Mexican Migrants: New Hypotheses and Tests," *Social Forces* 82, no. 2 (2003): 671–701; Jacqueline Maria Hagan, "Social Networks, Gender, and Immigrant Incorporation: Resources and Constraints," *American Sociological Review* 63, no. 1 (1998): 55–67; and Louise Ryan et al., "Social Networks, Social Support and Social Capital: The Experiences of Recent Polish Migrants in London," *Sociology* 42, no. 4 (2008): 672–90.

9. See, for example, Johanna Avato, Johannes Koettl, and Rachel Sabates-Wheeler, "Social Security Regimes, Global Estimates, and Good Practices: The Status of Social Pro-

tection for International Migrants," *World Development* 38, no. 4 (2010): 455–66; and Tanja Bastia, ed., *Migration and Inequality* (London: Routledge, 2015).

10. Sylvia Chant and Nikki Craske, *Gender in Latin America* (New Brunswick, NJ: Rutgers University Press, 2003); and Cathy McIlwaine, "Migrant Machismos: Exploring Gender Ideologies and Practices among Latin American Migrants in London from a Multi-Scalar Perspective," *Gender, Place & Culture* 17, no. 3 (2010): 281–300.

11. It has recently been announced that this will change so that migrants can apply as soon as they receive permanent residency.

12. Ministerio de Vivienda y Urbanismo, "Ley No. 18.101, 1982," *BNC*, 2003, http://www.leychile.cl/Navegar?idNorma=29526.

13. Land categorization as "urban" or "rural" is periodically revised in Chile, which has consequences for tenure, municipal service provision, and valuation.

14. Techo-Chile, "Monitor de Campamentos | CIS," 2015, http://chile.techo.org/cis/monitor/.

15. Techo-Chile, "TECHO realiza catastro de inmigrantes en campamento," TECHO | UN TECHO PARA MI PAÍS, 2013, http://www.techo.org/paises/chile/informate/techo-realiza-catastro-de-inmigrantes-en-campamento/.

16. For a brief introduction to the history of *campamentos* in Chile, see Ministerio de Vivienda y Urbanismo, "Mapa social de campamentos," VII Política Habitacional y Planificación, 2013, http://www.ministeriodesarrollosocial.gob.cl/btca/txtcompleto/mapasocial-campamentos.pdf. For a useful overview of informal settlements in the global South more broadly, and of changing policy approaches to such settlements, see Sylvia Chant and Cathy McIlwaine, *Geographies of Development in the 21st Century: An Introduction to the Global South* (Cheltenham, UK: Edward Elgar, 2009), 115–33.

17. Chant and McIlwaine, *Geographies of Development*.

18. Fernando Jiménez Cavieres, *Chilean Housing Policy: A Case of Social and Spatial Exclusion* (Münster, Germany: LIT Verlag, 2008); and Ministerio de Vivienda y Urbanismo, "Mapa social de campamentos."

19. Darío Oyarzún, "Entrevista a Darío Oyarzún: El MINVU no sólo debe poner a disposición el suelo que tiene, sino que comprar suelo," *Revista Planeo*, no. 8 (2012), http://revistaplaneo.cl/2012/11/07/entrevista-dario-oyarzun-el-minvu-no-solo-debe-poner-a-disposicion-el-suelo-que-tiene-sino-que-comprar-suelo/; Techo-Chile, "Modelo de intervención," TECHO | UN TECHO PARA MI PAÍS, 2015, http://www.techo.org/paises/chile/techo/modelo-de-intervencion/.

20. James Holston, *Insurgent Citizenship: Disjunctions of Democracy and Modernity in Brazil* (Princeton, NJ: Princeton University Press, 2008), 204.

21. Baltica Cabieses and Helena Tunstall, "Socioeconomic Vulnerability and Access to Healthcare among Migrants in Chile," in *Migration, Health and Inequality*, ed. Felicity Thomas and Jasmine Gideon (London: Zed Books, 2013), 80.

22. Guillermo Paraje and Felipe Vásquez, "Health Equity in an Unequal Country: The Use of Medical Services in Chile," *International Journal for Equity in Health* 11 (2012), doi:10.1186/1475-9276-11-81.

23. CASEN, "Salud: Síntesis de resultados," Observatorio del Ministerio de Desarrollo Social, 2013, http://observatorio.ministeriodesarrollosocial.gob.cl/documentos/Casen2013_Salud.pdf.

24. Ministerio de Desarrollo Social, "Informe de política social 2012," 2012, http://www.ministeriodesarrollosocial.gob.cl/ipos-2012/media/ipos_2012_pp_94-125.pdf.

25. Ministerio de Desarrollo Social, "Informe de política social 2012"; and Cabieses and Tunstall, "Socioeconomic Vulnerability and Access to Healthcare."

26. Ministerio de Salud, "ORD. A 14 No. 3229," 2008, http://www.extranjeria.gob.cl/files app/Of_%203229_MINSAL.pdf.

27. Emmanuel Scheppers et al., "Potential Barriers to the Use of Health Services among Ethnic Minorities: A Review," *Family Practice* 23, no. 3 (2006): 325–48.

28. Jasmine Gideon, *Gender, Globalization, and Health in a Latin American Context* (London: Palgrave Macmillan, 2014).

29. Gideon, *Gender, Globalization, and Health*; Cabieses and Tunstall, "Socioeconomic Vulnerability and Access to Healthcare"; and Lorena Núñez Carrasco, "Necesidades de las mujeres migrantes y la oferta de atención en salud reproductiva. Discrepancias y distancias de una relación no resuelta," in *Mujeres inmigrantes en Chile: ¿Mano de obra o trabajadoras con derechos?*, ed. Carolina Stefoni (Santiago, Chile: Universidad Alberto Hurtado, 2013).

30. CASEN, "Salud: Síntesis de resultados."

31. Cabieses and Tunstall, "Socioeconomic Vulnerability and Access to Healthcare."

32. Cabieses and Tunstall, "Socioeconomic Vulnerability and Access to Healthcare"; and Núñez Carrasco, "Living on the Margins."

33. This corresponds with findings in other research. See, for example, Demoscópica, "Diagnóstico y factibilidad global para la implementación de políticas locales de salud para inmigrantes en la Zona Norte de la Región Metropolitana," Demoscópica/OIM, 2009, http://web.minsal.cl/portal/url/item/71841d2e91f518a1e04001011f015cc6.pdf; Yoice Díaz Donoso et al., "Situación de salud en mujeres inmigrantes de la macro-región andina en el sistema público de salud de la ciudad de Arica" (undergraduate thesis, Universidad de Tarapacá, 2013); Gideon, *Gender, Globalization, and Health*; Cabieses and Tunstall, "Socioeconomic Vulnerability and Access to Healthcare"; and Núñez Carrasco, "Living on the Margins."

34. World Bank, "Mortality Rate, Infant (per 1,000 Live Births)," *World Bank Databank*, 2016, http://data.worldbank.org/indicator/SP.DYN.IMRT.IN.

35. World Bank, "Maternal Mortality Ratio (Modeled Estimate, per 100,000 Live Births)," *World Bank Databank*, 2016, http://data.worldbank.org/indicator/SH.STA.MMRT.

36. Médicos del Mundo, "Proyecto | WAWACHAÑA—Partos en el techo del mundo," 2013, http://www.medicosdelmundo.es/partoseneltechodelmundo/proyecto; and Barbara Bradby and Jo Murphy-Lawless, *ILCA—Reducing Maternal Mortality and Morbidity in Bolivia* (La Paz, Bolivia: Instituto de Lengua y Cultura Aymara, 2002); and Médicos del Mundo, "Proyecto | WAWACHAÑA"; and Bradby and Murphy-Lawless, *ILCA*.

37. Médicos del Mundo, "Proyecto | WAWACHAÑA"; and Bradby and Murphy-Lawless, *ILCA*.

38. Díaz Donoso et al., "Situación de salud en mujeres inmigrantes."

39. See Lorena Binfa et al., "Assessment of the Implementation of the Model of Integrated and Humanized Midwifery Health Services in Chile," *Midwifery* 35 (2016): 53–61. This study analyzes the experiences and perceptions of 1,882 women who gave birth in the public health system in Santiago, Chile. It concludes that there is a high degree of obstetric intervention during births, midwifery practice does not align with World Health Organiza-

tion guidelines, and some of the women in the study felt "mistreated" during labor and birth.

40. Núñez Carrasco, "Living on the Margins."

41. Ministerio de Salud, "ORD. A 14 No. 3229."

42. Ironically, until 2017 abortion was illegal in Chile in all circumstances, including when the woman's health was in danger, when the fetus was unviable, or when pregnancy was a consequence of rape. Legislation has now been passed to allow abortion in these cases.

43. In its initial acute phase, which lasts from a few weeks to a month or more, if symptoms of Chagas' disease present they are similar to flu or other common illnesses. Thus, the disease often goes undetected at the acute phase, which is the phase at which it is curable. Once in the chronic phase, the infection may remain dormant. In around 30 percent of cases, however, people develop cardiac and intestinal complications. Cardiac complications can result in sudden death from heart attack.

44. Verónica Zapana, "Enfermedad de Chagas afecta a 33 de cada 100 bolivianos," *Página Siete* (La Paz), April 15, 2016, http://web.paginasiete.bo/sociedad/2016/4/15/enferme-dad-chagas-afecta-cada-bolivianos-93286.html.

45. Médecins Sans Frontières, "Bolivia's Bug Killers: Preventing the Spread of Chagas," February 18, 2004, http://www.msf.org/en/article/bolivias-bug-killers-preventing-spread-chagas.

46. Ana María Cevallos and Roberto Hernández, "Chagas Disease: Pregnancy and Congenital Transmission," *BioMed Research International* 2014 (2014), doi:10.1155/2014/401864.

47. Cevallos and Hernández, "Chagas Disease."

48. I recognize that it is common in many countries' health-care systems for the mother to be discharged from the hospital before the baby in such cases. This does not, however, lessen the impact that such a practice may have on some women, such as Rosa.

49. CASEN, "Inmigrantes: Principales resultados (versión extendida)," Observatorio del Ministerio de Desarrollo Social, 2015, http://observatorio.ministeriodesarrollosocial .gob.cl/casen-multidimensional/casen/docs/CASEN_2015_INMIGRANTES_21122016 _EXTENDIDA_publicada.pdf. These are the latest available CASEN data on the level of migrant education in Chile on average, but they do not show a breakdown of years of schooling by nationality.

50. Carolina Stefoni, "Perfíl Migratorio de Chile," Organización Internacional de Migra-ciones, 2011, http://priem.cl/wp-content/uploads/2015/04/Stefoni_Perfil-Migratorio-de -Chile.pdf. This remains the most up-to-date measure of years of schooling by nationality.

51. Observatorio Plurinacional de la Calidad Educativa and UNICEF, "Estudio del Sub-sistema de Educación Regular: Resúmen," UNICEF, 2011, http://www.unicef.org/bolivia /Microsoft_Word_-_RESUMEN_ESTUDIO_SUBSISTEMA_DE_EDUCACION_REGU LAR.pdf.

52. UNESCO, "Education for All 2000–2015: Achievements and Challenges," Education for All Global Monitoring Report 2015, 2015, http://unesdoc.unesco.org/images/0023/002322 /232205e.pdf.

53. Ministerio de Educación, "La Educación en Bolivia: Indicadores, cifras, y resulta-dos," 2004, 49, http://www.minedu.gob.bo/micrositios/biblioteca/disco-1/informacion_ins titucional/memorias_educacion/94.pdf.

54. Luca Bicocchi and Michele LeVoy, *Undocumented Children in Europe: Invisible Victims of Immigration Restrictions* (Brussels, Belgium: PICUM, 2008), http://picum.org/picum.org/uploads/publication/Undocumented%20Children%20in%20Europe%20EN.pdf.

55. Marcelo Suárez-Orozco et al., "Migrations and Schooling," *Annual Review of Anthropology* 40, no. 1 (2011): 311–28.

56. Lesley Bartlett and Ameena Ghaffar-Kucher, *Refugees, Immigrants, and Education in the Global South: Lives in Motion* (London: Routledge, 2013), 2.

57. Iskra Pavez Soto, "Inmigración y racismo: Experiencias de la niñez peruana en Santiago de Chile," *Si Somos Americanos* 12, no. 1 (2012): 87. See also María Emilia Tijoux, "Las escuelas de la inmigración en la ciudad de Santiago: Elementos para una educación contra el racismo," *Polis* 12, no. 35 (2013): 75–99.

58. UNICEF, "Los prejuicios en niños, niñas y adoloscentes: Survey 'La voz de los niños sobre convivencia escolar y prejuicios,'" 2004, http://www.unicef.cl/voz/docs/PPT%20prejuicios%20final.pps.

59. Cf. Pavez Soto, "Inmigración y racismo."

60. See, for example, Sara Joiko and Alba Vásquez, "Acceso y elección escolar de familias migrantes en Chile: 'No tuve problemas porque la escuela es abierta, porque acepta muchas nacionalidades'," *Calidad En Educación* 45 (2016): 132–73; and Jair Marín Alaniz, "Ayni: Por una infancia sin fronteras. Arteterapia con hijos de migrantes en el norte de Chile," *Arteterapia. Papeles de arteterapia y educación artística para la inclusión social* 9 (2014): 61–72.

61. Joiko and Vásquez, "Acceso y elección escolar de familias migrantes," 147 (author's translation).

62. Joiko and Vásquez, "Acceso y elección escolar de familias migrantes."

63. Pavez Soto, "Inmigración y racismo"; and Joiko and Vásquez, "Acceso y elección escolar de familias migrantes."

64. Pavez Soto, "Inmigración y racismo," 85.

65. Joiko and Vásquez, "Acceso y elección escolar de familias migrantes."

66. Gioconda Herrera, "Rethinking the Family through Migration: Gender Ideologies and Practices of Care in Ecuador," in *Cross-Border Migration among Latin Americans: European Perspectives and Beyond*, ed. Cathy McIlwaine (London: Palgrave Macmillan, 2011), 53–70.

67. For a critical review and summary, see Nicola Yeates, "Global Care Chains: A State-of-the-Art Review and Future Directions in Care Transnationalization Research," *Global Networks* 12, no. 2 (2012): 135–54.

68. Cathy McIlwaine, "Legal Latins: Creating Webs and Practices of Immigration Status among Latin American Migrants in London," *Journal of Ethnic and Migration Studies* 41, no. 3 (2015): 493–511.

69. Findings in other contexts have been similar. See, for example, Lan Anh Hoang and Brenda Yeoh, "Sustaining Families across Transnational Spaces: Vietnamese Migrant Parents and their Left-Behind Children," *Asian Studies Review* 36, no. 3 (2012): 307–25; Pierrette Hondagneu-Sotelo and Ernestine Avila, "'I'M HERE, BUT I'M THERE': The Meanings of Latina Transnational Motherhood," *Gender & Society* 11, no. 5 (1997): 548–71; Rhacel Salazar Parreñas, "Mothering from a Distance: Emotions, Gender, and Intergenerational Relations in Filipino Transnational Families," *Feminist Studies* 27, no. 2 (2001): 361–90.

70. Rhacel Salazar Parreñas, *Children of Global Migration: Transnational Families and Gendered Woes* (Stanford, CA: Stanford University Press, 2005).

71. See, for example, Joanna Dreby, "Children and Power in Mexican Transnational Families," *Journal of Marriage and Family* 69, no. 4 (2007): 1050–64; Hoang and Yeoh, "Sustaining Families across Transnational Spaces"; Parreñas, *Children of Global Migration*; and Peggy Levitt, *The Transnational Villagers* (Berkeley: University of California Press, 2001).

72. Cf. Hondagneu-Sotelo and Avila, "'I'M HERE, BUT I'M THERE'"; Mirca Madianou and Daniel Miller, "Mobile Phone Parenting: Reconfiguring Relationships between Filipina Migrant Mothers and their Left-behind Children," *New Media & Society* 13, no. 3 (2011): 457–70; and Parreñas, "Mothering from a Distance."

73. Dreby, "Children and Power in Mexican Transnational Families"; and Levitt, *The Transnational Villagers*.

74. Moreover, the use of *despierta* to describe young women seems demonstrative of a repressive attitude toward women's sexuality.

75. On the effects of time on social network development for migrants, see Ryan et al., "Social Networks, Social Support and Social Capital."

76. The importance of the relationship among employment, accommodation, and "instrumental," or "weak tie," networks, has been extensively analyzed in other migration contexts. For examples, see Ryan et al., "Social Networks, Social Support and Social Capital"; Aguilera and Massey, "Social Capital and the Wages of Mexican Migrants"; and Hagan, "Social Networks, Gender, and Immigrant Incorporation." It is also the subject of some research in Chile. See Carolina Stefoni and Rosario Fernández, "Mujeres migrantes en el trabajo dómestico: Entre el servilismo y los derechos," in *Mujeres inmigrantes en Chile: ¿Mano de obra o trabajadoras con derechos?*, ed. Carolina Stefoni, Kindle ed. (Santiago, Chile: Universidad Alberto Hurtado, 2013).

77. Ryan et al., "Social Networks, Social Support and Social Capital."

78. It seems this is not uncommon. See, for example, Ryan et al., "Social Networks, Social Support and Social Capital."

79. Ryan et al., "Social Networks, Social Support and Social Capital."

6. "¿DE DÓNDE SOMOS?" "¡DE BOLIVIA!"

1. For further discussion of this point, see Niva Yuval-Davis and Prina Werbner, eds., *Women, Citizenship and Difference* (London: Zed Books, 1999).

2. Marco Martiniello, "Political Participation, Mobilisation, and Representation of Immigrants and Their Offspring in Europe" (Willy Brandt Series of Working Papers on International Migration and Ethnic Relations, 2005), http://muep.mah.se/bitstream/handle/2043/1495/WB_1-05.pdf?sequence=1&isAllowed=y. See also Eva Østergaard-Nielsen, "The Politics of Migrants' Transnational Political Practices," *International Migration Review* 37, no. 3 (2003): 760–86.

3. Examples of work on extraterritorial voting include Cathy McIlwaine and Anastasia Bermudez, "Ambivalent Citizenship and Extraterritorial Voting among Colombians in London and Madrid," *Global Networks* 15, no. 4 (2015): 305–482.; Jean-Michel Lafleur, *Transnational Politics and the State: The External Voting Rights of Diasporas* (London: Routledge, 2013); Paolo Boccagni, "Reminiscences, Patriotism, Participation: Approaching External

Voting in Ecuadorian Immigration to Italy," *International Migration* 49, no. 3 (2011): 76–98; and José Itzigsohn and Daniela Villacrés, "Migrant Political Transnationalism and the Practice of Democracy: Dominican External Voting Rights and Salvadoran Home Town Associations," *Ethnic and Racial Studies* 31, no. 4 (2008): 664–86. Studies on hometown associations include Ayse Caglar, "Hometown Associations, the Rescaling of State Spatiality and Migrant Grassroots Transnationalism," *Global Networks* 6, no. 1 (2006): 1–22; Claire Mercer and Ben Page, "African Home Associations in Britain: Between Political Belonging and Moral Conviviality," *African Diaspora* 3, no. 1 (2010): 110–30; and Roger Waldinger, Eric Popkin, and Hector Aquiles Magana, "Conflict and Contestation in the Cross-Border Community: Hometown Associations Reassessed," *Ethnic and Racial Studies* 31, no. 5 (2008): 1177–95.

4. Such as in work by Davide Però, "Policy Change from below: Recognising Migrants' Political Agency among Latin Americans in London," in *Cross-Border Migration among Latin Americans: European Perspectives and Beyond*, ed. Cathy McIlwaine (London: Palgrave Macmillan, 2011), 119–38; and Peter Nyers, "No One Is Illegal: Between City and Nation," *Studies in Social Justice* 4, no. 2 (2011): 127–43.

5. See, for example, Anastasia Bermúdez, "The Transnational Political Practices of Colombians in Spain and the United Kingdom: Politics 'here' and 'there,'" *Ethnic and Racial Studies* 33, no. 1 (2010): 75–91; Alejandro Portes, Cristina Escobar, and Renelinda Arana, "Bridging the Gap: Transnational and Ethnic Organizations in the Political Incorporation of Immigrants in the United States," *Ethnic and Racial Studies* 31, no. 6 (2008): 1211–48.

6. Robert Smith, *Mexican New York: Transnational Lives of New Immigrants* (Berkeley: University of California Press, 2006).

7. For a gendered approach, see, for example, Michael Jones-Correa, "Different Paths: Gender, Immigration and Political Participation," *International Migration Review* 32, no. 2 (1998): 326–49; and Lisa Montoya, Carol Hardy-Fanta, and Sonia Garcia, "Latina Politics: Gender, Participation, and Leadership," *PS: Political Science and Politics* 33, no. 3 (2000): 555–61. An intersectional approach can be found in Cathy McIlwaine and Anastasia Bermúdez, "The Gendering of Political and Civic Participation among Colombian Migrants in London," *Environment and Planning A* 43, no. 7 (2011): 1499–1513.

8. Michael Collyer and Zana Vathi, "Patterns of Extra-Territorial Voting," Sussex Centre for Migration Research, 2007, http://citeseerx.ist.psu.edu/viewdoc/download?doi=10.1.1.36 2.4065&rep=rep1&type=pdf.

9. Lafleur, *Transnational Politics and the State*.

10. Lafleur, *Transnational Politics and the State*, 47.

11. Alfonso Hinojosa Gordonava, Eduardo Domenech, and Jean-Michel Lafleur, "Surgimiento y desarrollo del 'voto en el exterior' en el 'proceso de cambio' boliviano," in *Diáspora y voto en el exterior: La participación política de los emigrantes bolivianos en las elecciones de su país de origen*, ed. Jean-Michel Lafleur (Barcelona: CIDOB, 2012), 39–64.

12. Hinojosa Gordonava, Domenech, and Lafleur, "Surgimiento y desarrollo," 57.

13. Jean-Michel Lafleur, ed., *Diáspora y voto en el exterior: La participación política de los emigrantes bolivianos en las elecciones de su país de origen* (Barcelona: CIDOB, 2012).

14. McIlwaine and Bermudez, "Ambivalent Citizenship."

15. Salvador Schavelzon, "La reelección de Evo Morales en São Paulo: Análisis de la votación," in *Diáspora y voto en el exterior: La participación política de los emigrantes*

bolivianos en las elecciones de su país de origen, ed. Jean-Michel Lafleur (Barcelona: CIDOB, 2012), 111–28; and Elisa Brey, Eduardo Inara Stürckow, and Jean-Michel Lafleur, "'¡Todos Con Evo!' El voto boliviano en Buenos Aires," in *Diáspora y voto en el exterior: La participación política de los emigrantes bolivianos en las elecciones de su país de origen*, ed. Jean-Michel Lafleur (Barcelona: CIDOB, 2012), 91–110.

16. A sense of disappointment was also apparent in conversations I had in Bolivia with those who had voted for the MAS. For a discussion of reactions to the MAS and Evo Morales since his rise to power, see Linda Farthing and Benjamin Kohl, *Evo's Bolivia: Continuity and Change* (Austin: University of Texas Press, 2014); and Nancy Postero, *The Indigenous State: Race, Politics, and Performance in Plurinational Bolivia* (Berkeley: University of California Press, 2017).

17. Fabiola Egüez Rojas, "Importante participación del voto boliviano en el exterior," *El Deber* (La Paz), October 13, 2014, http://www.eldeber.com.bo/bolivia/importante-participacion-del-voto-boliviano.html.

18. Órgano Electoral Plurinacional, "Resultados finales del cómputo—voto en el exterior," Órgano Electoral Plurinacional Tribunal Supremo Electoral, October 18, 2014, http://www.oep.org.bo/computo/index.html.

19. El Mercurio, "Bolivianos residentes en Chile votaron en el referéndum que permitiría la reelección de Evo Morales," *Emol* (Santiago, Chile), February 21, 2016, http://www.emol.com/noticias/Nacional/2016/02/21/789365/Referendum-constitucional-de-Bolivia-se-vivieron-en-calma-en-Santiago.html.

20. Formerly the Concertación de Partidos por la Democracia (Coalition of Parties for Democracy), known as the "Concertación."

21. I suggest that this is indicative of the difficulty of accessing the Bolivian migrant population, and potentially of their vulnerability and isolation, given that we spoke with migrants of various other nationalities, including people from much smaller migrant groups such as Ecuadorians and Dominicans.

22. Len Doyal and Ian Gough, *A Theory of Human Need* (London: Palgrave Macmillan, 1991).

23. For some examples, see José Itzigsohn, "Immigration and the Boundaries of Citizenship: The Institutions of Immigrants' Political Transnationalism," *International Migration Review* 34, no. 4 (2000): 1126–54; Luis Guarnizo, Alejandro Portes, and William Haller, "Assimilation and Transnationalism Determinants of Transnational Political Action among Contemporary Migrants," *American Journal of Sociology* 108, no. 6 (2003): 1211–48; Caglar, "Hometown Associations"; Claire Mercer, Ben Page, and Martin Evans, *Development and the African Diaspora: Place and the Politics of Home* (London: Zed Books, 2008); Bermúdez, "The Transnational Political Practices of Colombians"; Davide Però and John Solomos, "Introduction: Migrant Politics and Mobilization; Exclusion, Engagements, Incorporation," *Ethnic and Racial Studies* 33, no. 1 (2010): 1–18; and Milena Chimienti, "Mobilization of Irregular Migrants in Europe: A Comparative Analysis," *Ethnic and Racial Studies* 34, no. 8 (2011): 1338–56.

24. Bermúdez, "The Transnational Political Practices of Colombians."

25. Però and Solomos, "Introduction."

26. Però and Solomos, "Introduction," 5.

27. Però and Solomos, "Introduction," 6.

28. Thomas Wright and Rody Oñate Zúñiga, "Chilean Political Exile," *Latin American Perspectives* 34, no. 4 (2007): 31–49.

29. Verónica Schild, "Engendering the New Social Citizenship in Chile: NGOs and Social Provisioning under Neoliberalism," in *Gender, Justice, Development and Rights: Substantiating Rights in a Disabling Environment*, ed. Shahra Ravazi and Maxine Molyneux (Oxford: Oxford University Press, 2002), 170–203.

30. Joe Foweraker, "Grassroots Movements and Political Activism in Latin America: A Critical Comparison of Chile and Brazil," *Journal of Latin American Studies* 33, no. 4 (2001): 839–65. See also Jorge Larrain, "Changes in Chilean Identity: Thirty Years after the Military Coup," *Nations and Nationalism* 12, no. 2 (2006): 321–38.

31. Columbus Day in the United States and English-speaking world, it is officially known now in Chile as El Día del Encuentro de Dos Mundos (Day of the Meeting of Two Worlds); however, it is generally still referred to as El Día de la Raza (literally, Race Day), its title throughout the Spanish-speaking world since 1914.

32. James Dunkerley, "Evo Morales, the 'Two Bolivias' and the Third Bolivian Revolution," *Journal of Latin American Studies* 39, no. 1 (2007): 137.

33. Charles Tilly and Sidney Tarrow, *Contentious Politics* (Oxford: Oxford University Press, 2006). On the importance of collective identity for social movement formation see, for example, Alberto Melucci, "Liberation or Meaning? Social Movements, Culture and Democracy," *Development and Change* 23, no. 3 (1992): 43–77; and Francesca Polletta and James Jasper, "Collective Identity and Social Movements," *Annual Review of Sociology* 27, no. 1 (2001): 283–305.

34. As discussed in the Latin American context by, for example, Deborah Yashar, "Contesting Citizenship: Indigenous Movements and Democracy in Latin America," *Comparative Politics* 31, no. 1 (1998): 23–42.

35. For discussion of an increase in hometown associations in Bolivia, see Kaitlin Yarnall and Marie Price, "Migration, Development and a New Rurality in the Valle Alto, Bolivia," *Journal of Latin American Geography* 9, no. 1 (2010): 107–24. Results from the 2005 survey referred to can be found in Manuel Orozco, "Transnationalism: Trends and Opportunities in Latin America," in *Remittances: Development Impact and Future Prospects*, ed. Samuel Munzele Maimbo and Dilip Ratha (Washington, DC: World Bank, 2005), 324.

36. They declined to be interviewed.

37. Marco Martiniello and Jean-Michel Lafleur, "Ethnic Minorities' Cultural and Artistic Practices as Forms of Political Expression: A Review of the Literature and a Theoretical Discussion on Music," *Journal of Ethnic and Migration Studies* 34, no. 8 (2008): 1207.

38. See, for example, Mauro van Aken, "Dancing Belonging: Contesting Dabkeh in the Jordan Valley, Jordan," *Journal of Ethnic and Migration Studies* 32, no. 2 (2006): 203–22; Laura Edmondson, "Marketing Trauma and the Theatre of War in Northern Uganda," *Theatre Journal* 57, no. 3 (2005): 452–74; Tania Kaiser, "Songs, Discos and Dancing in Kiryandongo, Uganda," *Journal of Ethnic and Migration Studies* 32, no. 2 (2006): 183–202; Jan Sverre Knudsen, "Dancing Cueca 'with Your Coat On': The Role of Traditional Chilean Dance in an Immigrant Community," *British Journal of Ethnomusicology* 10, no. 2 (2001): 61–83; Paul Scolieri, "Global/Mobile: Re-Orienting Dance and Migration Studies," *Dance Research Journal* 40, no. 2 (2008): v–xx; and Julie Taylor, *Paper Tangos* (Durham, NC: Duke University Press, 1998).

39. Knudsen, "Dancing Cueca 'with Your Coat On,'" 81.

40. Jan Cohen-Cruz, *Radical Street Performance: An International Anthology* (London: Routledge, 1998); and Daniel Goldstein, *The Spectacular City: Violence and Performance in Urban Bolivia* (Durham, NC: Duke University Press, 2004).

41. Mikhail Bakhtin, *Rabelais and His World* (Bloomington: Indiana University Press, 1984), 10.

42. Setha Low, *On the Plaza: The Politics of Public Space and Culture* (Austin: University of Texas Press, 2000), 184.

43. As discussed by, for example, Gavin Carver, "The Effervescent Carnival: Performance, Context, and Mediation at Notting Hill," *New Theatre Quarterly* 16, no. 1 (2000): 34–49; Clare Lewis, "Woman, Body, Space: Rio Carnival and the Politics of Performance," *Gender, Place & Culture* 3, no. 1 (1996): 23–42; Abner Cohen, *Masquerade Politics: Explorations in the Structure of Urban Cultural Movements* (Berkeley: University of California Press, 1993); and Peter Jackson, "The Politics of the Streets: A Geography of Caribana," *Political Geography* 11, no. 2 (1992): 130–51.

44. Sian Lazar, *El Alto, Rebel City: Self and Citizenship in Andean Bolivia* (Durham, NC: Duke University Press, 2008), 118.

45. Lazar, *El Alto, Rebel City*, 118.

46. A young novice at the Jesuit house in Oruro, who had participated in carnival before joining the order, also offered me detailed explanations about the meanings of many dances and the beliefs surrounding carnival, for which I am very grateful.

47. Thomas Abercrombie, *Pathways of Memory and Power: Ethnography and History among an Andean People* (Madison: University of Wisconsin Press, 1997); and Alejandro Grimson, *Relatos de la diferencia y la igualdad: Los bolivianos en Buenos Aires* (Buenos Aires: Eudeba, 1999); and Lazar, *El Alto, Rebel City*.

48. Goldstein, *The Spectacular City*, 20. See also Lazar, *El Alto, Rebel City*.

49. Karsten Paerregaard, "The Show Must Go On: The Role of Fiestas in Andean Transnational Migration," *Latin American Perspectives* 37, no. 5 (2010): 62.

50. Henry Stobart, *Music and the Poetics of Production in the Bolivian Andes* (Aldershot, UK: Ashgate, 2006).

51. Olivia Harris, *To Make the Earth Bear Fruit: Essays on Fertility, Work and Gender in Highland Bolivia* (London: Institute of Latin American Studies, 2000), 147.

52. Harris, *To Make the Earth Bear Fruit*.

53. Harris, *To Make the Earth Bear Fruit*; and Stobart, *Music and the Poetics of Production*.

54. Stobart, *Music and the Poetics of Production*, 134.

55. Grimson, *Relatos de la diferencia y la igualdad*, 61.

56. For a pertinent comparison with the importance of beauty pageants in Bolivia and the type of beauty that is prized, see Andrew Canessa, "Sex and the Citizen: Barbies and Beauty Queens in the Age of Evo Morales," *Journal of Latin American Cultural Studies* 17, no. 1 (2008): 41–64.

57. Lazar, *El Alto, Rebel City*. See also Paerregaard, "The Show Must Go On."

58. Costumes change on a yearly basis and are imported from Bolivia.

59. Lazar, *El Alto, Rebel City*, 145.

60. Grimson, *Relatos de la diferencia y la igualdad*, 63.

61. As also analyzed by Jane Cowan, *Dance and the Body Politic in Northern Greece* (Princeton, NJ: Princeton University Press, 1990); Knudsen, "Dancing Cueca 'with Your Coat On'"; and Lazar, *El Alto, Rebel City*.

62. Something similar was expressed by participants in research by Grimson, *Relatos de la diferencia y la igualdad*.

63. A point of comparison is offered in Olga Nájera Ramírez, "Social and Political Dimensions of Folklorico Dance: The Binational Dialectic of Residual and Emergent Culture," *Western Folklore* 48, no. 1 (1989): 15–32.

64. Francisca Fernández Droguett and Roberto Fernández Droguett, "El *tinku* como expresión política: Contribuciones hacia una ciudadanía activista en Santiago de Chile," *Psicoperspectivas* 14, no. 2 (2015): 62–71.

65. Fernández Droguett and Fernández Droguett, "El *tinku* como expresión política," 64.

66. Renato Rosaldo, "Cultural Citizenship in San Jose, California," *PoLAR: Political and Legal Anthropology Review* 17, no. 2 (1994): 57–64.

67. Arnold van Gennep, *The Rites of Passage* (London: Psychology Press, [1909] 1960); and Victor Turner, *The Forest of Symbols: Aspects of Ndembu Ritual* (Ithaca, NY: Cornell University Press, 1967).

68. On the performance of gender identity, see Judith Butler, *Gender Trouble: Feminism and the Subversion of Identity* (London: Routledge, 2006).

69. Canessa, "Sex and the Citizen," 54.

70. Kerry Robinson and Cristyn Davies, "'She's Kickin' Ass, That's What She's Doing!,'" *Australian Feminist Studies* 23, no. 57 (2008): 349.

71. Canessa, "Sex and the Citizen"; and Bret Gustafson, "Spectacles of Autonomy and Crisis: Or, What Bulls and Beauty Queens Have to Do with Regionalism in Eastern Bolivia," *Journal of Latin American Anthropology* 11, no. 2 (2006): 351–79.

72. On the problematic use of indigenous dress by white beauty queens in Bolivia, see Canessa, "Sex and the Citizen."

73. Lazar, *El Alto, Rebel City*, 117.

74. Bakhtin, *Rabelais and His World*.

75. David Slater, "The Geopolitical Imagination and the Enframing of Development Theory," *Transactions of the Institute of British Geographers* 18, no. 4 (1993): 419–37.

76. It is important to note that while I have chosen to cover them in other chapters of this book, I recognize that other acts of some migrants—such as Cata and Marta leaving a situation of trafficking (see chapter 4)—could also be interpreted as profoundly "political." My intention here is not to falsely dichotomize the "personal" and the "collective," the "private" and the "public" in relation to what can be considered political. Rather, I use the framing of this chapter as a means of bringing together particular literatures on political citizenship through analysis of certain practices I became aware of during research. This is consistent with the framing of this book more generally, which seeks to acknowledge the complexity of overlap among legal, economic, social, and political spaces of citizenship.

CONCLUSION

1. Doyal and Gough, *A Theory of Human Need*.

2. For a summary of the 2016 incident, see Camilo Carreño, "Piñera: 'Muchas de las bandas de delincuentes en chile son de extranjeros,'" *La Tercera* (Santiago, Chile), November 29, 2016, http://www.latercera.com/noticia/pinera-muchas-las-bandas-delincuentes -chile-extranjeros/.

3. Joel Robbins, "Beyond the Suffering Subject: Toward an Anthropology of the Good," *Journal of the Royal Anthropological Institute* 19 (2013): 458.

4. A similar incremental approach is also advocated by Jonathan Darling, "Asylum and the Post-political: Domopolitics, Depoliticisation and Acts of Citizenship," *Antipode* 46, no. 1 (2013): 72–91.

5. El Mostrador, "Expertos tildan la 'ordenada' reforma a la migración como 'racista y restrictiva,'" *El Mostrador* (Santiago, Chile), April 21, 2018, http://www.elmostrador.cl/noti cias/pais/2018/04/21/expertos-tildan-la-ordenada-reforma-a-la-migracion-como-racista -y-restrictiva/.

BIBLIOGRAPHY

Abercrombie, Thomas. *Pathways of Memory and Power: Ethnography and History among an Andean People*. Madison: University of Wisconsin Press, 1997.

Acosta, Elaine. *Ciudados en crisis: Mujeres migrantes hacia España y Chile*. Santiago, Chile: Universidad Alberto Hurtado, 2015.

Aguilera, Michael, and Douglas Massey. "Social Capital and the Wages of Mexican Migrants: New Hypotheses and Tests." *Social Forces* 82, no. 2 (2003): 671–701.

Alaniz, Jair Marín. "Ayni: Por una infancia sin fronteras; Arteterapia con hijos de migrantes en el norte de Chile." *Arteterapia: Papeles de arteterapia y educación artística para la inclusión social* 9 (2014): 61–72.

Alba, Richard, and Victor Nee. "Rethinking Assimilation Theory for a New Era of Immigration." *International Migration Review* 31, no. 4 (1997): 826–74.

Albó, Xavier, Tomás Greaves, and Godofredo Sandóval. *Chukiyawu: La cara aymara de La Paz*. Vol. 1, *El paso a la ciudad*. La Paz, Bolivia: Centro de Investigación y Promoción del Campesinado, 1981.

Amelina, Anna, and Thomas Faist. "De-Naturalizing the National in Research Methodologies: Key Concepts of Transnational Studies in Migration." *Ethnic and Racial Studies* 35, no. 10 (2012): 1707–24.

Anderson, Bridget. "Battles in Time: The Relation Between Global and Labour Mobilities." Oxford Centre on Migration, Policy and Society. 2007. www.compas.ox.ac.uk/fileadmin/files/Publications/working_papers/WP_2007/WP0755%20Bridget%20Anderson.pdf.

———. "Migration, Immigration Controls and the Fashioning of Precarious Workers." *Work, Employment & Society* 24, no. 2 (2010): 300–317.

———. *Us and Them? The Dangerous Politics of Immigration Control*. Oxford: Oxford University Press, 2013.

Anderson, Bridget, and Martin Ruhs. "Researching Illegality and Labour Migration." *Population, Space and Place* 16, no. 3 (2010): 175–79.

Andolina, Robert, Nina Laurie, and Sarah Radcliffe. *Indigenous Development in the Andes: Culture, Power, and Transnationalism*. Durham, NC: Duke University Press, 2009.

Andrijasevic, Rutvica. *Migration, Agency and Citizenship in Sex Trafficking*. London: Palgrave Macmillan, 2010.

Anthias, Floya. "Transnational Mobilities, Migration Research and Intersectionality." *Nordic Journal of Migration Research* 2, no. 2 (2012): 102–10.

Arriagada, Irma, and Marcela Moreno. "La constitución de cadenas globales de ciudado y las condiciones laborales de las trabajadoras peruanas en Chile." In *Mujeres inmigrantes en Chile: ¿Mano de obra o trabajadoras con derechos?*, edited by Carolina Stefoni. Santiago, Chile: Universidad Alberto Hurtado, 2013. Kindle.

Assiter, Alison. "Citizenship Revisisted." In *Women, Citizenship and Difference*, edited by Nira Yuval-Davis and Prina Werbner, 41–53. London: Zed Books, 1999.

Avato, Johanna, Johannes Koettl, and Rachel Sabates-Wheeler. "Social Security Regimes, Global Estimates, and Good Practices: The Status of Social Protection for International Migrants." *World Development* 38, no. 4 (2010): 455–66.

Bakhtin, Mikhail. *Rabelais and His World*. Bloomington: Indiana University Press, 1984.

Balibar, Étienne. *Nous, citoyens d'Europe? Les frontières, l'État, le people*. Paris: La Découverte, 2001.

Ballard, Roger. "Remittances and Economic Development in India and Pakistan." In *Remittances: Development Impact and Future Prospects*, edited by Samuel Munzele Maimbo and Dilip Ratha, 103–18. Washington, DC: World Bank Publications, 2005.

Banco Central de Bolivia. "Nivel de remesas de trabajadores—mes de febrero de 2017." 2017. www.bcb.gob.bo/webdocs/10_notas_prensa/NP_20_REMESAS-FEBRERO.pdf.

Bartlett, Lesley, and Ameena Ghaffar-Kucher, *Refugees, Immigrants, and Education in the Global South: Lives in Motion*. London: Routledge, 2013.

Basch, Linda, Nina Glick-Schiller, and Cristina Szanton-Blanc. *Nations Unbound: Transnational Projects, Postcolonial Predicaments, and Deterritorialized Nation-States*. London: Routledge, 1994.

Bastia, Tanja. "From Mining to Garment Workshops: Bolivian Migrants in Buenos Aires." *Journal of Ethnic and Migration Studies* 33, no. 4 (2007): 655–69.

———. "'I Am Going, with or without You': Autonomy in Bolivian Transnational Migrations." *Gender, Place & Culture* 20, no. 2 (2013): 160–77.

———, ed. *Migration and Inequality*. London: Routledge, 2015.

———. "'Should I Stay or Should I Go?' Return Migration in Times of Crisis." *Journal of International Development* 23 (2011): 583–95.

Bastia, Tanja, and Siobhan McGarth. "Temporality, Migration, and Unfree Labour: Migrant Garment Workers." Manchester Papers in Political Economy, Working Paper No. 6. University of Manchester, 2011.

Berganza Setién, Isabel, and Mauricio Cerna Rivera. *Dinámicas migratorias en la frontera Perú-Chile: Arica, Tacna e Iquique*. Lima, Peru: Universidad Antonio Ruiz de Montoya, 2011. http://centroderecursos.alboan.org/ebooks/0000/0783/11_BER_DIN.pdf.

Bermúdez, Anastasia. "The Transnational Political Practices of Colombians in Spain and the United Kingdom: Politics 'Here' and 'There.'" *Ethnic and Racial Studies* 33, no. 1 (2010): 75–91.

Berriane, Mohamed, and Hein de Haas. *African Migrations Research*. London: Africa World Press, 2012.

Bibler Coutin, Susan. "Illegality, Borderlands, and the Space of Non-Existence." In *Globalization under Construction: Governmentality, Law, and Identity*, edited by Richard Warren Perry and Bill Maurer, 171–203. Minneapolis: Minnesota University Press, 2003.

Biblioteca del Congreso Nacional de Chile. "Trajadoras y trabajadores de casa particiular (nueva ley)." BCN. 2015. www.bcn.cl/leyfacil/recurso/trabajadoras-y-trabajadores -de-casa-particular-(nueva-ley).

Bicocchi, Luca, and Michele LeVoy. *Undocumented Children in Europe: Invisible Victims of Immigration Restrictions*. Brussels, Belgium: PICUM, 2008. http://picum.org/picum .org/uploads/publication/Undocumented%20Children%20in%20Europe%20EN.pdf.

Binfa, Lorena, Loreto Pantoja, Jovita Ortiz, Marcela Gurovich, and Gabriel Cavada. "Assessment of the Implementation of the Model of Integrated and Humanized Midwifery Health Services in Chile." *Midwifery* 35 (2016): 53–61.

Black, Richard. "Breaking the Convention: Researching the 'Illegal' Migration of Refugees to Europe." *Antipode* 35, no. 1 (2003): 34–54.

Black, Richard, Michael Collyer, Ronald Skeldon, and Claire Waddington. "Routes to Illegal Residence: A Case Study of Immigration Detainees in the United Kingdom." *Geoforum* 37, no. 4 (2006): 552–64.

Bloch, Alice, and Milena Chimienti. "Irregular Migration in a Globalizing World." *Ethnic and Racial Studies* 34, no. 8 (2011): 1271–85.

Bloch, Alice, Nando Sigona, and Roger Zetter. "Migration Routes and Strategies of Young Undocumented Migrants in England: A Qualitative Perspective." *Ethnic and Racial Studies* 34, no. 8 (2011): 1286–1302.

Boccagni, Paolo. "Reminiscences, Patriotism, Participation: Approaching External Voting in Ecuadorian Immigration to Italy." *International Migration* 49, no. 3 (2011): 76–98.

Bolivia Cultural. "Las parcelas de la explotación: La migración de Bolivia en Sao Paulo." 2013. http://www.boliviacultural.com.br/ver_noticias.php?id=364.

Bondi, Liz. "The Place of Emotions in Research: From Partitioning Emotion and Reason to the Emotional Dynamics of Research Relationships." In *Emotional Geographies*, edited by Joyce Davidson, Mick Smith, and Liz Bondi, 231–46. Aldershot, UK: Ashgate, 2007.

Bondi, Liz, Joyce Davidson, and Mick Smith. "Introduction: Geography's 'Emotional Turn.'" In *Emotional Geographies*, edited by Joyce Davidson, Mick Smith, and Liz Bondi, 1–18. Aldershot, UK: Ashgate, 2007.

Bradby, Barbara, and Jo Murphy-Lawless. *ILCA—Reducing Maternal Mortality and Morbidity in Bolivia*. La Paz, Bolivia: Instituto de Lengua y Cultura Aymara, 2002.

Brey, Elisa, Eduardo Inara Stürckow, and Jean-Michel Lafleur. "'¡Todos con Evo!' El voto boliviano en Buenos Aires." In *Diáspora y voto en el exterior: La participación política de los emigrantes bolivianos en las elecciones de su país de origen*, edited by Jean-Michel Lafleur, 91–110. Barcelona, Spain: CIDOB, 2012.

Briones Valentín, Viviana. "Arica colonial: Libertos y esclavos negros entre El Lumbanga y Las Maytas." *Chungará* (Arica) 36 (2004): 813–16.

Buechler, Simone. "Sweating it in the Brazilian Garment Industry: Korean and Bolivian Immigrants and Global Economic Forces in São Paulo." *Latin American Perspectives* 136, no. 3 (2004): 99–119.

Butler, Judith. *Gender Trouble: Feminism and the Subversion of Identity*. London: Routledge, 2006.

Cabieses, Batica, and Helena Tunstall. "Socioeconomic Vulnerability and Access to Health-care among Migrants in Chile." In *Migration, Health and Inequality*, edited by Felicity Thomas and Jasmine Gideon, 79–93. London: Zed Books, 2013.

Caglar, Ayse. "Hometown Associations, the Rescaling of State Spatiality and Migrant Grass-roots Transnationalism." *Global Networks* 6, no. 1 (2006): 1–22.

Caldeira, Teresa. *City of Walls: Crime, Segregation and Citizenship in Sao Paulo*. Berkeley: University of California Press, 2001.

"Canciller de Bolivia: El gobierno de Bachelet es peor que el de Pinochet." *CNN Español*, March 28, 2017. http://cnnespanol.cnn.com/2017/03/28/canciller-de-bolivia-el-gobierno-de-bachelet-es-peor-que-el-de-pinochet/.

Canessa, Andrew. "Conflict, Claim and Contradiction in the New 'Indigenous' State of Bolivia." *Critique of Anthropology* 34, no. 2 (2014): 153–73.

———. "Sex and the Citizen: Barbies and Beauty Queens in the Age of Evo Morales." *Journal of Latin American Cultural Studies* 17, no. 1 (2008): 41–64.

Cano, Verónica, Magdalena Soffia, and Jorge Martínez Pizarro. "Conocer para legislar y hacer política: Los desafíos de Chile ante un nuevo escenario migratorio." CEPAL. February 2009. www.cepal.org/es/publicaciones/7228-conocer-legislar-hacer-politica-desafios-chile-un-nuevo-escenario-migratorio.

Carreño, Camilo. "Piñera: 'Muchas de las bandas de delincuentes en chile son de extran-jeros.'" *La Tercera* (Santiago, Chile), November 29, 2016. www.latercera.com/noticia/pinera-muchas-las-bandas-delincuentes-chile-extranjeros/.

Carver, Gavin. "The Effervescent Carnival: Performance, Context, and Mediation at Not-ting Hill." *New Theatre Quarterly* 16, no. 1 (2000): 34–49.

CASEN. "Inmigrantes: Principales resultados (versión extendida)." Observatorio del Min-isterio de Desarrollo Social. 2015. http://observatorio.ministeriodesarrollosocial.gob.cl/casen-multidimensional/casen/docs/CASEN_2015_INMIGRANTES_21122016_EXTENDIDA_publicada.pdf.

———. "Pueblos indígenas: Sintesis de resultados." Observatorio del Ministerio de Desar-rollo Social. 2015. http://observatorio.ministeriodesarrollosocial.gob.cl/documentos/Casen2013_Pueblos_Indigenas_13mar15_publicacion.pdf.

———. "Salud: Síntesis de resultados." Observatorio del Ministerio de Desarrollo Social. 2013. http://observatorio.ministeriodesarrollosocial.gob.cl/documentos/Casen2013_Salud.pdf.

Castles, Stephen. "Nation and Empire: Hierarchies of Citizenship in the New Global Order." *International Politics* 42, no. 2 (2005): 203–24.

Castles, Stephen, and Alastair Davidson, *Citizenship and Migration: Globalization and the Politics of Belonging*. New York: Routledge, 2000.

CEDIB. "Indígenas: Quién gana, quién pierde." 2013. www.cedib.org/wp-content/uploads/2013/08/Tabla-Poblacion-Indigena1.pdf.

CEPAL. "CEPALSTAT: Base de datos y publicaciones estadísticas." CEPALSTAT. 2015. http://interwp.cepal.org/cepalstat/WEB_cepalstat/Perfil_nacional_social.asp?pais=CHL&idioma=e.

Cevallos, Ana María, and Roberto Hernández. "Chagas Disease: Pregnancy and Congenital Transmission." *BioMed Research International* 2014 (2014): doi:10.1155/2014/401864.

Chant, Sylvia, and Nikki Craske. *Gender in Latin America*. New Brunswick, NJ: Rutgers University Press, 2003.

Chant, Sylvia, and Cathy McIlwaine, *Geographies of Development in the 21st Century: An Introduction to the Global South*. Cheltenham, UK: Edward Elgar, 2009.

Chatterjee, Partha. *The Politics of the Governed: Reflections on Popular Politics in Most of the World*. New York: Columbia University Press, 2006.

Chilean National Commission on Truth and Reconciliation. "Report for the Chilean National Commission on Truth and Reconciliation." Translated by the Center of Civil and Human Rights of the Notre Dame Law School. Notre Dame, IN: University of Notre Dame Press, 1993. www.usip.org/files/resources/collections/truth_commissions/Chile 90-Report/Chile90-Report.pdf.

Chimienti, Milena. "Mobilization of Irregular Migrants in Europe: A Comparative Analysis." *Ethnic and Racial Studies* 34, no. 8 (2011): 1338–56.

Cohen, Abner. *Masquerade Politics: Explorations in the Structure of Urban Cultural Movements*. Berkeley: University of California Press, 1993.

Cohen-Cruz, Jan. *Radical Street Performance: An International Anthology*. London: Routledge, 1998.

Collier, Simon, and William Sater. *A History of Chile, 1808–1994*. Cambridge, UK: Cambridge University Press, 1996.

Collyer, Michael, and Zana Vathi. "Patterns of Extra-Territorial Voting." Sussex Centre for Migration Research. 2007. http://citeseerx.ist.psu.edu/viewdoc/download?doi=10.1.1.36 2.4065&rep=rep1&type=pdf.

Comisión Nacional sobre Prisión Política y Tortura. *Nómina de personas reconocidad como víctimas en etapa de reconsideración*. Santiago, Chile: Comisión Nacional sobre Prisión Política y Tortura, 2005. www.archivochile.com/Derechos_humanos/com_valech /Informe_complementario.pdf.

Cooper, Elizabeth, and David Patten, eds. *Ethnographies of Uncertainty in Africa*. London: Palgrave Macmillan, 2015.

Cowan, Jane. *Dance and the Body Politic in Northern Greece*. Princeton, NJ: Princeton University Press, 1990.

Crang, Mike, and Ian Cook. *Doing Ethnographies*. London: SAGE, 2007.

Creese, Gillian, and Brandy Wiebe. "'Survival Employment': Gender and Deskilling among African Immigrants in Canada." *International Migration* 50, no. 5 (2012): 404–32.

Crush, Jonathan, and Sujata Ramachandran. "Xenophobia, International Migration and Development." *Journal of Human Development and Capabilities* 11, no. 2 (2010): 209–28.

Dagnino, Evelina. "Citizenship in Latin America: An Introduction." *Latin American Perspectives* 30, no. 2 (2003): 211–25.

Darling, Jonathan. "Asylum and the Post-political: Domopolitics, Depoliticisation and Acts of Citizenship." *Antipode* 46, no. 1 (2013): 72–91.

Datta, Kavita. "Money Matters: Exploring Financial Exclusion among Low-Paid Migrant Workers in London." Queen Mary University of London. 2007. http://citeseerx.ist.psu .edu/viewdoc/download?doi=10.1.1.462.3580&rep=rep1&type=pdf, 24.

Datta, Kavita, Cathy McIlwaine, Jane Wills, Yara Evans, Joanna Herbert, and Jon May. "The New Development Finance or Exploiting Migrant Labour? Remittance Sending among

Low-Paid Migrant Workers in London." *International Development Planning Review* 29, no. 1 (2007): 43–67.

De Genova, Nicholas. "Migrant 'Illegality' and Deportability in Everyday Life." *Annual Review of Anthropology* 31, no. 1 (2002): 419–47.

de Haas, Hein. "Migration and Development: A Theoretical Perspective." University of Oxford International Migration Institute Working Papers 9. Oxford: University of Oxford International Migration Institute, 2008.

———. "Remittances, Migration and Social Development: A Conceptual Review of the Literature." Social Policy and Development Programme Paper. UNRISD. 2007. www.unrisd.org/80256B3C005BCCF9/%28httpAuxPages%29/8B7D005E37FFC77EC12573A 600439846/$file/deHaaspaper.pdf.

Demoscópica. "Diagnóstico y factibilidad global para la implementación de políticas locales de salud para inmigrantes en la Zona Norte de la Región Metropolitana." Demoscópica /OIM. 2009. http://web.minsal.cl/portal/url/item/71841d2e91f518a1e04001011f015cc6.pdf.

Departamento de Extranjería y Migración. "Tipos de permanencia definitiva." 2014. www.extranjeria.gob.cl/permanencia-definitiva/permiso-de-permanencia-definitiva/tipos -de-permanencia-definitiva/.

———. "Tipos de residencia temporaria." 2014. www.extranjeria.gob.cl/residencia-tempo raria/tipos-de-residencia-temporaria/.

———. "Migración en Chile 2005–2014." 2016. http://www.extranjeria.gob.cl/media/2016 /02/Anuario-Estad%C3%ADstico-Nacional-Migraci%C3%B3n-en-Chile-2005-2014.pdf

Díaz Donoso, Yoice, María Montoya Araya, Leonardo Núñez Oropeza, and Sandra Sáez Zegarra. "Situación de salud en mujeres inmigrantes de la macro-región andina en el sistema público de salud de la ciudad de Arica." Undergraduate thesis, Universidad de Tarapacá, 2013.

Doyal, Len, and Ian Gough, *A Theory of Human Need*. London: Palgrave Macmillan, 1991.

Dreby, Joanna. "Children and Power in Mexican Transnational Families." *Journal of Marriage and Family* 69, no. 4 (2007): 1050–64.

———. *Everyday Illegal: When Policies Undermine Immigrant Families*. Berkeley: University of California Press, 2015.

Drinot, Paulo. "Website of Memory: The War of the Pacific (1879–84) in the Global Age of YouTube." *Memory Studies* 4, no. 4 (2011): 370–85.

Dunkerley, James. *Bolivia: Revolution and the Power of History in the Present*. London: Institute for the Study of the Americas, 2007.

———. "The Bolivian Revolution at 60: Politics and Historiography." *Journal of Latin American Studies* 45, no.2 (2013): 325–50.

———. "Evo Morales, the 'Two Bolivias' and the Third Bolivian Revolution." *Journal of Latin American Studies* 39, no. 1 (2007): 133–66.

Durin, Séverine, María Eugenia de la O, and Santiago Bastos, eds. *Trabajadoras en la sombra: Dimensiones del servicio doméstico latinoamericano*. Monterrey, Mexico: CIESAS, 2014.

Duvell, Franck, and Bill Jordan. *Irregular Migration: The Dilemmas of Transnational Mobility*. Cheltenham, UK: Edward Elgar, 2003.

Dwyer, Peter. *Understanding Social Citizenship: Themes and Perspectives for Policy and Practice*. Bristol, UK: Policy Press, 2010.

Edmondson, Laura. "Marketing Trauma and the Theatre of War in Northern Uganda." *Theatre Journal* 57, no. 3 (2005): 452–74.

Egüez Rojas, Fabiola. "Importante participación del voto boliviano en el exterior." *El Deber* (La Paz), October 13, 2014. www.eldeber.com.bo/bolivia/importante-participacion-del -voto-boliviano.html.

El Mercurio. "Bolivianos residentes en Chile votaron en el referéndum que permitiría la reelección de Evo Morales." *Emol* (Santiago, Chile), February 21, 2016. www.emol.com /noticias/Nacional/2016/02/21/789365/Referendum-constitucional-de-Bolivia-se-vivi eron-en-calma-en-Santiago.html.

El Mostrador. "Expertos tildan la 'ordenada' reforma a la migración como 'racista y restrictiva'." *El Mostrador* (Santiago, Chile), April 21, 2018. http://www.elmostrador.cl/noticias /pais/2018/04/21/expertos-tildan-la-ordenada-reforma-a-la-migracion-como-racista-y -restrictiva/.

Faist, Thomas. "Transnational Social Spaces out of International Migration: Evolution, Significance, and Future Prospects." *European Journal of Sociology* 39, no. 2 (1998): 213–47.

Farcau, Bruce. *The Ten Cents War: Chile, Peru, and Bolivia in the War of the Pacific, 1879–1884*. Westport, CT: Praeger, 2000.

Farthing, Linda, and Benjamin Kohl. *Evo's Bolivia: Continuity and Change*. Austin: University of Texas Press, 2014.

Ferguson, James, and Akhil Gupta, "Spatializing States: Toward an Ethnography of Neoliberal Governmentality." *American Ethnologist* 29, no. 4 (2002): 981–1002.

Fernández Droguett, Francisca, and Roberto Fernández Droguett. "El *tinku* como expresión política: Contribuciones hacia una ciudadanía activista en Santiago de Chile," *Psicoperspectivas* 14, no. 2 (2015): 62–71.

Foweraker, Joe. "Grassroots Movements and Political Activism in Latin America: A Critical Comparison of Chile and Brazil." *Journal of Latin American Studies* 33, no. 4 (2001): 839–65.

Freeman, Cordelia. "Violence on the Chile-Peru Border, Arica 1925–2015." PhD thesis, University of Nottingham, 2016. http://eprints.nottingham.ac.uk/33556/.

Gideon, Jasmine. *Gender, Globalization, and Health in a Latin American Context*. London: Palgrave Macmillan, 2014.

Gill, Lesley. *Precarious Dependencies: Gender, Class, and Domestic Service in Bolivia*. New York: Columbia University Press, 1994.

Glazer, Nathan, and Daniel Moynihan. *Beyond the Melting Pot: The Negroes, Puerto Ricans, Jews, Italians, and Irish of New York City*. 2nd ed. Cambridge, MA: The MIT Press, 1970.

Glenn, Evelyn. "Caring and Inequality." In *Women's Labour in the Global Economy*, edited by Sharon Harley, 46–61. New Brunswick, NJ: Rutgers University Press, 2007.

Glick-Schiller, Nina, Linda Basch, and Cristina Szanton-Blanc. "From Immigrant to Transmigrant: Theorizing Transnational Migration." *Anthropological Quarterly* 68, no. 1 (1995): 48–63.

Goldring, Luin. "The Gender and Geography of Citizenship in Mexico-U.S. Transnational Spaces." *Identities* 7, no. 4 (2001): 501–37.

Goldring, Luin, and Patricia Landolt. *Producing and Negotiating Non-Citizenship: Precarious Legal Status in Canada*. 3rd ed. Toronto: University of Toronto Press, 2013.

Goldstein, Daniel. *The Spectacular City: Violence and Performance in Urban Bolivia.* Durham, NC: Duke University Press, 2004.

González Miranda, Sergio. "Patrioteros, marzorqueros, nativos y cowboys en el conflict peruano-chileno por Tacna y Arica." *Si Somos Americanos* 6, no. 5 (2004): 107–22.

Gough, Ian. "What Are Human Needs?" In *Social Policy and Social Justice: The IPPR Reader,* edited by Jane Franklin, 50–56. Oxford: Polity Press, 1998.

Grimson, Alejandro. *Relatos de la diferencia y la igualdad: Los bolivianos en Buenos Aires.* Buenos Aires, Argentina: Eudeba, 1999.

Guarnizo, Luis, Alejandro Portes, and William Haller, "Assimilation and Transnationalism: Determinants of Transnational Political Action among Contemporary Migrants." *American Journal of Sociology* 108, no. 6 (2003): 1211–48.

Gustafson, Bret. "Spectacles of Autonomy and Crisis: Or, What Bulls and Beauty Queens Have to Do with Regionalism in Eastern Bolivia." *Journal of Latin American Anthropology* 11, no. 2 (2006): 351–79.

Hagan, Jacqueline Maria. "Social Networks, Gender, and Immigrant Incorporation: Resources and Constraints." *American Sociological Review* 63, no. 1 (1998): 55–67.

Hale, Charles. "Does Multiculturalism Menace? Governance, Cultural Rights and the Politics of Identity in Guatemala." *Journal of Latin American Studies* 34, no. 3 (2002): 485–524.

Han, Clara. *Life in Debt: Times of Care and Violence in Neoliberal Chile.* Berkeley: University of California Press, 2012.

Hardy-Fanta, Carol. *Latina Politics, Latino Politics: Gender, Culture, and Political Participation in Boston.* Philadelphia, PA: Temple University Press, 1993.

Harris, Olivia. *To Make the Earth Bear Fruit: Essays on Fertility, Work and Gender in Highland Bolivia.* London: Institute of Latin American Studies, 2000.

Herrera, Gioconda. "Rethinking the Family through Migration: Gender Ideologies and Practices of Care in Ecuador." In *Cross-Border Migration among Latin Americans: European Perspectives and Beyond,* edited by Cathy McIlwaine, 53–70. London: Palgrave Macmillan, 2011.

Hinojosa Gordonava, Alfonso. "La visibilización de las migraciones transnacionales en Bolivia." *Tinkazos* 11, no. 25 (2008): 89–106.

Hinojosa Gordonava, Alfonso, Eduardo Domenech, and Jean-Michel Lafleur. "Surgimiento y desarrollo del 'voto en el exterior' en el 'proceso de cambio' boliviano." In *Diáspora y voto en el exterior: La participación política de los emigrantes bolivianos en las elecciones de su país de origen,* edited by Jean-Michel Lafleur, 39–64. Barcelona, Spain: CIDOB, 2012.

Ho, Elaine. "Citizenship, Migration and Transnationalism: A Review and Critical Interventions." *Geography Compass* 2, no. 5 (2008): 1286–1300.

———. "Constituting Citizenship through the Emotions: Singaporean Transmigrants in London." *Annals of the Association of American Geographers* 99, no. 4 (September 17, 2009): 788–804.

Hoang, Lan Anh, and Brenda Yeoh. "Sustaining Families across Transnational Spaces: Vietnamese Migrant Parents and their Left-Behind Children." *Asian Studies Review* 36, no. 3 (2012): 307–25.

Hochschild, Arlie. "Global Care Chains and Emotional Surplus Value." In *On the Edge: Globalization and the New Millennium,* edited by Anthony Giddens and Will Hutton, 130–46. London: SAGE, 2000.

Holmes, Seth. *Fresh Fruit, Broken Bodies: Migrant Farmworkers in the United States.* Berkeley: University of California Press, 2013.

Holston, James. *Insurgent Citizenship: Disjunctions of Democracy and Modernity in Brazil.* Princeton, NJ: Princeton University Press, 2008.

Hondagneu-Sotelo, Pierrette. *Doméstica: Immigrant Workers Cleaning and Caring in the Shadows of Affluence.* 2nd ed. Berkeley: University of California Press, 2007.

Hondagneu-Sotelo, Pierrette, and Ernestine Avila. "'I'M HERE, BUT I'M THERE': The Meanings of Latina Transnational Motherhood." *Gender & Society* 11, no. 5 (1997): 548–71.

Hopper, Elizabeth, and José Hidalgo. "Invisible Chains: Psychological Coercion of Human Trafficking Victims." *Intercultural Human Rights Law Review* 1 (2006): 185–209.

Hubbard, Phil, Rob Kitchin, and Gill Valentine, eds. *Key Thinkers on Space and Place.* London: SAGE, 2004.

Hujo, Katja, and Nicola Piper. "South–South Migration: Challenges for Development and Social Policy." *Development* 50, no. 4 (2007): 19–25.

Hylton, Forrest, and Sinclair Thomson. *Revolutionary Horizons: Past and Present in Bolivian Politics.* London: Verso, 2007.

Imaña, Gabriela. "Las remesas crecieron en 8% en 2013." *La Razón* (La Paz), February 11, 2014. www.la-razon.com/index.php?_url=/economia/remesas-crecieron_0_1996600357 .html.

Instituto Nacional de Estadísticas Bolivia. "Intituto Nacional de Estadística Bolivia: Nota de prensa." 2012. http://censosbolivia.ine.gob.bo/webine/sites/default/files/archivos_adj untos/N%204%20Area%20urbanas%20y%20rurales_1.pdf.

Internet Live Stats. "Internet Users by Country (2016)." www.internetlivestats.com/inter net-users-by-country/.

Isin, Engin. *Being Political: Genealogies of Citizenship.* Minneapolis: University of Minnesota Press, 2002.

Isin, Engin, and Kim Rygiel. "Abject Spaces: Frontiers, Zones, Camps." In *The Logics of Biopower and the War on Terror: Living, Dying, Surviving*, edited by Elizabeth Dauphinee and Cristina Masters, 181–203. London: Palgrave Macmillan, 2007.

Itzigsohn, José. "Immigration and the Boundaries of Citizenship: The Institutions of Immigrants' Political Transnationalism." *International Migration Review* 34, no. 4 (2000): 1126–54.

Itzigsohn, José, and Daniela Villacrés. "Migrant Political Transnationalism and the Practice of Democracy: Dominican External Voting Rights and Salvadoran Home Town Associations." *Ethnic and Racial Studies* 31, no. 4 (2008): 664–86.

Jackson, Peter. "The Politics of the Streets: A Geography of Caribana." *Political Geography* 11, no. 2 (1992): 130–51.

Jackson, Peter, Philip Crang, and Claire Dwyer. *Transnational Spaces.* London: Routledge, 2004.

Jelin, Elizabeth. "Women, Gender, and Human Rights." In *Constructing Democracy: Human Rights, Citizenship, and Society in Latin America*, edited by Elizabeth Jelin and Eric Hershberg, 177–224. Boulder, CO: Westview Press, 1996.

Jiménez Cavieres, Fernando. *Chilean Housing Policy: A Case of Social and Spatial Exclusion.* Münster, Germany: LIT Verlag, 2008.

Joiko, Sara, and Alba Vásquez. "Acceso y elección escolar de familias migrantes en Chile: 'No tuve problemas porque la escuela es abierta, porque acepta muchas nacionalidades.'" *Calidad en Educación* 45 (2016): 132–73.

Jones-Correa, Michael. "Different Paths: Gender, Immigration and Political Participation." *International Migration Review* 32, no. 2 (1998): 326–49.

Kaiser, Tania. "Songs, Discos and Dancing in Kiryandongo, Uganda." *Journal of Ethnic and Migration Studies* 32, no. 2 (2006): 183–202.

Kapur, Devesh. "Remittances: The New Development Mantra?" G-24 Discussion Paper Series. United Nations. 2003. www.cities-localgovernments.org/committees/fccd/Upload /library/gdsmdpbg2420045_en_en.pdf.

Kessler-Harris, Alice. "In Pursuit of Economic Citizenship." *Social Politics: International Studies in Gender, State and Society* 10, no. 2 (2003): 157–75.

Klein, Herbert. *A Concise History of Bolivia*. Cambridge, UK: University of Cambridge, 2011.

Koser, Khalid. "Dimensions and Dynamics of Irregular Migration." *Population, Space and Place* 16, no. 3 (2010): 181–93.

———. "Irregular Migration, State Security and Human Security: A Paper Prepared for the Policy Analysis and Research Programme of the Global Commission on International Migration." Global Commission on International Migration. 2005, 5. www.iom .int/jahia/webdav/site/myjahiasite/shared/shared/mainsite/policy_and_research/gcim /tp/TP5.pdf.

Kymlicka, Will. *Multicultural Citizenship: A Liberal Theory of Minority Rights*. Oxford: Clarendon Press, 1996.

"La pelea entre Piñera y Morales que nos recordó el '¿Por qué no te callas?' de Hugo Chávez." *CNN Español*, June 26, 2017. http://cnnespanol.cnn.com/2017/06/26/la-pelea-entre-pin era-y-morales-que-nos-recordo-el-por-que-no-te-callas-a-hugo-chavez/.

Lafleur, Jean-Michel. *Transnational Politics and the State: The External Voting Rights of Diasporas*. London: Routledge, 2013.

———, ed. *Diáspora y voto en el exterior: La participación política de los emigrantes bolivianos en las elecciones de su país de origen*. Barcelona, Spain: CIDOB, 2012.

Larrain, Jorge. "Changes in Chilean Identity: Thirty Years after the Military Coup." *Nations and Nationalism* 12, no. 2 (2006): 321–38.

Lazar, Sian. *The Anthropology of Citizenship: A Reader*. Oxford: Wiley-Blackwell, 2013.

———. *El Alto, Rebel City: Self and Citizenship in Andean Bolivia*. Durham, NC: Duke University Press, 2008.

Lee, Charles. "Bare Life, Interstices, and the Third Space of Citizenship." *WSQ: Women's Studies Quarterly* 38, no. 1 (2010): 57–81.

Lefebvre, Henri. *The Production of Space*. Translated by Donald Nicholson-Smith. Oxford: Wiley-Blackwell, 1991.

Levitt, Peggy. *The Transnational Villagers*. Berkeley: University of California Press, 2001.

Levitt, Peggy, and Rafael de la Dehesa. "Transnational Migration and the Redefinition of the State: Variations and Explanations." *Ethnic and Racial Studies* 26, no. 4 (2003): 587–611.

Levitt, Peggy, and B. Nadya Jaworsky. "Transnational Migration Studies: Past Developments and Future Trends." *Annual Review of Sociology* 33, no. 1 (2007): 131–32.

Lewis, Clare. "Woman, Body, Space: Rio Carnival and the Politics of Performance." *Gender, Place & Culture* 3, no. 1 (1996): 23–42.

Lewis, Hannah, Peter Dwyer, Stuart Hodkinson, and Louise Waite. "Hyper-Precarious Lives: Migrants, Work and Forced Labour in the Global North." *Progress in Human Geography* 39, no. 5 (2014): 580–600.

Lister, Ruth. *Citizenship: Feminist Perspectives.* 2nd ed. New York: New York University Press, 2003.

Low, Setha. *On the Plaza: The Politics of Public Space and Culture.* Austin: University of Texas Press, 2000.

Lube-Guizardi, Menara, and Alejandro Garcés. "Circuitos migrantes. Itinerarios y formación de redes migratorias entre Perú, Bolivia, Chile y Argentina en el norte grande chileno." *Papeles de Población* 19, no. 78 (2013): 65–110.

Madianou, Mirca, and Daniel Miller. "Mobile Phone Parenting: Reconfiguring Relationships between Filipina Migrant Mothers and Their Left-behind Children." *New Media & Society* 13, no. 3 (2011): 457–70.

Mahler, Sarah, and Patricia Pessar. "Gendered Geographies of Power: Analyzing Gender across Transnational Spaces." *Identities* 7, no. 4 (2001): 441–59.

Marcus, George. "Ethnography in/of the World System: The Emergence of Multi-Sited Ethnography." *Annual Review of Anthropology* 24 (1995): 95–117.

Marshall, Thomas Humphrey. *Citizenship and Social Class, and Other Essays.* Cambridge, UK: Cambridge University Press, 1950.

Martínez Pizarro, Jorge. *Migración internacional en América Latina y el Caribe: Nuevas tendencias y nuevos enfoques.* Santiago, Chile: CEPAL, 2011.

Martiniello, Marco. "Political Participation, Mobilisation, and Representation of Immigrants and their Offspring in Europe." Willy Brandt Series of Working Papers on International Migration and Ethnic Relations. 2005. http://muep.mah.se/bitstream/handle/2043/1495/WB_1-05.pdf?sequence=1&isAllowed=y.

Martiniello, Marco, and Jean-Michel Lafleur. "Ethnic Minorities' Cultural and Artistic Practices as Forms of Political Expression: A Review of the Literature and a Theoretical Discussion on Music." *Journal of Ethnic and Migration Studies* 34, no. 8 (2008): 1191–1215.

Masi de Casanova, Erynn. "Embodied Inequality: The Experience of Domestic Work in Urban Ecuador." *Gender and Society* 27, no. 4 (2013): 561–85.

Massey, Doreen. *For Space.* London: SAGE, 2005.

McDowell, Linda. "Thinking through Work: Complex Inequalities, Constructions of Difference and Trans-National Migrants." *Progress in Human Geography* 32, no. 4 (2008): 491–507.

McIlwaine, Cathy. "Constructing Transnational Social Spaces among Latin American Migrants in Europe: Perspectives from the UK." *Cambridge Journal of Regions, Economy and Society* 5, no. 2 (2012): 289–304.

McIlwaine, Cathy. "From Local to Global to Transnational Civil Society: Re-Framing Development Perspectives on the Non-State Sector." *Geography Compass*, no. 6 (2007): 1252–81.

———. "Legal Latins: Creating Webs and Practices of Immigration Status among Latin American Migrants in London." *Journal of Ethnic and Migration Studies* 41, no. 3 (2015): 493–511.

———. "Migrant Machismos: Exploring Gender Ideologies and Practices among Latin American Migrants in London from a Multi-Scalar Perspective." *Gender, Place & Culture* 17, no. 3 (2010): 281–300.

McIlwaine, Cathy, and Anastasia Bermúdez. "Ambivalent Citizenship and Extraterritorial Voting among Colombians in London and Madrid." *Global Networks* 15, no. 4 (2015): 305–482.

McIlwaine, Cathy, and Anastasia Bermúdez. "The Gendering of Political and Civic Participation among Colombian Migrants in London." *Environment and Planning A* 43, no. 7 (2011): 1499–1513.

Médecins Sans Frontières. "Bolivia's Bug Killers: Preventing the Spread of Chagas." February 18, 2004. www.msf.org/en/article/bolivias-bug-killers-preventing-spread-chagas.

Médicos del Mundo. "Proyecto | WAWACHAÑA—Partos en el techo del mundo." 2013. www.medicosdelmundo.es/partoseneltechodelmundo/proyecto.

Melde, Susanne, Rudolf Anich, Jonathan Crush, and John Oucho. "Introduction: The South-South Migration and Development Nexus." In *A New Perspective on Human Mobility in the South*, edited by Rudolf Anich, Jonathan Crush, Susanne Melde, and John Oucho, 1–20. New York: Springer, 2014.

Mellafe, Rolando. *La esclavitud en Hispanoamérica*. Buenos Aires, Argentina: Editorial Universitaria de Buenos Aires, 1964.

Meller, Patricio. *The Unidad Popular and the Pinochet Dictatorship: A Political Economy Analysis*. Translated by Tim Ennis. London: Palgrave Macmillan, 2000.

Melucci, Alberto. "Liberation or Meaning? Social Movements, Culture and Democracy." *Development and Change* 23, no. 3 (1992): 43–77.

Menjívar, Cecilia. "Liminal Legality: Salvadoran and Guatemalan Immigrants' Lives in the United States." *American Journal of Sociology* 111, no. 4 (2006): 99–1037.

Mercer, Claire, and Ben Page. "African Home Associations in Britain: Between Political Belonging and Moral Conviviality." *African Diaspora* 3, no. 1 (2010): 110–30.

Mercer, Claire, Ben Page, and Martin Evans. *Development and the African Diaspora: Place and the Politics of Home*. London: Zed Books, 2008.

MERCOSUR. "En pocas palabras." n.d. http://www.mercosur.int/innovaportal/v/3862/2/innova.front/en-pocas-palabras

Meza, Patricio. "Buscar arriendo: Las insólitas exigencias que hoy convierten el trámite en una pesadilla interminable." *La Segunda* (Santiago, Chile), February 15, 2014. www.lasegunda.com/Noticias/Nacional/2014/02/914573/buscar-arriendo-las-insolitas-exigencias-que-hoy-convierten-el-tramite-en-una-pesadilla-interminable.

Ministerio de Desarrollo Social. "Informe de política social 2012." 2012. www.ministeriodesarrollosocial.gob.cl/ipos-2012/media/ipos_2012_pp_94-125.pdf.

Ministerio de Educación. "La Educación en Bolivia: Indicadores, cifras, y resultados." 2004, 49. www.minedu.gob.bo/micrositios/biblioteca/disco-1/informacion_institucional/memorias_educacion/94.pdf.

Ministerio de Relaciones Exteriores de Chile. "Recomendaciones para ingresar a Chile." 2014. www.minrel.gob.cl/minrel/site/artic/20080619/pags/20080619154047.html.

Ministerio de Salud. "ORD. A 14 No. 3229." 2008. www.extranjeria.gob.cl/filesapp/Of_%203229_MINSAL.pdf.

Ministerio de Vivienda y Urbanismo. "Ley No. 18.101, 1982." BNC. 2003. www.leychile.cl/Navegar?idNorma=29526.

———. "Mapa social de campamentos." VII Política Habitacional y Planificación. 2013. www.ministeriodesarrollosocial.gob.cl/btca/txtcompleto/mapasocial-campamentos.pdf.

Ministerio del Interior y Seguridad Pública. "Resolución Exenta No 64819." June 10, 2014. www.extranjeria.gob.cl/media/2013/09/Valores-Visas.pdf.

Mohan, Giles, and A. B. Zack Williams. "Globalisation from Below: Conceptualising the Role of the African Diasporas in Africa's Development." *Review of African Political Economy* 29, no. 92 (2002): 211–36.

Molina, Fernando. "El himno al mar que canta Bolivia e irrita a Chile." *El País*, February 23, 2015. https://elpais.com/internacional/2015/02/23/actualidad/1424727376_935994.html.

Moller Okin, Susan. *Justice, Gender, and the Family*. New York: Basic Books, 2008.

Mondaca Plaza, Jorge. "Migración laboral y los flujos migratorios." In *Mirada sobre la migración boliviana: Aportes para el informe sobre las migraciones*, edited by Jorge Evangelista, 23–36. La Paz, Bolivia: Capítulo Boliviano de Derechos Humanos, Democracia y Desarrollo, 2007.

Montoya, Lisa, Carol Hardy-Fanta, and Sonia Garcia. "Latina Politics: Gender, Participation, and Leadership." *PS: Political Science and Politics* 33, no. 3 (2000): 555–61.

Nájera Ramírez, Olga. "Social and Political Dimensions of Folklorico Dance: The Binational Dialectic of Residual and Emergent Culture." *Western Folklore* 48, no. 1 (1989): 15–32.

Ngai, Pun. *Made in China: Women Factory Workers in a Global Workplace*. Durham, NC: Duke University Press, 2005.

Núñez Carrasco, Lorena. "Living on the Margins: Illness and Healthcare among Peruvian Migrants in Chile." PhD thesis, Leiden University, 2008. https://openaccess.leidenuniv.nl/handle/1887/13105.

———. "Necesidades de las mujeres migrantes y la oferta de atención en salud reproductiva: Discrepancias y distancias de una relación no resuelta." In *Mujeres inmigrantes en Chile: ¿Mano de obra o trabajadoras con derechos?*, edited by Carolina Stefoni. Santiago, Chile: Universidad Alberto Hurtado, 2013. Kindle.

Nyers, Peter. "Community without Status: Non-Status Migrants and Cities of Refuge." In *Renegotiating Community: Interdisciplinary Perspectives, Global Contexts*, edited by Diana Brydon and William Coleman, 123–38. Vancouver: University of British Columbia Press, 2008.

Nyers, Peter. "No One Is Illegal: Between City and Nation." *Studies in Social Justice* 4, no. 2 (2011): 127–43.

Observatorio Plurinacional de la Calidad Educativa and UNICEF. "Estudio del subsistema de educación regular: Resúmen." UNICEF. 2011. www.unicef.org/bolivia/Microsoft_Word_-_RESUMEN_ESTUDIO_SUBSISTEMA_DE_EDUCACION_REGULAR.pdf.

OECD. "Society at a Glance 2014: OECD Social Indicators." OECD Publishing, 2014. http://dx.doi.org-10.1787/soc_glance-2014-en.

———. "Society at a Glance 2016: OECD Social Indicators." OECD Publishing, 2016. http://dx.doi.org/10.1787/9789264261488-en.

———. "Statistics / OECD Factbook / 2013 / Income Inequality." OECD iLibrary. 2013. www.oecd-ilibrary.org/sites/factbook-2013-en/03/02/01/index.html?itemId=/content/chapter/factbook-2013-25-en.

Ong, Aihwa. "Cultural Citizenship as Subject-Making." *Current Anthropology* 37, no. 5 (1996): 737–62.

———. *Flexible Citizenship: The Cultural Logics of Transnationality*. Durham, NC: Duke University Press, 1999.

———. *Spirits of Resistance and Capitalist Discipline*. 2nd ed. New York: State University of New York Press, 2010.

Órgano Electoral Plurinacional. "Resultados finales del cómputo—Voto en el exterior." Órgano Electoral Plurinacional Tribunal Supremo Electoral. October 18, 2014. www .oep.org.bo/computo/index.html.

Orozco, Manuel. "Transnationalism: Trends and Opportunities in Latin America." In *Remittances: Development Impact and Future Prospects*, edited by Samuel Munzele Maimbo and Dilip Ratha, 307–29. Washington, DC: World Bank, 2005.

Østergaard-Nielsen, Eva. "The Politics of Migrants' Transnational Political Practices." *International Migration Review* 37, no. 3 (2003): 760–86.

Oviedor Treiber, Victor. *Rural Poverty, Vulnerability and Food Insecurity: The Case of Bolivia*. Potsdam, Germany: Universitätsverlag Potsdam, 2012.

Oyarzún, Darío. "Entrevista a Darío Oyarzún: El MINVU no sólo debe poner a disposición el suelo que tiene, sino que comprar suelo." *Revista Planeo*, no. 8 (2012). http://revista planeo.cl/2012/11/07/entrevista-dario-oyarzun-el-minvu-no-solo-debe-poner-a-dis posicion-el-suelo-que-tiene-sino-que-comprar-suelo/.

Paerregaard, Karsten. "The Show Must Go On: The Role of Fiestas in Andean Transnational Migration." *Latin American Perspectives* 37, no. 5 (2010): 50–66.

Paley, Julia. *Marketing Democracy: Power and Social Movements in Post-Dictatorship Chile*. Berkeley: University of California Press, 2001.

Paraje, Guillermo, and Felipe Vásquez. "Health Equity in an Unequal Country: The Use of Medical Services in Chile." *International Journal for Equity in Health* 11 (2012): doi:10.1186/1475-9276-11-81.

Pateman, Carole. *The Disorder of Women: Democracy, Feminism, and Political Theory*. Stanford, CA: Stanford University Press, 1990.

———. *The Sexual Contract*. Stanford, CA: Stanford University Press, 1988.

Pavez Ojeda, Jorge. "Affecciones afrocolombianas: Transnacionalización y racialización del mercado del sexo en las ciudades mineras del norte de Chile." *Latin American Research Review* 51, no.2 (2016): 24–45.

Pavez Soto, Iskra. "Inmigración y racismo: Experiencias de la niñez peruana en Santiago de Chile." *Si Somos Americanos* 12, no. 1 (2012): 75–99.

Peredo Beltrán, Elizabeth. *Trabajadoras asalariadas del hogar en Bolivia: Aprendizajes de una larga lucha*. La Paz, Bolivia: Red de Mujeres Transformanda la Economía, 2015.

Pereira Morató, René. "Perfil migratorio de Bolivia." Organización Internacional de Migraciones. 2011, 9. http://publications.iom.int/system/files/pdf/perfil_migratorio_de_bolivia .pdf.

Però, Davide. "Policy Change from below: Recognising Migrants' Political Agency among Latin Americans in London." In *Cross-Border Migration among Latin Americans: European Perspectives and Beyond*, edited by Cathy McIlwaine, 119–38. London: Palgrave Macmillan, 2011.

Però, Davide, and John Solomos. "Introduction: Migrant Politics and Mobilization: Exclusion, Engagements, Incorporation." *Ethnic and Racial Studies* 33, no. 1 (2010): 1–18.

Polletta, Francesca, and James Jasper. "Collective Identity and Social Movements." *Annual Review of Sociology* 27, no. 1 (2001): 283–305.

Portes, Alejandro. "Introduction: Toward a Structural Analysis of Illegal (Undocumented) Immigration." *International Migration Review* 12, no. 4 (1978): 469–84.

Portes, Alejandro, Cristina Escobar, and Renelinda Arana. "Bridging the Gap: Transnational and Ethnic Organizations in the Political Incorporation of Immigrants in the United States." *Ethnic and Racial Studies* 31, no. 6 (2008): 1056–90.

Portes, Alejandro, Luis Guarnizo, and Patricia Landolt. "The Study of Transnationalism: Pitfalls and Promise of an Emergent Research Field." *Ethnic and Racial Studies* 22, no. 2 (1999): 217–37.

Postero, Nancy. *The Indigenous State: Race, Politics, and Performance in Plurinational Bolivia.* Berkeley: University of California Press, 2017.

———. *Now We Are Citizens: Indigenous Politics in Postmulticultural Bolivia.* Stanford, CA: Stanford University Press, 2007.

Pries, Ludger. "Configurations of Geographic and Societal Spaces: A Sociological Proposal between 'Methodological Nationalism' and the 'Spaces of Flows.'" *Global Networks* 5, no. 2 (2005): 167–90.

Ratha, Dilip, and William Shaw. "South-South Migration and Remittances." World Bank Working Papers. 2007. https://elibrary.worldbank.org/doi/abs/10.1596/978-0-8213-7072-8.

Redstone Akresh, Ilana. "Occupational Mobility among Legal Immigrants to the United States." *International Migration Review* 40, no. 4 (2006): 854–84.

Reed-Danahay, Deborah, and Caroline Brettell. *Citizenship, Political Engagement, and Belonging: Immigrants in Europe and the United States.* New Brunswick, NJ: Rutgers University Press, 2008.

Riaño, Yvonne. "Drawing New Boundaries of Participation: Experiences and Strategies of Economic Citizenship among Skilled Migrant Women in Switzerland." *Environment and Planning A* 43, no. 7 (2011): 1530–46.

Richards, Patricia. *Pobladoras, Indígenas and the State: Conflicts over Women's Rights in Chile.* New Brunswick, NJ: Rutgers University Press, 2004.

———. *Race and the Chilean Miracle: Neoliberalism, Democracy and Indigenous Rights.* Pittsburgh, PA: University of Pittsburgh Press, 2013.

Robbins Joel. "Beyond the Suffering Subject: Toward an Anthropology of the Good." *Journal of the Royal Anthropological Institute* 19 (2013): 447–62.

Roberts, Bryan. *The Making of Citizens: Cities of Peasants Revisited.* London: Arnold, 1995.

Robinson, Kerry, and Cristyn Davies, "'She's Kickin' Ass, That's What She's Doing!'" *Australian Feminist Studies* 23, no. 57 (2008): 343–58.

Rojas Pedemonte, Nicolás, and Sebastián Bueno Moya. "Redes de inclusión: Estudio estadístico de las condiciones socio-laborales de migrantes en Arica." In *Migración y trabajo: estudio y propuestas para la inclusión sociolaboral de migrantes en Arica*, edited by José Tomás Vicuña Undurraga SJ and Nicolás Rojas Pedemonte, 56–100. Santiago, Chile: Ciudadano Global y Organización Internacional para las Migraciones, 2014. http://creas.uahurtado.cl/2014/11/libro-migracion-y-trabajo-es-editado.html.

Rojas Pedemonte, Nicolás, and Omar Miranda. "Dínamica sociopolítica del conflicto y la violencia en territorio mapuche: Particularidades históricas de un nuevo ciclo en las relaciones contenciosas." *Revista de Sociología* 30 (2015): 33–69.

Rojas Pedemonte, Nicolás, and Claudia Silva Dittborn. "La migración en Chile: Breve reporte y caracterización." Obersvatorio Iberoamericano sobre Movilidad Humana, Migraciones y Desarrollo. 2016. www.extranjeria.gob.cl/media/2016/08/informe_julio_agosto_2016.pdf.

Rosaldo, Renato. "Cultural Citizenship in San Jose, California." *PoLAR: Political and Legal Anthropology Review* 17, no. 2 (1994): 57–64.

Ryan, Louise, Rosemary Sales, Mary Tilki, and Bernadette Siara. "Social Networks, Social Support and Social Capital: The Experiences of Recent Polish Migrants in London." *Sociology* 42, no. 4 (2008): 672–90.

Ryburn, Megan. "Living the Chilean Dream? Bolivian Migrants' Incorporation in the Space of Economic Citizenship." *Geoforum* 76 (2016): 48–58.

Salazar Parreñas, Rhacel. *Children of Global Migration: Transnational Families and Gendered Woes.* Stanford, CA: Stanford University Press, 2005.

———. "Migrant Filipina Domestic Workers and the International Division of Reproductive Labor." *Gender & Society* 14, no. 4 (2000): 560–80.

———. "Mothering from a Distance: Emotions, Gender, and Intergenerational Relations in Filipino Transnational Families." *Feminist Studies* 27, no. 2 (2001): 361–90.

Sandel, Michael. "The Procedural Republic and the Unencumbered Self." *Political Theory* 12, no. 1 (1984): 81–96.

Sarti, Raffaella, and Francesca Scrinzi. "Introduction to the Special Issue: Men in a Woman's Job, Male Domestic Workers, International Migration and the Globalization of Care." *Men and Masculinities* 13, no. 1 (2010): 4–15.

Sassen, Saskia. "The Repositioning of Citizenship: Emergent Subjects and Spaces for Politics." *CR: The New Centennial Review* 3, no. 2 (2003): 41–66.

Satie Bermudes, Leticia. "Two Little Bolivias: The Reality of Bolivian Immigrants in the Cities of Buenos Aires and São Paulo." Master's thesis, Columbia University, 2012. http://academiccommons.columbia.edu/catalog/ac:145491.

Schavelzon, Salvador. "La reelección de Evo Morales en São Paulo: Análisis de la votación." In *Diáspora y voto en el exterior: La participación política de los emigrantes bolivianos en las elecciones de su país de origen*, edited by Jean-Michel Lafleur, 111–28. Barcelona, Spain: CIDOB, 2012.

Scheppers, Emmanuel, Els van Dongen, Jos Dekker, Jan Geertzen, and Joost Dekker. "Potential Barriers to the Use of Health Services among Ethnic Minorities: A Review." *Family Practice* 23, no. 3 (2006): 325–48.

Schild, Verónica. "Engendering the New Social Citizenship in Chile: NGOs and Social Provisioning under Neoliberalism." In *Gender, Justice, Development and Rights: Substantiating Rights in a Disabling Environment*, edited by Shahra Ravazi and Maxine Molyneux, 170–203. Oxford: Oxford University Press, 2002.

Scolieri, Paul. "Global/Mobile: Re-Orienting Dance and Migration Studies." *Dance Research Journal* 40, no. 2 (2008): v–xx.

SD Online. "Weaving the Rebellion: Plan 3000, Center of Resistance in Eastern Bolivia | Socialism and Democracy." *Socialism and Democracy Online* (2011). http://sdonline.org/51/weaving-the-rebellion-plan-3000-center-of-resistance-in-eastern-bolivia/.

Shields, Rob. *Places on the Margin: Alternative Geographies of Modernity.* London: Psychology Press, 1992.

Skrivankova, Klara. "Between Decent Work and Forced Labour: Examining the Continuum of Exploitation." JF Programme Paper: Forced Labour. Joseph Rowntree Foundation. 2010. www.prostitutionresearch.info/pdfs_all/trafficking%20all/forced-labour-exploitation-full.pdf.

Skuban, William. *Lines in the Sand: Nationalism and Identity on the Peruvian-Chilean Frontier.* Albuquerque: University of New Mexico Press, 2007.

Slater, David. "The Geopolitical Imagination and the Enframing of Development Theory." *Transactions of the Institute of British Geographers* 18, no. 4 (1993): 419–37.

Smith, Michael. "Transnational Urbanism Revisited." *Journal of Ethnic and Migration Studies* 31, no. 2 (2005): 235–44.

Smith, Robert. *Mexican New York: Transnational Lives of New Immigrants.* Berkeley: University of California Press, 2006.

Soy Arica. "Colombianos lideran lista de extranjeros que ingresan ilegalmente a Chile." December 5, 2014. www.soychile.cl/Arica/Sociedad/2014/05/12/248540/Colombianos -lideran-la-lista-de-extranjeros-que-ingresan-ilegalmente-a-Chile-a-traves-de-Arica .aspx.

Staeheli, Lynn, Patricia Ehrkamp, Helga Leitner, and Caroline Nagel. "Dreaming the Ordinary: Daily Life and the Complex Geographies of Citizenship." *Progress in Human Geography* 36, no. 5 (2012): 628–44.

Stark, Oded, and Edward Taylor. "Relative Deprivation and International Migration." *Demography* 26, no. 1 (1989): 1–14.

Stefoni, Carolina. "Perfíl migratorio de Chile." Organización Internacional de Migraciones. 2011. http://priem.cl/wp-content/uploads/2015/04/Stefoni_Perfil-Migratorio-de-Chile .pdf.

Stefoni, Carolina, and Rosario Fernández. "Mujeres migrantes en el trabajo dómestico: Entre el servilismo y los derechos." In *Mujeres inmigrantes en Chile: ¿Mano de obra o trabajadoras con derechos?*, edited by Carolina Stefoni. Santiago, Chile: Universidad Alberto Hurtado, 2013. Kindle.

Stern, Peter. *The Memory Box of Pinochet's Chile.* Durham, NC: Duke University Press, 2010.

Stobart, Henry. *Music and the Poetics of Production in the Bolivian Andes.* Aldershot, UK: Ashgate, 2006.

Strauss, Kendra. "Coerced, Forced and Unfree Labour: Geographies of Exploitation in Contemporary Labour Markets." *Geography Compass* 6, no. 3 (2012): 137–48.

Suárez-Orozco, Marcelo, Tasha Darbes, Sandra Dias, and Matt Sutin. "Migrations and Schooling." *Annual Review of Anthropology* 40, no. 1 (2011): 311–28.

Sverre Knudsen, Jan. "Dancing Cueca 'with Your Coat On': The Role of Traditional Chilean Dance in an Immigrant Community." *British Journal of Ethnomusicology* 10, no. 2 (2001): 61–83.

Tadeu de Oliveira, Antônio. "O perfil geral dos imigrantes no Brasil a partir dos censos demográficos 2000 e 2010." *Caderna Obmigra—Revista Migrações Internacionais* 1, no. 2 (2015): http://periodicos.unb.br/index.php/obmigra/article/view/14895/10661.

Tamburini, Leonardo. "Bolivia Censo 2012: Algunas claves para entender la variable indígena." SERVINDI. 2013. https://www.servindi.org/actualidad/94399.

Taylor, Edward. "The New Economics of Labour Migration and the Role of Remittances in the Migration Process." *International Migration* 37, no. 1 (1999): 63–88.

Taylor, Julie. *Paper Tangos.* Durham, NC: Duke University Press, 1998.

Techo-Chile. "Modelo de intervención." TECHO | UN TECHO PARA MI PAÍS. 2015. www .techo.org/paises/chile/techo/modelo-de-intervencion/.

———. "Monitor de Campamentos | CIS." 2015. http://chile.techo.org/cis/monitor/.

———. "TECHO realiza catastro de inmigrantes en campamento." TECHO | UN TECHO PARA MI PAÍS. 2013. www.techo.org/paises/chile/informate/techo-realiza-catastro-de -inmigrantes-en-campamento/.

Thieme, Tatiana Adeline. "The Hustle Economy: Informality, Uncertainty and the Geographies of Getting By." *Progress in Human Geography* (2017). http://journals.sagepub.com /doi/pdf/10.1177/0309132517690039.

Thrift, Nigel. "Space: The Fundamental Stuff of Geography." In *Key Concepts in Geography*, edited by Sarah Holloway, Stephen Rice, and Gill Valentine, 95–107. London: SAGE, 2003.

Tijoux Merino, María Emilia. "Las escuelas de la inmigración en la ciudad de Santiago: Elementos para una educación contra el racismo." *Polis* 12, no. 35 (2013): 287–307.

———. *Racismo en Chile: La piel como marca de la inmigración*. Santiago, Chile: Ediciones Universitaria, 2016.

Tilly, Charles, and Sidney Tarrow, *Contentious Politics*. Oxford: Oxford University Press, 2006.

Turner, Victor. *The Forest of Symbols: Aspects of Ndembu Ritual*. Ithaca, NY: Cornell University Press, 1967.

Twine, Fred. *Citizenship and Social Rights: The Interdependence of Self and Society*. London: SAGE, 1994.

UNESCO. "Education for All 2000–2015: Achievements and Challenge." Education for All Global Monitoring Report 2015. UNESCO. 2015. http://unesdoc.unesco.org/images /0023/002322/232205e.pdf.

UNICEF. "Los prejuicios en niños, niñas y adoloscentes. Survey 'La voz de los niños sobre convivencia escolar y prejuicios.'" UNICEF. 2004. www.unicef.cl/voz/docs/PPT%20pre juicios%20final.pps.

Ustubici, Aysen. *Export-Processing Zones and Gendering the Resistance: "Women's Strike" in Antalya Free Zone in Turkey*. London: London School of Economics, Gender Institute, 2009.

Valenzuela Fernández, Rodrigo. "Inequidad, ciudadanía y pueblos indígenas en Bolivia." CELADE/CEPAL. 2004. http://repositorio.cepal.org/bitstream/handle/11362/6070 /S043147_es.pdf?sequence=1.

van Aken, Mauro. "Dancing Belonging: Contesting Dabkeh in the Jordan Valley, Jordan." *Journal of Ethnic and Migration Studies* 32, no. 2 (2006): 203–22.

van Gennep, Arnold. *The Rites of Passage*. London: Psychology Press, (1909) 1960.

Vertovec, Steven. "Migrant Transnationalism and Modes of Transformation." *International Migration Review* 38, no. 3 (2004): 970–1001.

Vigh, Henrik. "Motion Squared: A Second Look at the Concept of Social Navigation." *Anthropological Theory* 9, no. 4 (2009): 419–38.

Villalba, Gabi. "Fragmentos de ciudad: El cité." Plataforma Urbana. September 22, 2006. www.plataformaurbana.cl/archive/2006/09/22/fragmentos-de-ciudad-el-cite/.

Viveros Vigoya, Mara. "Sexuality and Desire in Racialised Contexts." In *Understanding Global Sexualities: New Frontiers*, edited by Peter Aggleton, 218–31. Oxford: Routledge, 2012.

Wade, Peter. *Race and Ethnicity in Latin America*. London: Pluto Press, 1997.

Waldinger, Roger, and David Fitzgerald. "Transnationalism in Question." *American Journal of Sociology* 109, no. 5 (2004): 1177–95.

Waldinger, Roger, Eric Popkin, and Hector Aquiles Magana. "Conflict and Contestation in the Cross-Border Community: Hometown Associations Reassessed." *Ethnic and Racial Studies* 31, no. 5 (2008): 843–70.

Webber, Jeffrey. *From Rebellion to Reform in Bolivia: Class Struggle, Indigenous Liberation, and the Politics of Evo Morales.* Chicago: Haymarket Books, 2011.

Whyte, Susan. "Uncertain Undertakings: Practicing Health Care in the Subjunctive Mood." In *Managing Uncertainty: Ethnographic Studies of Illness, Risk, and the Struggle for Control,* edited by Richard Jenkins, Hanne Jessen, and Vibeke Steffen, 245–64. Copenhagen, Denmark: Museum Tusculanum Press, 2005.

Widmark, Charlotta. *To Make Do in the City: Social Identities and Cultural Transformations among Aymara Speakers in La Paz.* Uppsala, Sweden: Uppsala University Press, 2003.

Wills, Jane, Jon May, Kavita Datta, Yara Evans, Joanna Herbert, and Cathy McIlwaine. "London's Migrant Division of Labour." *European Urban and Regional Studies* 16, no. 3 (2009): 257–71.

Wimmer, Andreas, and Nina Glick Schiller. "Methodological Nationalism and beyond: Nation-State Building, Migration and the Social Sciences." *Global Networks* 2, no. 4 (2002): 301–34.

Winn, Peter, ed. *Victims of the Chilean Miracle: Workers and Neoliberalism in the Pinochet Era.* Durham, NC: Duke University Press, 2004.

World Bank. "Country Profile: Bolivia." *World Bank Databank.* 2017. http://databank.world bank.org/data/Views/Reports/ReportWidgetCustom.aspx?Report_Name=CountryProf ile&Id=b450fd57&tbar=y&dd=y&inf=n&zm=n&country=BOL.

World Bank. "Maternal Mortality Ratio (modeled estimate, per 100,000 live births)." *World Bank Databank.* 2016. http://data.worldbank.org/indicator/SH.STA.MMRT.

———. "Mortality Rate, Infant (per 1,000 live births)." *World Bank Databank.* 2016. http://data.worldbank.org/indicator/SP.DYN.IMRT.IN.

Wright, Thomas, and Rody Oñate Zúñiga. "Chilean Political Exile." *Latin American Perspectives* 34, no. 4 (2007): 31–49.

Yarnall, Kaitlin, and Marie Price. "Migration, Development and a New Rurality in the Valle Alto, Bolivia." *Journal of Latin American Geography* 9, no. 1 (2010): 107–24.

Yashar, Deborah. "Contesting Citizenship: Indigenous Movements and Democracy in Latin America." *Comparative Politics* 31, no. 1 (1998): 23–42.

Yeates, Nicola. "Global Care Chains: A State-of-the-Art Review and Future Directions in Care Transnationalization Research." *Global Networks* 12, no. 2 (2012): 135–54.

Young, Iris Marion. "The Ideal of Community and the Politics of Difference." *Social Theory and Practice* 12, no. 1 (1986): 1–26.

Yuval-Davis, Niva, and Prina Werbner, eds. *Women, Citizenship and Difference.* London: Zed Books, 1999.

Zapana, Verónica. "Enfermedad de Chagas afecta a 33 de cada 100 bolivianos." *Página Siete* (La Paz), April 15, 2016. http://web.paginasiete.bo/sociedad/2016/4/15/enfermedad-chagas -afecta-cada-bolivianos-93286.html.

Zeiderman, Austin. *Endangered City: The Politics of Security and Risk in Bogotá.* Durham, NC: Duke University Press, 2016.

Zeiderman, Austin, Sobia Ahmad Kaker, Jonathan Silver, and Astrid Wood. "Uncertainty and Urban Life." *Public Culture* 72, no. 2 (2015): 281–304.

Zloniski, Christian. "Economic Globalization and Changing Capital-Labor Relations in Baja California's Fresh-Produce Industry." In *The Anthropology of Labor Unions,* edited by E. Paul Durrenberger and Karaleah Reichart, 157–88. Boulder: University Press of Colorado, 2010.